Disaster Handbook

Robert Brown Butler

© 2014

Robert Brown Butler

c ISBN-13: 978-1-497-52818-5

Published by Robert Brown Butler

Soft cover, 216 pages, 7.5 x 9.25 in (19.1 x 23.5 cm)

Drawings and photos by the author except as otherwise noted.

Cover design, book design, and page layout design by the author.

Books by Robert Brown Butler

The Ecological House (Morgan & Morgan)
Architectural and Engineering Calculations Manual (McGraw-Hill)
Standard Handbook of Architectural Engineering (McGraw-Hill)
Architectural Engineering Design: Structural Systems (McGraw-Hill)
Architectural Engineering Design: Mechanical Systems (McGraw-Hill)
Architectural Engineering Formulas (McGraw-Hill)
Architecture Laid Bare! (Robert Brown Butler)
Disaster Handbook (Robert Brown Butler)

This book has won the following literary awards

2014 Great Midwest Book Festival: How-To Books, Runner-Up
2014 New England Book Festival: How-To Books, Honorable Mention
2014 Great Northwest Book Festival: How-To Books, Winner
2014 Great Southwest Book Festival: How-To Books, Winner
2014 Great Southeast Book Festival: How-To Books, Runner-Up
2014 New York Book Festival: How-To Books, Honorable Mention

About the Author

Since graduating from the Cornell School of Architecture in 1964, Robert Brown Butler has been involved in every aspect of architectural design and construction for fifty years. From 1967 to 1973 he worked as a carpenter in California and Colorado. Since 1973 he has lived in New York where he has worked somewhat chronologically as a carpenter, contractor, registered architect, and author. In 1981 he wrote his first book, *The Ecological House*, which describes how to design and build houses that minimize damage to the environment. Between 1984 and 2002 he authored five books on architectural engineering for McGraw-Hill, and in 2012 he wrote *Architecture Laid Bare*, a book for laymen that describes the latest environmental and technical issues that face American architecture today. Mr. Butler's environmental and engineering expertise as expressed in his previous publications are relevant in the *Disaster Handbook*, for most disasters are a clash between the outer forces of the environment and the inner forces of building engineering. Mr. Butler's seventh book has a website: architecturelaidbare.com, and his typography has a website, bufontforge.com. The present book also has a website, http://thedisasterhandbook.com.

Consider how slight a shelter is absolutely necessary.

Henry Thoreau

Note

For a few important subjects this book employs a quick-find notation, as follows:

If you are reading a passage on page 114 that says something like "If you have pets, provide what they need as listed at **M** on page 173," go to page 173 to where you will see beside the referred text a prominently visible icon that looks like → FROM **M** 114 This notation lets you find important information quickly without having to look all over the page for it, and it eliminates the need to repeat the information and take up extra space.

Contents

110 Deaths

On the night of October 29, 2012, America's most populous metropolitan area was struck by hurricane Sandy, the worst natural disaster in its history, causing 110 citizens to die.[4] A grim list of these deaths shows that …

30 drowned.

6 died when trees fell on their homes.

5 died of carbon monoxide poisoning while operating gasoline generators in their homes.

3 more died of carbon monoxide poisoning in their homes or apartments.

5 died when storm-damaged trees fell on them while they were clearing debris.

4 died in their homes due to hypothermia from the cold.

4 died in falls down stairs in homes with no electricity.

3 died from falls elsewhere indoors when the power was out.

2 died of cardiac arrest.

2 died when their oxygen machines ran out of oxygen.

M. P. died when struck by a falling tree while helping his family into their car to evacuate.

V. B. died when struck by a falling tree while moving his car.

E. M. and C. M. died after being swept away from their mother by a surge of water.

I. V. died when a surge of water swept him off a sidewalk.

R. P. was found dead at the base of a wet stairwell in his home.

K. J. died when his car stalled in flooding water and he got out to flee and slipped in the water.

K. G. died when he lost his balance and fell in a strong wind.

T. W. died when he fell on the steps outside his home.

K. J. died after his motorcycle crashed at an intersection whose traffic light didn't work.

V. G. died when he was struck by a car while crossing a street where a traffic light was out.

G. U. died when a strong wind blew part of a roof from a mobile home into the windshield of her car.

U. H. and F. H. died when a falling tree crushed their car.

W. I. died when his car struck a tree fallen across a road.

J. R. died when he lost his footing in the dark.

D. G. died when a tree fell on her tent while she was camping in a wooded area.

M. V. and M. Y. were killed by a falling tree while they were walking a dog.

H. Y. died when she was swept out to sea while walking her dog on a beach.

N. C. died when she cut her arm and bled to death after shutting off the gas to her house.

D. S. died of carbon monoxide poisoning from a charcoal grill she was using in her home.

J. D. and L. D. died in a fire in their home.

M. S. and N. S. died in a fire started by a candle.

N. E. died from being burned by a kerosene lantern in his home.

D. N. was electrocuted while wading through floodwater in his basement.

M. H. and N. H. were crushed by falling debris in their basement.

O. D. was killed when she stepped on a fallen power line in front of her home while taking photos of the damage.

R. T. died when a tree fell on her as she was walking to a neighbor's house.

G. I. died after being struck in the head by a broken tree limb.

D. J. died while trimming a tree that had partly fallen during the storm.

W. H. died of a chainsaw accident while clearing storm debris.

T. K. died when hit by a truck while cleaning up storm debris.

These 110 people didn't die because they failed as survivalists, or were inept at using weapons, or fell at the hands of marauders.

They died because they didn't observe a few rules of safety.

This book gives you these rules, and much more.

It reveals the mistakes that led these victims into the lairs of death.

It describes the foods, tools, and other "calamity commodities" you will need when Nature gets wrathful.

It asserts that the part of your home or workplace that will serve as shelter must be nearly indestructible. For what use is it to have everything you would need in a disaster if where you store and use it is destroyed?

It says the biggest danger of a disaster is that it prevents you from performing those simple, everyday, taken-for-granted tasks that keep you alive. Hence the heart of this book reveals how to cook, wash the dishes, clean your clothes, bathe, go to the bathroom, and keep everything sanitary when you have no power and no pure water. When misfortune knocks your life ajar, these are the links that form a chain of survival.

Nearly as important is what you *don't* need in a disaster. You don't need a generator. You don't need to know wilderness survival skills. And you don't need an arsenal of weapons or knowledge of hand-to-hand combat. When facing these challenges, far more citizens know the need for teamwork and friendship and try to help each other, and would rather be known as Samaritans than Survivalists.

To overcome a disaster you also don't need to be young or strong. During two major disasters the author performed many tasks that appear in these pages when he was past the age of seventy. Absent youth and strength, he exercised the kind of creativity and cleverness everyone has regardless of age, strength, or gender.

You'd think everyone would want to know these things. But many customers will skip the shopping cart or cash-out clerk because they have seen so many disasters on TV they've acquired a panic mentality when they think of these events. "Disasters scare me to death!" they cry. "I don't want to read about them!" But really, learning how to defeat a disaster is as easy as deciding to go out to dinner. Remove the dread that bars your doors of perception, and you will enjoy a banquet of treats that will make the difference between suffering and safety. You will enter a brave new world that will erase your panic, and release you from the grip of terror, and remove you from the deadening effects of indifference —and you will find that switch of initiative that will energize your intelligence, empower your imagination, and arouse your sense of vigilance in ways that will tilt the odds of danger from being forever against you to being always in your favor. Indeed, here the delight of defeating a disaster awaits you.

To Begin With ...

Though every disaster that covers a large area and claims a number of lives is different from every other, each has three elemental phases: *Before, During, After* ....

Before is everything you do before a disaster may strike. This is divided into *Well Before, Days Before, Just Before,* and *Suddenly.*

Well Before is the time you have —weeks, months, years perhaps— to analyze your needs, lay in supplies, establish routines, and practice drills so you are prepared for whatever may transpire.

Days Before is the time between when the National Weather Service (or perhaps strangely barking dogs or erratically flying birds) forecasts a hurricane, blizzard, or similar disaster and when it arrives. This is your chance to drive to a service station and local stores and buy what you and the others in your party may need while sequestered in your safe room or similar sanctuary.

Just Before is the time you have to find a safe place when a tornado, tsunami, wildfire, or similar disaster is approaching.

Suddenly is a disaster that strikes without warning —earthquake, explosion, toxic spill.

Wide variations may occur among these markers of time. Hours before a tornado touches down in your area the sky may fill with dark clouds. A day before a wildfire reaches your property the horizon may billow with smoke. Weeks before Mount St. Helens erupted in 1980 seismologists warned that the mountain was experiencing minor tremors and its north slope was bulging —but no one knew when or even if an eruption would occur. [4]

During covers the time between when a disaster begins and when its ravaging ends. This may be seconds for an earthquake, minutes for a tornado, hours for a hurricane, or years after a nuclear reactor meltdown. Sadly, many disasters spawn further disasters. Consider the levees that failed after hurricane Katrina struck New Orleans in 2005; the tsunamis that caused nuclear reactors to explode after the earthquake off the coast of Japan in 2011; the mudflows, flash floods, earthquakes, and wildfires that raged over hundreds of square miles after the eruption of Mount St. Helens in 1980. Hence in some disasters you may experience more than one "during" before the coast is clear.

After begins when the disaster ends and ends when all is reasonably restored. This is divided into *Just After* and *Well After*.

   Just After is the time that you spend coping with the destruction until things return to normal, which may be minutes if you do little more than put away the candles after a blackout, or months after a major hurricane.

   Well After begins when things have returned to normal and spans the time you may spend cleaning up and repairing any damage.

This practical primer also emphasises that defeating disasters is largely an ***Architectural Matter.*** For what good is it to have everything you would need in a disaster if where you would store and use everything is destroyed? Hence this reference, in addition to describing what you will need in a disaster, details how to design and construct a building's areas of disaster storage and use as indestructibly as you can make them with architectural drawings you can take to a professional designer or builder.

   Viewing disasters through an architectural lens has another advantage. It will shift your concerns from worrying about what on earth could happen to you to envisioning those constructions that will keep you safe — and this will shift your thinking from *fear-oriented* to *task-oriented*. This will replace paralysis with strength, and you will be able to steer your life more quickly and surely back to normal.

Well Before

I suppose you're reading this in a comfortable place. Likely the temperature is around 70 degrees, the air isn't too dry or humid, the lighting is bright, and you have plenty of room around you.

You can be nearly this comfortable in almost any disaster you may face if you think ahead a little. There's no reason to get afraid or panicky about it. It's like eating: you don't wait until five before six to get your food for dinner; long before this you will have shopped for and stored what you will eat so it will all be there when six o'clock rolls around. It's the same with disasters. You think ahead a little, then everything is there when you need it. Nothing to get afraid or panicky about. First you obtain what you will need (easy if you have accurate lists which this book provides). Second, you store what you've obtained in a safe place (this usually involves some precautionary architectural design and construction which this book describes in professional detail, especially since it is authored by an architect). Third, you use what you've obtained and stored (which this book describes in language a ten-year-old can understand). Again, there's no need to get afraid or panicky about it.

Another reason why disasters seem so needlessly frightening is because many victims tend to see them as a whole rather than divide them into much smaller and more manageable problems. A disaster can seem overwhelming when you are confronted with everything at once —but if you break it down to the 50 or 60 little things you need to do and knock them off one at a time, the whole thing can be as easy as eating a lavish dinner one bite at a time. So if a disaster ever bangs on your roof and walls, dice it into tiny parts until each is as easy to do as your normal routines during more tranquil hours.

In these ways you can remain nearly as comfortable during a disaster as during normal times, and if you are seriously inconvenienced these misfortunes will be much less painful. Usually you needn't be afraid or panicky over what could transpire.

So let's prepare.

1. DISASTER AMULET (L.E.D. PEN LIGHT)

Create communication networks

One of the simplest and most effective ways you can prepare for any disaster that could occur at any time is to develop as many methods of communication with others as you can as described below. Then when you quickly need help you can quickly get it.

Gather information ... Contact local crisis managers, civil defense facilities, fire stations, libraries, the red cross, town hall, and the like, and collect whatever information they have. Contact these authorities *well before* a disaster may strike, as during one they may be swamped with requests for help. Bring a tote bag to carry what they give you. The first of many questions to ask are ...

☞ What disasters could occur in your community?
☞ How would you be warned?
☞ How should you prepare for each?

Make a list of emergency contacts ... Every home and workplace should have emergency addresses and phone numbers near each phone. The more contacts you have, the better your chances of getting help. At the end of this book is a blank page for listing these contacts ...

☞ *Family, friends, and co-workers.*
☞ *Local sources of information* ... hospitals, police, fire houses, radio stations and TV channels that broadcast local disaster updates.
☞ *Your childrens' schools* ... teachers, nurses, office staff.
☞ *Overnight accommodations* ... hotels, motels, bed-and-breakfasts, relatives, friends, and other places you could stay at in an emergency.
☞ *Daytime shelters* ... schools, churches, civic organizations (Elks Club, etc.), health clubs (many allow nonmembers to shower during emergencies), libraries (they have local newspapers and often let citizens recharge electronic devices).
☞ *Service providers* ... ministers, doctors, vets, insurers, plumbers, electricians, carpenters, tree services, hardware stores, and garbage collectors. Home Depot, Lowes, and Sears often have building construction specialists who can help.

Share information with others ... Your family if at home, co-workers if at work. Groups that prepare together usually fare better than those who don't.

☞ Discuss the disasters that could occur at your home or place of work, and how you should prepare and respond to each.
☞ Ask your family and co-workers how they would react in a disaster. Discuss how it could affect each person physically and emotionally.
☞ Discuss what to do if you evacuate.
☞ Discuss what supplies and equipment you should have and where to store and use it.

Team with neighbors who are responsible and you can trust. Plan how your neighborhood could work together in a disaster.

☞ Know each neighbor's skills and needs: what they can and can't contribute, physically and psychologically.
☞ Discuss how to help people with special needs: the elderly, disabled, etc.
☞ Make plans for child care if parents can't get home.
☞ Make plans for neighbors' pet care if their owners can't get home.

Train yourself … Almost every community has fire stations, civic groups, the Red Cross, and ambulance corps units that teach first aid, fire suppression, rescue operations, team organization, and other aspects of disaster preparedness. You will also meet experienced people, local assistance offices, and useful resources in your community as well as other enrollees who have similar interests as yours. As a sample of the surprises you may discover, the other day I drove past a fire station with a large sign in front that said, "Need volunteers, will pay college tuition." Also consider enrolling in a local CERT (Community Emergency Response Team) training program. For more info visit www.citizencorps.gov/cert.

Create a family contact card … Remember the credit card ad that said, "Don't leave home without it?" The same goes for the **Family Contact Card** on the right. This "disaster dogtag" is about the size of a business card folded over. It will help everyone in your family reunite if disaster strikes when they aren't together —say if Mom is at work, Dad is shopping, one kid is at band practice and another is playing soccer. It lists personal information plus a friend or relative who lives some distance away who can serve as a contact for everyone to call, and it has space to describe a local meeting place if you can't return home. Every family member, including school children, should carry one in a wallet, purse, or school knapsack. Also send a copy to each school to keep on file, put a copy in your personal relief kit, and send a copy to your distant contact. Four more **Family Contact Cards** appear at the end of this book so you can easily photocopy or remove them.

Other Important Information

Family Contact Card

Contact Name
Address
Phone
Distant Contact Name
Address
Phone
Meeting Place
Phone

Dial 9-1-1 for Emergencies!

2. THE FAMILY CONTACT CARD[5]. ON PAGE 215 ARE REMOVABLE COPIES OF THIS CARD

Have useful transportation … This wheeled communication is useful *before* and *after* a disaster, but rarely during one, as during most disasters the worst thing you can do is drive somewhere —and possibly be prey to flying debris, falling trees, blocked roads, and a host of other horrors, plus you'll get in the way of police cars, fire trucks, ambulances, and other emergency responders.

So what's the best vehicle to have? A picture is worth a paragraph of words, as appears in figure 3. Part of owning a useful vehicle is knowing where to drive it, which varies according to the disaster. If a hurricane is two days away, you may want to drive 150 miles northwest. If a blizzard will blanket you, you may drive 150 miles south. A good plan is to *know four different escape routes*: i.e. north, east, south, west; or NE, SE,

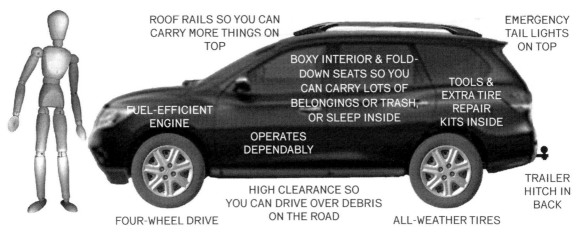

ROOF RAILS SO YOU CAN CARRY MORE THINGS ON TOP

EMERGENCY TAIL LIGHTS ON TOP

BOXY INTERIOR & FOLD-DOWN SEATS SO YOU CAN CARRY LOTS OF BELONGINGS OR TRASH, OR SLEEP INSIDE

TOOLS & EXTRA TIRE REPAIR KITS INSIDE

FUEL-EFFICIENT ENGINE

OPERATES DEPENDABLY

TRAILER HITCH IN BACK

HIGH CLEARANCE SO YOU CAN DRIVE OVER DEBRIS ON THE ROAD

FOUR-WHEEL DRIVE

ALL-WEATHER TIRES

3. A DEPENDABLE CAR IN A DISASTER

SW, NW —you get the idea. Obtain a local roadmap and mark these routes on it (for a published example see figure 4 on the right). If you are incapacitated, someone else — even a hitchhiker— can use your map to drive you and rest of your party to safety.

Prepping your house and grounds

Though many of the procedures below are routine house maintenance, keeping up with them can yield big dividends if a disaster suddenly bangs on your roof and walls …

4. GEORGIA ROADMAP SHOWING HURRICANE EVACUATION ROUTES NEAR SAVANNAH [7]

☞ *Make an emergency escape plan of each floor.*
If you have floorplans of your home or place of work, get some paper and trace each floor. No plans? Sketch a plan of each floor, including the walls, windows, doors, and stairs. Dimensions needn't be accurate. Label the rooms, then with colored pens or pencils mark two escape routes, preferably in opposite directions from each room (especially bedrooms) in case of fire or other crisis. Test each escape window to make sure it opens easily, is low enough to climb into, and large enough to climb through. Post a copy of each floor at eye level in each child's bedroom, make sure each child understands it, and on each plan write

where everyone should meet after fleeing the building, (such as the Smith's front porch next door). Do practice drills with them, like fire drills at school. The experience of practicing an escape drill will reinforce the lesson better than simply studying a drawing. Learning these routines when you don't need to is also more fun when no lives are at stake, and practices are more forgiving if you make a mistake.

5. ESCAPE PLAN MOUNTED ON A BEDROOM DOOR

☞ *Install carbon monoxide alarms and smoke alarms* on each floor of your home or place of work, especially outside bedroom doors. A fire creates three dangerous things: flames, smoke, and carbon monoxide (a colorless, odorless, deadly gas). *Ionization alarms* are best at detecting flames (i.e. paper burning in a wastebasket), *photoelectric alarms* are best at sensing smoke (i.e. a smoldering mattress or burning plastic), and *CO alarms* are best at sensing carbon monoxide (i.e. leaky furnaces and gas stoves). Some alarms detect any two of these killers, but none presently warn of all three. Two such products appear in figure 6 and 7. You really need to understand their capabilities when you buy them. Discuss this with a knowledgeable salesperson, or you can read First Alert's *Smoke and Carbon Monoxide Detectors Guide* (go to amazon.com) and *Consumer Report's CO & Smoke Alarms* (go to http://www.consumerreports.org/cro/co-and-smoke-alarms/buying-guide.htm).

6. FIRST ALERT SMOKE & FIRE ALARM [9]

7. KIDDE SMOKE & CO ALARM [10]

A quick way to install the right alarm in the right area in your home or workplace is to go from room to room and think *flame, smoke,* or *CO?* In each bedroom you'd likely say *smoke.* In your furnace room and garage you're apt to say *CO.* In your kitchen you need to think of two *more* things: the kind of stove you have (gas? electric?) and how any food on them could ignite (flame from grease? smoke from burnt food?). As *Consumer Reports* says, "Effective protection from fire and CO remains far too complicated." [11] At least now you know.

All this points to another big problem with disaster preparation: it's often a two-step process: (1) Learning the problem. (2) Forming the solution. Sometimes one is easy and the other is hard, and vice versa. One thing you don't want to do is form a solution before learning the problem. Bil-

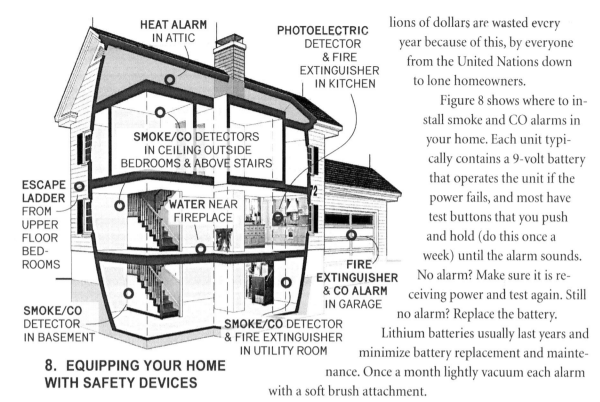

HEAT ALARM
IN ATTIC

PHOTOELECTRIC
DETECTOR
& FIRE
EXTINGUISHER
IN KITCHEN

SMOKE/CO DETECTORS
IN CEILING OUTSIDE
BEDROOMS & ABOVE STAIRS

ESCAPE
LADDER
FROM
UPPER
FLOOR
BED-
ROOMS

WATER NEAR
FIREPLACE

FIRE
EXTINGUISHER
& CO ALARM
IN GARAGE

SMOKE/CO
DETECTOR
IN BASEMENT

SMOKE/CO DETECTOR
& FIRE EXTINGUISHER
IN UTILITY ROOM

lions of dollars are wasted every year because of this, by everyone from the United Nations down to lone homeowners.

Figure 8 shows where to install smoke and CO alarms in your home. Each unit typically contains a 9-volt battery that operates the unit if the power fails, and most have test buttons that you push and hold (do this once a week) until the alarm sounds. No alarm? Make sure it is receiving power and test again. Still no alarm? Replace the battery. Lithium batteries usually last years and minimize battery replacement and maintenance. Once a month lightly vacuum each alarm with a soft brush attachment.

8. EQUIPPING YOUR HOME WITH SAFETY DEVICES

☞ *Know if you live or work in a flood-prone area.* Ask your local government office about your area's flood history, and if your property is above not the "maximum previous flood-stage level" but the "maximum future-ever" level. Find an expert if you can, and analyze a U.S. Geodetic Survey map (topographic map) of the acreage around your property. Obtain a copy of your flood evacuation plan if there is one, and locate the safest route from your home to the nearest shelter or high ground. A little foresight here might save your house and life someday.

☞ *Inspect gas lines for corrosion, leaks, and dips.* If a gas line dips (runs down and up again) when it passes through a crawl space or other unheated area where the temperature could fall below freezing, the water vapor in propane and other fuel gases can settle in the dip where it may freeze, crack the line, and leak —then boom, there goes the house. If a gas line has a dip, remount it so it runs continuously either up or down until it enters heated areas indoors.

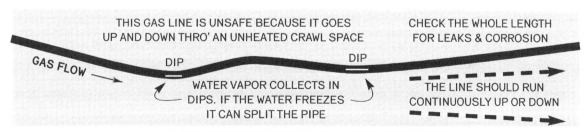

THIS GAS LINE IS UNSAFE BECAUSE IT GOES
UP AND DOWN THRO' AN UNHEATED CRAWL SPACE

CHECK THE WHOLE LENGTH
FOR LEAKS & CORROSION

GAS FLOW

DIP

DIP

WATER VAPOR COLLECTS IN
DIPS. IF THE WATER FREEZES
IT CAN SPLIT THE PIPE

THE LINE SHOULD RUN
CONTINUOUSLY UP OR DOWN

9. A BIG REASON WHY GAS LINES EXPLODE

☞ *Mount storm shutters on each window*, or cut pieces of $3/4$ inch exterior-grade plywood (not sheets of OSB because water ruins it) and have them ready to fit if a disaster threatens. Installing plywood panels is not as easy as internet videos make it look; because the method of fastening the panel over the glass depends on (1) the frame around the glass, (2) the exterior finish around the frame, (3) whether the frame projects beyond the exterior finish or is inside it, (4) whether the window has a projecting sill, and (5) how high the window's top is above the ground (if this is more than 7 feet you'll need to install ladders or scaffolds). In short, this seemingly simple "Sunday chore" for laymen is typically a time-consuming job for professionals.

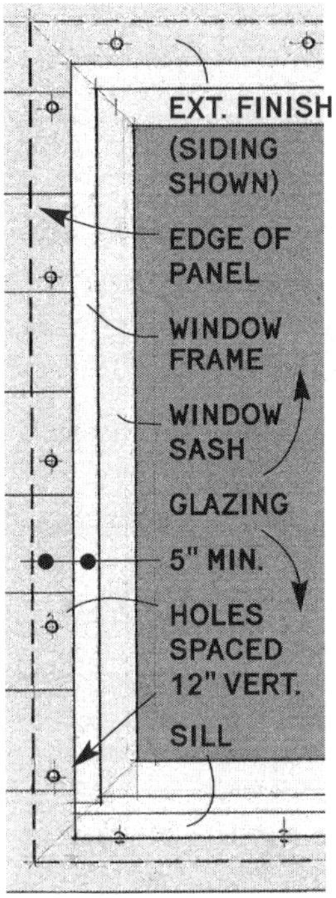

INSTALLATION DEPENDS ON

A
FROM
82

TYPE OF CONSTRUCTION AROUND OPENING
WOOD FRAMING ... INSERT $1/4$ IN. LAG BOLTS INTO WOOD FRAMING
CONCRETE ... FIT $5/16$ IN. LAG BOLTS INTO EXPANSION BOLTS MOUNTED IN CONCRETE

TYPE OF EXTERIOR FINISH AROUND OPENING
WOOD OR VINYL ... INSERT $1/4$ IN. LAG BOLTS THRO' SIDING INTO SOLID CONSTRUCTION
BRICK OR STONE ... FIT $5/16$ IN. LAG BOLTS INTO EXPANSION BOLTS IN MASONRY

TYPE OF WINDOW FRAME
PROJECTING ... INSERT 4 IN. LAG BOLTS INTO FRAME
INSET ... CUT PANEL TO FIT INSIDE FRAME & HOLD IN PLACE WITH SPRING CLIPS
FLUSH ... INSERT 3 IN. LAG BOLTS INTO WOOD FRAMING OR MASONRY

TYPE OF SILL
FLUSH ... FASTEN BOTTOM OF PANEL 4 IN. BELOW WINDOW.
PROJECTING ... BOTTOM OF PANEL RESTS ON SILL, NO CONNECTORS ALONG BASE

LOCATION ABOVE GROUND
IF TOP OF WINDOW IS MORE THAN 7 FT ABOVE GROUND, USE LADDERS OR SCAFFOLDS

ANY OBSTRUCTIONS IN FRONT OF WINDOW
IF SHRUBS, FUEL TANKS, ETC. ARE IN FRONT, INSTALL LADDERS &/OR SCAFFOLDS

FOR ANY INSTALLATION

1. USE EXTERIOR GRADE PLYWOOD; DO NOT USE OSB (WATER RUINS IT).
2. WHEN CUTTING PANELS, ADD 5" TO EACH SIDE, TOP, & BOTTOM IF NO SILL.
3. PRIME & PAINT ALL SURFACES SO PANEL CAN BE REUSED REPEATEDLY.
4. LABEL EACH PANEL SO YOU WILL KNOW WHAT OPENING IT FITS ON.
5. CALL A PROFESSIONAL TO INSTALL.

Diagram labels:
EXT. FINISH (SIDING SHOWN)
EDGE OF PANEL
WINDOW FRAME
WINDOW SASH
GLAZING
5" MIN.
HOLES SPACED 12" VERT.
SILL

10. FITTING PLYWOOD SHUTTERS OVER WINDOWS

☞ *Know your utility cutoffs.* These are the master switches or valves in every building that has running water, electricity, or gas. If you don't know where they are, contact a utility company, contractor, or other knowledgeable person, then show their locations to your family and co-workers. If you fail to turn them off, your later discomforts may include a short-circuit that burns down the building, a flooded basement, or a ruptured gas line that causes an explosion. Clear the area around each cutoff so it will be easy to reach, make sure nothing is stored in any hallways or other routes you would walk through to reach them, and plan an escape route outdoors in case a disaster leaves you trapped near the cutoff. You could paint the area around each (not the cutoff itself as paint can damage it) with white or fluorescent paint to make it more visible: perhaps create a bullseye with red arrows in the surrounding white that point to the valve in the center. Create an indelible impression in the memory of anyone who would use it. Since these disconnects are usually located in the darkest, dankest, buggiest part of a building, carry a flashlight when you visit them. Three common switches and valves are described below.

The *water supply shutoff valve* is near where the main pipe enters the building. Its round handle, known to plumbers as a handwheel valve, looks like the hose spigot outside your house. If you live in an apartment or condo, or work in a building leased by several tenants, find this valve and learn how to use it, or know how to contact the building custodian. Two verbal guides that will help you remember which direction turns the water off are "clockwise close" and "rightsy-tightsy leftsy-loosy."

The *electrical master switch* is typically a wide black "snap switch" near the top of a metal box resembling a medicine cabinet located indoors near where the electrical primary cable enters the building. This switch is fairly hard to turn on and off, and below it is a metal door that opens to vertical rows of circuit breakers that protect every electrical outlet in the building. If a light illuminates the area in front of the panel box, turn it on before operating this switch; the light should go out when you turn the switch off.

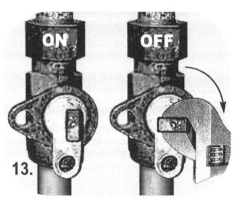

If your home or workplace has a *gas line shutoff valve*, it is usually near where the gas line enters the building or in a metal box a couple feet below the ground out front near the street. Indoors, this valve usually is a rectangular stub about $1/4$ x $3/4$ inches in size that you can turn with a special tool or crescent wrench, as appears at left. Outdoors, the valve may require a long tool resembling a walking cane with a fitting on its end that you fit over the valve and turn. Either way, get the right tool at your local gas company or hardware store and learn how to use it.

☞ **If your plumbing has a septic system, know where the septic tank and leaching field are located on your property.** You may need to know where these systems are if your plumbing fixtures don't drain properly or your property has been flooded. If you don't have a site plan of these systems, your local building department should have one.

☞ *Eliminate areas of moisture in the building.* You wouldn't want to find the mess that appears on the right in your house or workplace someday. Extensive decay like this is caused by little drops of water seeping slowly into wood framing. The reason you're seeing this damage in a disaster handbook is because the rotted wood framing on the right will hardly support its own weight —and if a disaster impacts this weak construction it is far more likely to collapse and injure anyone inside than if the construction is dry and strong. Hence one of the surest ways to protect your house and everything inside in a disaster is, in advance, *keep moisture out of the construction.* Any leaky plumbing inside vanities or counters? Call a plumber. Any damp areas around the base of toilets? Call a plumber. Any moisture under water heaters? Call a plumber. Any mold around bathtubs or the bottoms of walls? Call a plumber or carpenter. Any cracks in any masonry either indoors or outdoors? Call a mason. To prevent mold and mildew, (1) indoors, remove any old mattresses and piles of newspapers and clothes; (2) outdoors, remove grass clippings, tree trimmings, trash, weeds, etc. near the house; and (3) trim back the shrubbery so at least two feet of open space exists between the foliage and the facades —because air circulation is public enemy number one to mold. Then your home or place of work will remain strong and give you maximum protection when you need it most.

14.[12]
WHAT A LITTLE MOISTURE CAN DO

☞ *Anchor large indoor items that could shift or fall.* Large mirrors or pictures on the walls (especially if covered with glass), tall furniture like bookcases, heavy furniture like pianos, and large pieces of mechanical equipment can move around in earthquakes, explosions, tornados, and hurricanes. Bolt these large objects to solid construction in the walls behind or floors below with bolts, **L** brackets, and other strong connectors as described on page 92. Also …

- Place large or heavy objects on low shelves, hang mirrors and heavy pictures away from beds and chairs, brace overhead light fixtures, and install clips, locks, or latches on cabinet doors.
- Fill any deep cracks in foundations with mortar. These are weak seams where the construction on each side will most readily shake apart in a violent disaster.
- Connect gas water heaters to flexible gas lines; these are far less likely to break if the heater is knocked around. Gas stoves are less desirable in earthquake and tornado country because these disasters can sever municipal gas lines.

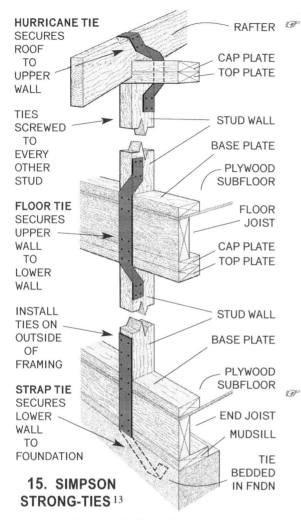

HURRICANE TIE SECURES ROOF TO UPPER WALL — RAFTER

CAP PLATE
TOP PLATE

TIES SCREWED TO EVERY OTHER STUD — STUD WALL

BASE PLATE

PLYWOOD SUBFLOOR

FLOOR TIE SECURES UPPER WALL TO LOWER WALL — FLOOR JOIST

CAP PLATE
TOP PLATE

STUD WALL

INSTALL TIES ON OUTSIDE OF FRAMING — BASE PLATE

PLYWOOD SUBFLOOR

STRAP TIE SECURES LOWER WALL TO FOUNDATION — END JOIST

MUDSILL

TIE BEDDED IN FNDN

15. SIMPSON STRONG-TIES [13]

☞ *Strengthen your house with Simpson strong-ties.* When wood framing is violently shaken it splits at corners, ridges, and edges because the nails holding these seams together do little more than keep them in place under the force of gravity. But *hurricane ties, floor ties,* and *strap ties* like the ones on the left firmly hold roofs to walls, walls to floors, floors to lower walls, and walls to foundations. These fasteners are especially effective in hurricanes, tornadoes, and earthquakes, which are some of the strongest forces that damage buildings. Admittedly it is hard to add these fasteners to existing construction; but if you ever give your house a dressier exterior, between removing the old and adding the new, fit its framing with these inexpensive connectors. A few hundred dollars' worth could save you a few hundred thousand dollars of construction someday.

☞ *Make sure your radio and cellphone work in your safe room.* If the walls are concrete, radio and cellphone signals may not transmit through them. Don't wait until you're huddled inside these walls during an emergency to learn about this. If necessary install an antenna outside, and test it for reception.

☞ *Store flammable liquids* in safe containers with tight lids away from living or sleeping areas. Indoors, store them in a ventilated area, against an exterior wall (if they ignite they'll damage less of the building), near the floor (if they fall and break they'll splash less), and away from heat sources. In earthquake country, secure shelves of containers with bungee cords to minimize falling and spills, as appears below.

NAIL IN WALL

← BUNGEE CORD →

16. HOLDING SHELVED ITEMS IN PLACE WHEN THE BUILDING SHAKES

☞ *If you live in an area where lightning often strikes, mount lightning rods on your roof.* A grounded TV antenna is not a lightning rod. An effective system has pointed terminals mounted on the highest parts of your roof from which thick stranded cables descend to the ground. A licensed electrical contractor should install these systems. Also plug your computer, microwave oven, and every other piece of electronic equipment you have into a surge protector, or, better yet, a universal power source, known as a UPS. A serious lightning strike can "jump" the terminals in a surge protector and fry your computer, but it won't do this with a UPS.

☞ *Make sure the grounds around your house are safe.* Keep all lawn furniture, power equipment, and the like inside strong construction. A shed resting on concrete blocks is not strong construction, but a basement or a garage with concrete walls is. Label hazardous materials and fuel gas or oil tanks you can't move. Spray paint is a better label than a taped piece of paper which can peel away in a high wind. If possible, chain the tanks securely to auger anchors, as appears in figure 19 on the opposite page, or other solid construction. Figure 17 below shows a number of ways you can protect your house or place of work from a disaster well before it may arrive.

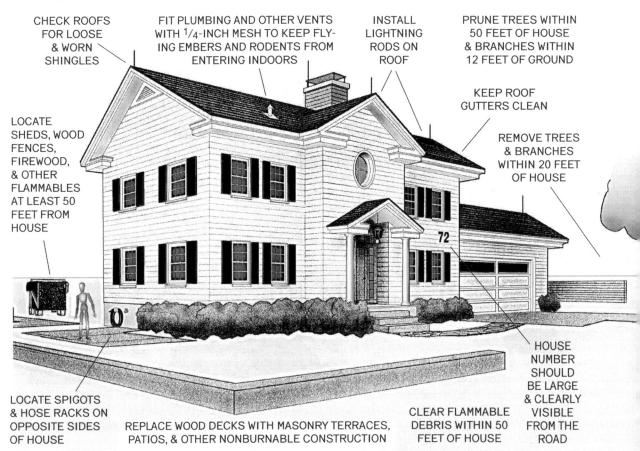

CHECK ROOFS FOR LOOSE & WORN SHINGLES

FIT PLUMBING AND OTHER VENTS WITH 1/4-INCH MESH TO KEEP FLYING EMBERS AND RODENTS FROM ENTERING INDOORS

INSTALL LIGHTNING RODS ON ROOF

PRUNE TREES WITHIN 50 FEET OF HOUSE & BRANCHES WITHIN 12 FEET OF GROUND

KEEP ROOF GUTTERS CLEAN

LOCATE SHEDS, WOOD FENCES, FIREWOOD, & OTHER FLAMMABLES AT LEAST 50 FEET FROM HOUSE

REMOVE TREES & BRANCHES WITHIN 20 FEET OF HOUSE

HOUSE NUMBER SHOULD BE LARGE & CLEARLY VISIBLE FROM THE ROAD

LOCATE SPIGOTS & HOSE RACKS ON OPPOSITE SIDES OF HOUSE

REPLACE WOOD DECKS WITH MASONRY TERRACES, PATIOS, & OTHER NONBURNABLE CONSTRUCTION

CLEAR FLAMMABLE DEBRIS WITHIN 50 FEET OF HOUSE

17. FOILING DISASTERS AROUND FACADES

18. "TUMBLING TUMBLEWEEDS" … MOBILE HOMES IN HIGH WINDS

☞ *If you live in a mobile home,* a violent disaster may make you pay dearly for your economical accommodations. These dwelling's shells are thin and light, their narrow widths make them tip over easily, and they are poorly connected to the ground. Most mobile homes have little more than leveling blocks fitted under their floors while a typical wood frame house is fastened to a concrete foundation with long thick anchor bolts every six linear feet, each of which ballasts the house with half a ton of weight.

B
FROM 98

TOP MOUNT

TURN-BUCKLE

BASE MOUNT

SIDE OF MOBILE HOME, SHED, ETC.

19. AUGER ANCHOR ASSEMBLY

THIS AUGER ANCHOR IS 30 IN. LONG

LEAVE 40 FEET OF SPACE BETWEEN TREES WITHIN 100 FEET OF HOUSE

REMOVE BRANCHES HANGING OVER DRIVEWAYS; IF THEY FALL DUE TO WIND OR FIRE THEY COULD BLOCK THE ROAD

There's no practical way a mobile home can duplicate this anchorage. A few *auger anchors* with cable tiedowns as sketched on the right can help in a stiff breeze; but if the part of the home that holds the bolt that holds the cable that holds the auger that holds the earth it is buried in has little holding power, the weakest link in this chain of structure could kill you when things get extreme. Better to fly like the wind into a storm cellar you've built on your property. If you live in a "park" whose mobile homes are clustered ten to the acre, you'll need to worry about your neighbors' homes blowing on you.

SURROUND BUILDING AS MUCH AS POSSIBLE WITH DRIVEWAYS, TURNAROUNDS, POOLS, & OTHER NONFLAMMABLE SURFACES

☞ *If you live in a multistory building* … Contact the manager and request that a professional engineer inspect the building's foundation, structure, and resistance to flooding. Since your escape route possibilities are fewer when you're many floors above the ground, your best route to safety may lie inward —to a small area deep in your domicile that is strong, has lots of shelves stocked with emergency supplies, and is away from windows that could shatter glass on you yet is near a window that receives light during the day. Know if your windows are openable. If so and you have a rope that will reach the ground, you can tie a bucket to its end and haul food and water up and waste down to emergency personnel.

Prepping your place of work

The rules for prepping homes also apply to commercial buildings. Every business, library, church, health club, or other building you regularly visit should have a disaster plan for its occupants. Though these facilities vary greatly in size and shape, investigate the following:

☞ How safe is the building from fire? Does every floor have fire alarms, evacuation routes, and fire exits? How easily can you read the exit signs? If anything isn't right, ask the building manager to correct it.

☞ How strong is the building's structure? If the beams and columns are concrete, look for cracks and reddish stains on their surfaces. This may indicate that the reinforcing in the concrete is rusting. Rusting, cracks, and corrosion can weaken a structure to the breaking point in a disaster.

☞ Would indoor air remain breathable in a power failure? Ask the building manager how the HVAC (heating, ventilation and cooling) system works. Ask about "fresh air intakes" and "return air ducts". Ask other occupants what they know about these things.

☞ Is the building low-rise (two or three floors reached by stairs) or high-rise (several or more stories reached by elevators)? If the power fails or a disaster damages an elevator, you may need to use the stairs to go up or down. Disabled occupants are especially endangered by this.

☞ Does the floorspace you occupy have an exterior wall with openable windows? Big buildings often have central floor areas with no access to outdoor light or air. If your building is like this, find out what auxiliary lighting its interior spaces have if the power fails.

☞ Does the building have an emergency shelter? Visit it. Note its facilities. Toilets? Sinks? Shower? First aid supplies? Tables for eating and reading? Floorspace and blankets for sleeping? What else does it have? Write it down.

☞ Does the building have adequate tools, a three-day supply of pure water, nonperishable food, towels, sheets, and blankets for an average number of occupants? Is everything easily accessible?

After you've made sure the building is safe and solid, assemble a team of knowledgeable coworkers and prepare a detailed *disaster preparation and recovery program* for your business that clarifies the nature of possible disasters that could happen (i.e. define the problem) and how to cope with them during and after they happen (i.e. define the solution). This should include:

☞ Emergency shelters, exits, and evacuation routes. This includes plans of every floor and exit signage that is visible from every area on each floor.

☞ An insurance policy. Know what it does and doesn't cover. Take photos or videos of the building inside and out from two or three different angles, keep records of construction and maintenance costs to establish the validity of the building's assessed value, and store this information along with your financial records and other important documents in a fireproof and waterproof container.

☞ Arrangements to pay employees, preferably in cash, if disaster strikes, in case banks are closed.

☞ Crisis communications that include (1) a public announcement intercom for broadcasting emergency information, weather updates, and advisories, and (2) phones that enable occupants to contact families and friends outside. Having a TV for news events is also a good idea.

☞ Plans and schedules that detail the orderly operation and maintenance of mechanical systems. This includes keeping indoor air supply and return vents unclogged and periodically replacing air filters.

☞ An area to conduct disaster recovery operations. This includes food prep counters, sleeping space, first aid area, tool closet, and supply storage. The staff may use these spaces for normal activities everyday, but they should be easily convertible if disaster strikes.

☞ Methods of continuing business activities.

☞ Training, testing, and drills. Conduct a practice session every two months during which the alarm activates at, say, ten minutes before lunch break, then everyone sets up facilities to eat lunch from the supply room and locates where they would sleep and bathe. Roll over supplies so none will be more than six months old.

☞ A method of implementing, managing, administrating, and periodically evaluating the program.

If a violent weather event is forecast within the next few days, do the following if you can …

☞ Clean drains, gutters and downspouts.

☞ Remove antennas and any loose objects from the roof.

☞ Bring in display racks, signs, and objects usually left outside. In severe weather this could include anything smaller than a refrigerator.

☞ Secure all loose objects, such as trash cans, signs, and outdoor furniture, that might get tossed around in strong winds.

☞ If the building has store windows or large panes of glass, (1) clear the area 12 feet inside the glass as much as possible, (2) cover the glass with shutters or plywood if you can, and (3) duct-tape large **X**s on the inside of each pane to reduce shattering.

The day before a disaster is expected, do the following …

☞ Clear desks, tables, and shelves of books and other small loose objects.

☞ Take down all loosely hung pictures, plaques, hanging plants, etc.

☞ Secure everything in boxes, drawers, or other sturdy containers on the lowest floor in the innermost part of the building.

☞ If you put anything in drawers, duct-tape them shut.

☞ Move furniture, computers, file cabinets, and the like at least 12 feet away from windows and skylights to avoid damage from shattering glass and water, and cover the furnishings with tarpaulins or plastic sheeting secured with ropes, bungee cords, or duct tape.

☞ If flooding is a threat, place everything on desks, tables, or counters or carry them to an upper floor.

☞ If time permits, make an inventory of all moved items to ease unpacking after the disaster passes.

☞ Disconnect all electrical equipment except refrigeration. If you leave, turn off the electrical system's master circuit breaker.

☞ Close all windows and draw the blinds, curtains, and drapes.

☞ If you own equipment that could be useful after the disaster passes, such as pumps and generators, notify local emergency management officials.

The safe room

This book emphasizes repeatedly that more important than having everything you may need in a disaster is having a safe place to store and use it all. For what good would it be to have all you would need if where you would store and use it is destroyed? Even more than having everything you may need, where you would keep it all must be virtually indestructible. If you live where earthquakes, tornadoes, and other impactful disasters could occur, this construction must be built like a bank vault to satisfy this criteria. In less threatening areas, three other kinds of construction may be satisfactory, which are described below.

Another factor that influences a safe room's construction is a disaster's *duration*: how long it may last. An earthquake may last only a few seconds, a tornado a few minutes, a hurricane half a day, a chemical spill a day or more, a blizzard two days, and nuclear fallout for possibly years. And after the disaster passes you may be trapped until help arrives. The longer this total time may be, the larger your shelter must be for you to eat, sleep, bathe, go to the bathroom, and engage in other life-maintaining activities in reasonable comfort until rescuers can extricate you.

20. ENTRANCE TO A SAFEROOM [14]

Although disasters can happen while you are at work, on the road, or elsewhere away from home, if you have one safe room to build, think of your home first; because about 80 percent of the time you'll either be home or have enough warning to go home before the disaster arrives, and in your home you have more control over the preparations you may make.

Two disasters where a safe room is *not* a safe place to hide are *floods* and *wildfires*. If your property could be flooded, seeking shelter in the bowels of your house could lead you to drown. In a wildfire, if high temperatures don't fry you, lack of oxygen due to the fire consuming it could asphyxiate you.

The construction of your safe room or similar sanctuary has two aspects, **space** and **shell** …

Space … the floor area you and your party will need to cope with the disaster depending on its duration. *Quick disasters* require at least 5 square feet per sheltered person. *Long disasters* should have 10 to 15 square feet per person.

Shell … the strength of the construction enclosing the floor area depending on the disaster's severity. For *low-impact disasters* (power outages, snowfall, chemical spillages, etc.) strong wood construction may suffice. For *high-impact disasters* (ones that can crush or sweep away your house) you need 10-inch thick reinforced concrete below, around, and above.

Regarding high-impact disasters, a serious issue should be addressed that FEMA, Texas Tech, and related authorities have failed to consider. These officials say a high-impact disaster shelter must be built to withstand 250-mile-an-hour winds (i.e. F5 tornadoes). This criteria deludes you into thinking you are building something that is strong enough when it is not —as proven by this scary tale aired on Channel 2 after the tornado that struck Moore, Oklahoma, in May 2013, where a woman said ...

> "When I heard the siren, I had to decide whether my small son and I would hide in the bathroom or jump in the car and drive away from the tornado's path. I decided to drive away. When I returned, our house was demolished, and the tornado had lifted a metal dumpster and dropped it on the bathroom and crushed it. If we had hidden there, we would have been killed."

Obviously the chief criteria for constructing a high-impact safe room is NOT high winds, but a three-ton weight being dropped from fifty feet above. If you need further proof of this power, go to YouTube ➜ http://www.weather.com/video/tornado-picks-up-debris-near-dallas-26761, and watch thirty-foot truck trailers being tossed 90 feet into the sky like kleenex in a breeze, one of which appears on the right (this photo is blurry because it was taken directly from the video). THIS is the force a high-impact safe room must resist to be *truly safe* for you and your loved ones. Do this, and the high-wind requirement will vanish in a breeze.

Particularly important —and often overlooked— in such construction are *strong ceilings* and *strong corners*. If done professionally as described below, this work will cost *less*, not more, and be safe besides. Any construction that isn't strong enough will be a waste of money no matter how little was spent in building it.

21. THAT'S A TRUCK TRAILER BEING TOSSED INTO THE SKY BY A TORNADO [15]

Four important aspects of designing and building safe rooms are as follows ...

1. Although nearly every part of this book is written to be "family friendly" so a ten-year-old can read and discuss what its pages advise, this section is not. The directives on the next eleven pages can be described only in the technical and visual language *that will enable professional designers and builders to construct what you may need.* Hence these pages are written and drawn not so much so you can understand them but so you can take them to a professional designer or builder and say, "This is what I want." As a first step you might take these pages to a building contractor

22.[16]

and go through them line by line and ask what each unfamiliar term is. You don't know what pea gravel is? Ask. You don't know what toggle bolts or cellular metal decking are? Ask. Afterwards, pay your mentor a fee for the time s/he spent educating you.

2. A safe room should not be a place to hide when a disaster strikes and otherwise be unusable for normal living activities. A few spaces in most houses that could nicely double as a safe room are a den, TV room, dining room with a kitchen and bathroom close by, and a large walk-in closet off the master bedroom. Who is to know that behind such a room's attractive decor may lurk ten inches of solid reinforced concrete? Every domicile is different, and you can take these ideas where your imagination leads you and your pocketbook lets you.

3. In addition to protecting a family during such major disasters as earthquakes and hurricanes, a safe room should also protect occupants from such comparatively minor disruptions as burglaries, assaults, and other break-ins. Such spaces should have …

- A hidden entrance door, such as behind a bookcase or closet, under a staircase, etc. This portal should be solid sheet steel, kevlar, or similar material that can't be kicked in or shot through, and it should have at least two strongbox locks that fit into stronger frames.
- A phone, so you can call 911, with its wires located underground so they can't be cut outside.
- TV surveillance cameras outside. These can be patched into your TV set, then you can tell 911 what the intruder looks like, what s/he is wearing, and if s/he is armed.
- A safe or locked drawer for important papers. These include bank statements, social security and credit card numbers, passports (these sell on the street for close to a thousand dollars these days), plus credit card statements, and blank checks (all gold mines for identity thieves). A list of documents you should have appears on page 64.

4. A safe room needn't look like the inside of a jail cell. One can be made to look attractive in many ways, one example being the luxury bunker that appears in figure 23 on the opposite page.

Structurally speaking, there are four general kinds of disaster shelters, as follows …

Interior enclosures for low-impact disasters … If you don't live in such crisis corridors as Tornado Alley in the Midwest, the hurricane belt along the East and Gulf Coasts, the seismic zones of the Pacific Rim, or in hills where landslides can occur, you may need to do little more than partition an interior part of your abode so you will be safe until things return to normal. In fact, for many citizens the most common "disaster" is a blackout —like the Northeast blackout in August 2003 that left 55 million people without power

23.[17]

for up to three days. These occurrences are caused by public utility malfunctions, traffic accidents, storms, and the like that bring down power lines, depressurize plumbing systems, frustrate cell-phoning, shut down gas stations, and in other ways leave families helpless without their needing to burrow into cavelike enclosures to be safe. Many people also don't have the space or funds to construct a vaultlike sanctuary on their property. If this choice appeals to you, consider doing the following …

☞ Select an area that includes part of the kitchen and a nearby bathroom, or install near a bathroom a compact kitchen unit like the one appearing on the previous page. Include in this space plenty of shelves, a table for the family to sit at, a pantry, and beds or cots to sleep on.

☞ Install cabinets and shelves everywhere you can fit them. Much useful space usually exists high against the walls above doors and windows.

☞ Include an openable window or two to provide ample daylight and ventilation.

☞ Consider a heat source in regions of cold winter weather. Heat sources are covered on pages 38 to 44. This space's construction needn't be strong, but it should be cocooned in thick insulation.

☞ Include duct tape, caulking (and a caulking gun), and clear plastic sheeting (and a stapler) in case you need to seal the perimeters of windows, doors, and vents in the shell construction.

Strong wood framing for medium-impact disasters … If severe thunderstorms, mild tornadoes, inland hurricanes, and the like could tear away your roof or exterior finish or topple a tree on your house, you may want to strengthen the construction around a bathroom, walk-in closet, or other small

28

room on the lowest level of your house as described below, provided the area isn't subject to flooding. If so, strip the outer finish from the room's walls, then strengthen them as sketched in figure 24 and texted below. If you don't understand some of this construction, have a professional help you.

1. Anchor the base plate, typically a 2 x 4 beneath the base of the studs, to solid concrete below with anchor bolts or hurricane ties. This should keep the room from ripping off its foundation.
2. Double the studs all around. Where plumbing is between two studs, double both on the side away from the pipes. Glue each new stud to the old with panel adhesive, then screw-gun the two studs together with $2^5/_8$-inch drywall screws vertically spaced 12 inches apart on each side.
3. If no plumbing exists between two studs, cover the inside of each void between the studs with tarpaper. This includes the top of the bottom plate, the sides of the studs, and the wall surface between the studs. This will keep the wood from decaying when it contacts the cement after you've done the step below.

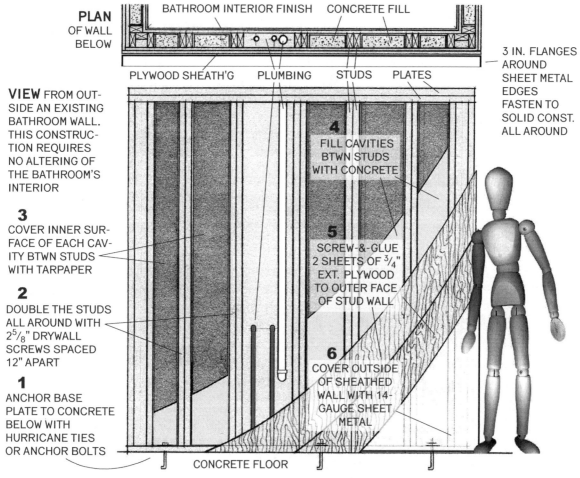

24. STRONG WOOD FRAMING FOR MEDIUM-IMPACT DISASTERS

4. Fill the spaces between the pairs of studs with no plumbing between them as follows. Nail 24-inch-high strips of plywood against the studs' bottoms and fill the cavities behind with concrete containing pea-gravel aggregate. Two days later reinstall the plywood 22 inches higher (the bottom two inches should overlap the hardened concrete below), again fill the cavities behind, and do this four times until a 6 to 8-inch space remains between the top of the plywood form and the underside of the top plate. In this space trowel in the final concrete.

5. Screw-and-glue $^3/_4$-inch sheets of exterior-grade plywood (*not* OSB) to the studs' outsides. Apply panel adhesive to the outer edges of each stud and plate, then screw the plywood to the studs and plates with $1^5/_8$-inch drywall screws spaced 24 inches apart, then screw-and-glue a second sheet of plywood to the first with $2^5/_8$-inch drywall screws 12 inches apart. Overlap all vertical seams.

6. Against the plywood install sheets of 14-gauge sheet steel with 3-inch flanges on the bottoms, tops, and the outer sides that will fasten to solid construction all around.

7. Install a steel solid-core door in a steel doorframe, and add two deadbolt locks that are operable from both sides.

8. When you're done, notify the local fire department so they'll know where to find you if disaster traps you inside.

This construction is kick-proof, ram-proof, and largely bullet-proof, and the concrete between the studs will keep the room from crushing if a tree falls on it. The room's interior finishes can also remain untouched and useable during this construction, a big plus when converting an existing bathroom.

Garage storm shelters for high-impact disasters of short duration ...

This construction will protect you from strong tornados, hurricanes, earthquakes, and other violent disasters briefly until rescuers arrive. These shelters are sheet steel containers about 4 feet wide, 6 feet long, and 5 feet deep that are installed in the floor of a garage, and they contain benches that can seat up to six people with room underneath to store food, water, blankets, first-aid kit, radio, flashlights, batteries, and a bathroom bucket with a tight lid. This construction is excellent for high-impact disasters of short duration, and is installed by companies who specialize in this work as follows. (1) A worker with a diamond-tipped power saw cuts a rectangular hole in the floor just inside the garage door. (2) A small backhoe removes the rectangle of concrete, excavates a cavity in the earth below, and lowers the sheet metal shelter into the cavity. (3) Concrete is poured into the space between the shelter and the surrounding earth and a sliding steel door is mounted on top. This labor takes about eight hours.

WIDTH ≈ 4 FT
LENGTH ≈ 8 FT
OUTLINE OF STEPS INSIDE
OUTLINE OF BENCHES INSIDE
HT ≈ 6 FT

25.[18]
GARAGE STORM SHELTER

Afterward, paint every interior surface white so the shelter's interior is as reflective as possible. Several other important details are described in the Youtube videos below.

Younker.coma/watch?v=Taghlik
Younker.coma/watch?v=Nekoma

Concrete vaults for high-impact disasters of long duration ... If you live in Tornado Alley or are threatened by hurricanes, earthquakes, landslides, explosions, or other high-impact disasters and want maximum protection, the next six pages are for you. Look a moment at figure 26 on the right. That 2 x 6 went right though an exterior wall and a refrigerator. You wouldn't want to meet a missile like that head-on in a serious disaster.

If a safe room must be built like a bank vault to protect you, a good way to build it is the way bank vaults are built —of thick reinforced concrete. Since this construction is heavy, it should rest on the ground. Any higher and it will cost *much* more to build the substructure needed to support it. To locate a safe room on the ground, have a set of plans of the parent building and first retain the services of a soil engineer to examine the earth below. If the building's lowest floor is concrete, rent a small jackhammer or masonry saw and remove a small part of the floor so the engineer can drill a hole

26.¹⁹

in the soil with a power auger and remove a soil test boring from 4 to 6 feet down. You want strong soil under your safe room walls, since every linear foot may weigh 1,500 pounds. Most clayey and rocky soils will support this weight, but you want to be sure. If the soil is weak, you will need a wider footing under the walls.

Whatever size a safe room may be, its floor area should not be square but a rectangle. If you need 144 square feet, don't make it 12 x 12 feet; make it something like 8 x 18 feet. The shorter span is the direction the ceiling structure should run, and the shorter this is the stronger and cheaper the ceiling is to build. For example, if the ceiling spans 8 feet and is reinforced concrete, it must be 10 inches deep to resist the impact of a serious disaster; but if it spans 12 feet it must be 15 inches deep to be equally as strong, which means more

TWO PLAN SHAPES OF EQUAL AREA:

SQUARE

144 SQ FT
SHORTER SPAN = 12 FEET
12 FT
12 FT

IN THE SQUARE PLAN THE SHORTER CEILING SPAN IS 12 FEET, WHICH MUST BE 15 IN. DEEP TO RESIST A SERIOUS DISASTER

RECTANGLE

144 SQ FT
SHORTER SPAN = 8 FEET
8 FT
18 FT

IN THE RECTANGULAR PLAN THE SHORTER CEILING SPAN IS 8 FEET, WHICH MUST BE ONLY 10 IN. DEEP TO BE EQUALLY AS STRONG AS THE 12 FOOT SPAN

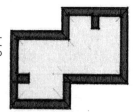

THE MORE CORNERS & FINS, THE STRONGER THE SHAPE

27. ECONOMICAL PLAN SHAPES

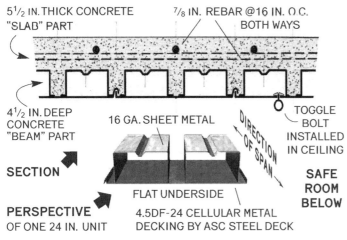

5½ IN. THICK CONCRETE "SLAB" PART

⅞ IN. REBAR @16 IN. O.C. BOTH WAYS

4½ IN. DEEP CONCRETE "BEAM" PART

16 GA. SHEET METAL

DIRECTION OF SPAN

TOGGLE BOLT INSTALLED IN CEILING

SECTION

SAFE ROOM BELOW

PERSPECTIVE OF ONE 24 IN. UNIT

FLAT UNDERSIDE

4.5DF-24 CELLULAR METAL DECKING BY ASC STEEL DECK

28. HOW TO CONSTRUCT THE CEILING

materials used and more money spent. A rectangular room can be made even stronger by dividing it into smaller rectangles that create more corners, which are stronger than straight walls, and extending fins from the walls as appears in figure 27. These shapes also give you more flexibility when trying to find the best place for this room in a building.

As for a safe room's ceiling, a fine way to build it both strongly and economically appears in figure 28 above. This is a reinforced concrete slab-and-beam structure whose concrete is poured onto lengths of formed sheet metal called *cellular metal decking*. The slab on top is $5\frac{1}{2}$ inches thick and reinforced with $\frac{7}{8}$-inch steel bars (known as #7 rebars) located 16 inches apart in both directions. The row of little beams below are $4\frac{1}{2}$ inches deep and reinforced by the steel deck around them, which conveniently acts as formwork while the concrete is being poured. If this floor is 10 inches deep and spans 8 feet, it will support more than 400 pounds per square foot and be virtually impenetrable. From the decking's flat underside you can also hang eyebolts and hooks for holding lights, shelves, and other useful objects from the ceiling.

A vital part of this structure is where two walls meet at a corner. All horizontal rebars must *continue through the corner*. They should never end at a corner, or the structure will not have the "seam strength" to resist the mightiest tornados and earthquakes. If the ends of two rebars must meet at a corner, reinforce them with *L-bars*: L-shaped rebars with 16-inch legs that tie to the rebar ends on each side, as sketched in figure 29 below. The same continuous reinforcing must connect the walls' bottoms to the floor and their tops to the ceiling.

In addition to being strong, a safe room should be fairly comfortable. One, it needs ventilating, so if several people must remain inside a few days they won't deplete the air of oxygen. A way to vent the space is to mount in opposite

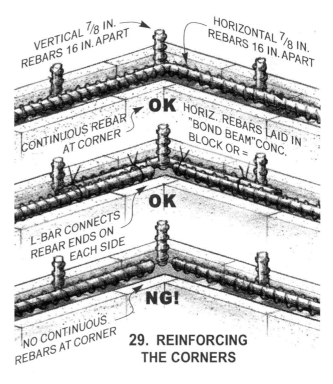

VERTICAL ⅞ IN. REBARS 16 IN. APART

HORIZONTAL ⅞ IN. REBARS 16 IN. APART

CONTINUOUS REBAR AT CORNER

OK HORIZ. REBARS LAID IN "BOND BEAM" CONC. BLOCK OR =

OK

L-BAR CONNECTS REBAR ENDS ON EACH SIDE

NG!

NO CONTINUOUS REBARS AT CORNER

29. REINFORCING THE CORNERS

walls short lengths of 8-inch-diameter steel pipe with elbows on the outside that turn down to keep debris from entering them. This $1/2$-inch thick steel pipe almost surely won't be crushed if heavy debris falls on it. Two, the room should have openings in its shell that allow some light to enter or the space will be dark during the day, and the less you use candles or batteries the better. One way to let light enter is to mount an 8 x 8 inch glass block every 8 linear feet at face height along the walls. To maximize light reflection inside, paint the walls and ceiling white and cover the floor with white ceramic tile. Three, in humid weather a safe room enclosed in thick concrete may be prey to mildew. If so, install a dehumidifier on the floor (if located any higher it will remove little moisture from levels below). When the utility power is on, this machine will keep musty microbes from spoiling stored foods, clothing, leather, and anything made of paper. From the humidifier's collection tank run a small hose to a nearby floor drain, another utility installation every safe room should have. Every safe room must also have an entrance door, a good choice being a 24-inch-wide solid-core metal door mounted in a metal frame. Mount it in the wall facing northwest, as this is the side least likely to be piled with debris in a tornado.

Now that we've covered the generalities, let's get to the specifics —most importantly, where you should locate a safe room in a house? You already know it should be on the ground and higher than a nearby body of water. There are three good places in most houses where this room can be built: a *basement, crawl-space*, or *concrete slab on grade*. Let's consider these possibilities.

A *basement*'s outer walls between the footing and the first floor are likely 8- to 10-inch-thick poured concrete or concrete blocks that contain little steel reinforcing, which will not support the kind of ceiling a safe room should have. The solution? Build a second concrete wall inside the first. The second wall need be only 8 inches thick if built next to the first, but its reinforcing should always be $7/8$-inch rebars placed 16 inches apart horizontally *and* vertically. Any open wall built on a basement floor should be 10 inches thick and contain the same reinforcing, as appears in figure 30 below.

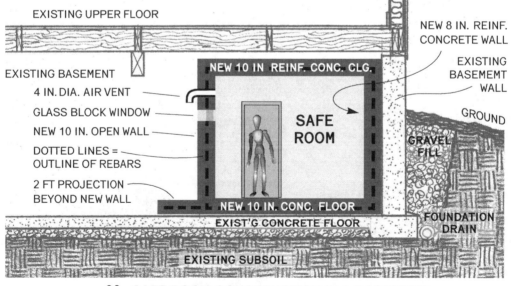

30. SAFE ROOM CONSTRUCTION IN A BASEMENT

Another crucial dimension is a basement's clear floor-to-ceiling height. Though this is normally about 96 inches, a safe room's clear height needs to be *only 80 inches*. If a safe room's floor and ceiling structure are only 10 inches thick you can fit a room this high, including its floor and ceiling, within the open height of a normal basement. If the basement has a concrete floor (typically 4 inches thick), rather than dig it up, build on top an 8-inch concrete floor with $7/8$-inch rebars spaced 16 inches both ways. The combined 12-inch concrete floor will almost always support a safe room's heavy walls. As you can see in figure 31 below, the 8-inch floor on top should extend two feet beyond the safe room walls except where a wall abuts an existing basement wall. If the safe room's walls are 80 inches high, enough room should exist above to construct a 10-inch thick ceiling under the basement ceiling. If you don't have room to do the construction, you can remove the floor joists above and raise the safe room's ceiling until its top aligns with the floor above and finish its top with ceramic floor tile, or reframe the wood floor as it was before.

If a dwelling's lowest level is a ***crawl space***, its first floor will likely be 18 to 30 inches above the ground and supported by perimeter walls of concrete and a few central piers. A tornado, hurricane, or earthquake can push the whole house off this flimsy foundation. But you can locate the crushproof box prescribed for basements inside this foundation, partly inside and outside, or against it outside. Wherever you place it, do not block any of the vents mounted in the crawlspace walls (the crawlspace is kept dry by air flowing through these openings). If the safe room is inside, its ceiling may be 4 or 5 feet above the dwelling's first floor, which may leave enough room above for a loft or storage under the existing ceiling.

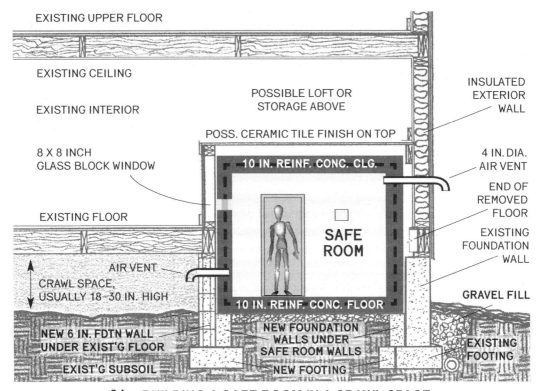

31. BUILDING A SAFE ROOM IN A CRAWL SPACE

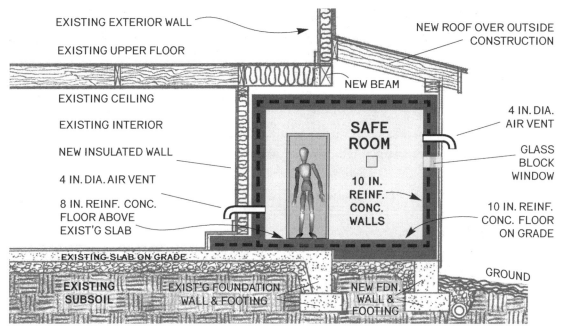

EXISTING EXTERIOR WALL

EXISTING UPPER FLOOR

NEW ROOF OVER OUTSIDE CONSTRUCTION

EXISTING CEILING

EXISTING INTERIOR

NEW INSULATED WALL

4 IN. DIA. AIR VENT

8 IN. REINF. CONC. FLOOR ABOVE EXIST'G SLAB

NEW BEAM

SAFE ROOM

10 IN. REINF. CONC. WALLS

4 IN. DIA. AIR VENT

GLASS BLOCK WINDOW

10 IN. REINF. CONC. FLOOR ON GRADE

EXISTING SLAB ON GRADE

GROUND

EXISTING SUBSOIL

EXIST'G FOUNDATION WALL & FOOTING

NEW FDN. WALL & FOOTING

32. SAFE ROOM CONSTRUCTION PARTLY ON A SLAB AND PARTLY OUTDOORS

If the existing dwelling's lowest level is a ***concrete slab on grade***, you could locate the safe room inside, outside, or even partly inside and outside. Since the last possibility is the most complicated, it is sketched in figure 32 above. From this drawing a contractor will know how to construct a safe room either inside or outside the dwelling or in between. Locate the entry door so you can enter from indoors.

If you have no practical place to put a safe room in your house, you could build it outdoors, per-haps 40 feet behind the house. Here it must be protected from the weather. You could do this by gussying up its exterior until it looks as inviting as a children's playhouse, as on the right. The curtained windows are faux.

If you have the funds and the space, you may want to build the "luxury suite" that appears in fig-ure 34 on the opposite page. This construction includes adequate

33. COULD THIS BE A SAFE ROOM? [20]

OUTER CONST. OF 10 IN. THICK REINFORCED CONC.

CHAMFERED CORNERS ARE STRONGER THAN SQUARE ONES

FLUE

TWO OR THREE BUNK BEDS & STORAGE UNDER LOWEST BUNK

WOOD STOVE

DEEP FL-CLG SHELVES

8 X 8 IN. GLASS BLOCK WINDOWS

LADDER TO UPPER BUNKS

CENTRAL FLOOR DRAIN

PLUMBING FOR KITCHEN SINK & BATHROOM

SHOWER, TOILET, & SINK

DEEP FLOOR-TO-CEILING SHELVES

SOLID-CORE METAL ENTRY DOOR W/ 3 DEAD-BOLT LOCKS

CURTAIN DOORS

CLOSET

TABLE & FOUR CHAIRS

4-IN. STEEL PIPE AIR VENT WITH ELBOWS TURNED DOWN TO OUTDOORS

CABINETS OVER KITCHENETTE

FLOOR PLAN: 8 × 18 FT   SCALE

0   1   2   4 FT   8

34. THE SAFE ROOM "LUXURY SUITE"

space and every furnishing you would need in nearly any disaster.

If you build a new home, you can do everything correctly from the start. But logistically it isn't possible for every family to vacate their existing abodes and build new homes with safe rooms. Thus governments, designers, and builders must strive to make *existing* homes safe for disasters —which is what this book recommends. How much would all this construction cost? There are so many variables, depending on where you live, local cost of materials, and local wages for construction workers, that the best way to get a handle on this is to discuss the situation with a few local contractors.

Now let's fill this sanctuary with what you will need in a disaster.

Furnishing the safe room

Since every person and property is different and since many disasters often occur only in certain areas, with every advisory in these pages you may want to prioritize it as *must have, should have,* or *nice to have.* As a sample, in every disaster you *must have* clean water, you *should have* a manual can opener, and it would *nice to have* a nuclear radiation detector on your keychain.

Water … Even more than food you need water. Your body needs it more, and much food is inedible without it. Plan to have two gallons per person per day for drinking, preparing food, and hygienic acts as washing your face and brushing your teeth. On pages 159 to 171 this book describes the five different kinds of water, how to conserve pure water, how to purify dirty water, and how to wash the dishes, clean your clothes, bathe, and flush toilets when you have no power or pure water.

You can store water in jugs or bottles that have been thoroughly washed and rinsed (make sure you clean inside the cap). Fill each to the very top, tightly close the cap, add a label with the date, store in a cool dark place, and replace every six months. Don't reservoir pure water in glass containers (they are heavy and can break), cardboard containers (they leak and aren't made for long-term storage), or milk or fruit juice containers (milk proteins and fruit sugars cannot be completely removed from the cardboard and will promote bacterial growth in water stored in them).

SUCKING END

35.[21]

DIPPING END

If your faucets fail and you have stored no pure water, know where the nearest creeks, ponds, or other water sources are (hopefully a short walk away) so you can collect what you need with a few buckets. Two effective water purifiers are *iodine tablets* and *unscented chlorinated bleach*. But anyone who's ever seen a **lifestraw personal water filter** in action will never forget it. This plastic tube is about one inch thick and seven inches long, looks like a thick soda straw and works like one too. You stick the bottom end into muddy water, then suck on the top and your mouth fills with pure water. Can't get simpler than this! This device has prevented the spread of water-borne diseases in developing countries for several years. One tube filters up to 250 gallons of water.[16] Considering the cylinder's price, that's about ten cents for a gallon of water. If the water contains debris, strain it first through a T-shirt folded twice over.

Food ... If a disaster is on the way, don't wait till the last day to buy food, or you may find only cans of creamed corn on the shelves. Buy it early, store a month's supply in a dry cool dark place, write the storage date on each container, and check and replenish regularly. Rotate them "first in, first out" so what you eat will be fresher. If you select a can or sealed package that has a "USE BY" date which has expired, this doesn't mean the food is unsafe to eat, only that its flavor and nutritional quality may be reduced. A few more tips...

☞ Eat high-calorie foods that are protein-rich and help build energy.
☞ Buy drinks that are prepackaged or in plastic bottles, and buy food in foil packets and foil-lined boxes. Avoid foods that are commercially dehydrated or sold in glass bottles (they can break) or large cans (after opening them and using a small amount the remaining contents can spoil).
☞ Avoid metal containers that may corrode and give their contents a bad taste.
☞ Select foods that require no refrigeration, little preparation or cooking, and little or no water.
☞ Keep foods in small containers or ones that hold one-meal supplies.
☞ Keep foods that could be eaten by mice and bugs in coolers or other large containers.

In figure 36 on the opposite page appears a pantry of foods you should stock up on well before a disaster comes knocking on your door. Most of them you can eat every day, but don't let your larder get below about two-thirds full as you chow them down. To read how to prepare food in a disaster, see pages 162 to 166.

You and your party will also need cookware and dinnerware. If you have the items appearing in figure 37 on page 38 you can serve breakfasts, lunches, and dinners whose delectability will be limited not by the severity of a disaster but by your ability as a chef. Many items may already be in your kitchen. Wherever they are, arrange them closely together in a strong place so you can use them easily in a small area.

Dry Foods

SALT & PEPPER
CEREALS
SUGAR
NUTS
FLOUR
MILKS
PASTAS
POPCORN

CORN MEAL
TEAS & COFFEES
RICE
OATS
BEANS
SPICES
RAISINS & OTHER DRIED FRUITS

Imperishables

TRAIL MIX
SOY SAUCE
CHOCOLATE SYRUP
VINEGAR
COOKING OIL
LEMON JUICE
PICKLES
PEANUT BUTTER

JERKY
POWER BARS
CURED SAUSAGE
JAMS & JELLIES

Canned Foods

JUICES
FRUITS
OLIVES
TUNA
SARDINES
SOUPS
TOMATOES

MRE (Meal Ready to Eat) full meal kits   Food rations for military and emergency relief activities. Buyable online, they are precooked, easy to open, and can be eaten after boiling in water for five minutes. If kept off the ground in a dry cool place they can last three to five years.

Dehydrated & freeze-dried foods   Meats, vegetables, and desserts from which most of the water is removed to reduce their volume and packaged in sealed containers that will last for years.

36. A PANTRY OF DISASTER FOODS

MECHANICAL CAN OPENER

CORKSCREW

"CHURCH KEY" BOTTLE OPENER

SCOURING PADS

PANCAKE TURNER, TO FLIP FOOD & FISH THINGS FROM FIRES. METAL ONES ARE STRONGER & WON'T MELT OR BURN

MEAT TENDERIZER, THIS ONE CAN PRY OPEN SHELLFISH & PULVERIZE NUTS

SWISS ARMY KNIFE SMALL & VERSATILE: WHAT YOU WANT IN A SURVIVAL KITCHEN

GRATER, FOR CHEESES, NUTS, & OTHER HARD FOODS

FLAME-RESISTANT HOT PADS

FISH SCALER THIS ONE IS MADE FROM A BOTTLECAP

EGG BEATER, TO FOODS, RE-MOVE CLOROX ODOR FROM WATER, ETC.

WOK, COOKS LOTS OF FOOD WITH LITTLE HEAT

PAPER CUPS & PLATES, PLUS PLASTIC UTENSILS

GRILLE

CHEESECLOTH, MANY CLEVER USES

SIEVES, COARSE, MEDIUM, & FINE

PRESSURE COOKER THIS AIRTIGHT CON-TAINER COOKS FOOD MORE QUICKLY WITH LESS FUEL

MEASURING CUPS & SPOONS

PLASTIC WRAP, WAX PAPER, ZIP-LOK BAGS, & TIN FOIL

37. A CABINET OF DISASTER COOKWARE

Heat source … In cold weather you need heat to keep warm, and in any weather you need it to cook food. Have more than one source, since none will work in every disaster. Here are the possibilities …

☞ *Gas stove* … This works when the power fails, unless the gas is supplied by a public utility and the disaster severs the supply main. Better may be a gas stove with a periodically filled tank of propane or other fuel gas located on the property.

☞ *Electric range* … Useless when the power fails.

☞ *Countertop gas stove* … These have two burners and sit on a noncombustible counter. They typically run on propane or other fuel gas and have instant-start ignition. Some have an oven below the burners that you can open to warm the room. These stoves are made for cooking outdoors in camps, so do not use one in a tightly closed space indoors, but some shelter is desirable because a draft or a breeze can blow out the flame. A popular model is the Camp Chef Ranger (figure 38). This stove cooks for five hours on a one-pound container of propane, which

38. CAMP TABLE STOVE[22]

should be stored six feet away. A five-pound jug lasts about two weeks. Have a professional install it unless you are familiar with adapters, hoses, regulators, and connectors.

☞ *Sterno stove* … This petite heater can be taken anywhere. You can also slip a pocket-size can of sterno fuel into an empty tin can like the two on the right. Poke holes around the tops and bottoms of the can's side with a can opener.

39.

☞ *Kerosene heater* … Though these are portable they are hard to cook on, are dangerously hot, emit a greasy odor, and need lots of ventilation. Never add fuel to a kerosene heater when hot, keep it from flammable objects, and have an ABC Class fire extinguisher close by.

☞ *Fireplace* … When the power fails this is a versatile heating and cooking source. It provides light at night, you can burn paper so you heat and clean at the same time, and in front of it you can dry wet clothes and build your morale. But creating a fireplace usually begins with creating the house. If you do this, make the firebox high, wide, and shallow, like the colonial kitchen fireplaces, and locate a crane high on one side to hold kettles over the fire (one of these hearths appears on page 96). If your home has a typical fireplace that is about a yard high, wide, and deep, you can set a pair of andirons on the hearth and lay a grate on top for grilling. But such a hearth is only about 20 percent efficient. Fireplace inserts bump this up to 50 to 60 percent, plus you can close the damper at night which keeps a lot of heat from flowing up the chimney; but inserts are hard to cook on.

☞ *Woodstove* … This hearth is less costly and more efficient than a fireplace, even one with an insert. Best is a cast iron model with a flat top you can cook on and glass doors in front so you can enjoy the flames. In a house with so-called "airtight" construction, a fireplace or woodstove should have an outdoor vent that brings fresh air to the hearth. Otherwise the fire could deprive the air indoors —and you— of oxygen.

Whatever heater or cooker you use, never burn charcoal in it unless it is outdoors. Charcoal emits deadly carbon monoxide —and it takes more than a draft of air blowing through a slightly open window to remove it. Failure to do this is why one victim in our grim list died "of carbon monoxide poisoning from a charcoal grill she was using in her home."

40. A WOODSTOVE YOU CAN COOK ON[23]

☞ *Solar cooker* … About all these devices do is throw a few sunrays into a box —highly inefficient, and often expensive. But a *parabolic dish* theoretically focuses the sun's rays onto a small area which becomes very hot. To test this theory, I made a parabolic dish by dividing its shape into eight octagonal parts, cutting each part out of art board, rubber-cementing aluminum foil onto one side, and assembling them as in figure 41. The dish is 28 inches across and 13 inches deep. The four wires extending from the rim hold the slightly floppy shape together and create a crosshair center that casts a shadow on the dish's "hot spot" which makes it easy to aim it at the sun. Late one sunny morning I took this burner out for a test drive. In the dish's base I mounted a paint can on a wire stand to serve as a frying pan (this appears in figure 61 on page 54), cracked an egg in the pan, and waited. A minute later a cloud passed over the sun and shut the thing down. Five minutes later the sun returned. Another five minutes later the egg yolk began to turn white. Another cloud came. A minute later a gust of wind blew the stove over, egg, pan and all. This is reality TV, folks. At this point I had performed enough onsite research to know that if I ever want to fry an egg, heat a cup of tea, or warm my fingers, I can do it cheaper with a can of sterno fuel ($4 compared to $31 for art board, rubber cement, and foil) and can use it any hour of the day, outdoors or indoors, and in rain sleet, snow, and the dark of night.

**41.
THE ILL-FATED SOLAR STOVE**

☞ *Campfire* … If you're roughing it in the rubble, this heat source may be your only choice. Since one typically builds this with materials found onsite just after a disaster has occurred, its construction is described on page 154 in the *Just After* section of this book.

Every heat source needs fuel, such as electricity, gases like propane and butane, maybe solar and kerosene, and firewood. Since you will likely gather, store, and prepare your own firewood, here are some pointers on how to do this effectively …

Make sure this fuel is seasoned and not green. Some texts say you should cure firewood for six months. Not true: it takes a *year* and six months for wood to be dry enough to ignite quickly. If it is green you will split it and re-split it into pieces nearly as thin as knitting needles before it will catch fire. After six months the pieces can be a half inch thick, but the fire will smoke and sputter before the flames take hold. After a year and six months the pieces can be an inch thick and in hardly the time it takes to strike a match the wood will sprout with flames. Softwoods (pines and other woods with needles) are best for starting a fire, and hardwoods (oaks and other woods with leaves) create hotter and longer-lasting coals. As for storing firewood, don't stack the logs against the house (this fosters mold and makes it easy for termites and other destructive bugs to enter the building). If the facade behind is masonry, this may get rid of the bugs but not the mold. Stack the logs several inches above the ground so the lowest logs won't rot, brace the ends so the logs won't roll down, and protect the wood from rain with a tarp or weighted tarpaper that won't blow away. Picture please? Figure 42 on the opposite page.

41

Wood also needs a means of lighting it. The quickest way to make a flame is a match. Three common kinds are *book matches* (these are mounted in a tiny folder and are usually free where cigarets are sold; keep a few books in a waterproof bag), *fireplace matches* (these are several inches long so you can thrust one under a stack of kindling without burning your fingers), and *safety matches* (these have half the ignition chemicals in the head and half in a sandpapery striker patch on the box). On a box of safety matches keep the striker patch dry or the matches will be worthless. You can waterproof a match by dipping its head a half inch into melted paraffin (candle wax). The match will also burn brighter and longer after it's lit. A clever way to start a fire with no matches at all is to hold a 9-volt flashlight battery's terminals against a piece of fine steel wool. The steel wool burns brightly and will ignite a cottonball or piece of newspaper if you blow on it. To witness this arson in action, visit www.youtube.com/watch?v=mj-jejT_QbeY.

Anytime you have a fire, you must have a method of extinguishing it. Chief possibilities are water and fire extinguishers, as appear on the next page …

PROTECT TOP WITH WEIGHTED TARPAPER THAT WON'T BLOW AWAY

DON'T STACK NEXT TO HOUSE

BRACE ENDS SO LOGS WON'T ROLL DOWN

EXPOSE ENDS OF LOGS TO SUN & AIR

STACK ABOVE GROUND SO AIR CAN CIRCULATE BELOW & PREVENT ROT

42. STACKING FIREWOOD

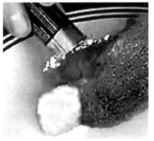
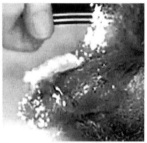

1 PRESS BATTERY INTO FINE STEEL WOOL —SPARKS APPEAR

2 LAY COTTON ON SPARKS & BLOW UNTIL COTTON BURSTS INTO FLAME

STARTING A FIRE WITH A 9-VOLT BATTERY

SAFETY MATCHES

WATERPROOF MATCHES
THE PART BEHIND THE HEAD IS SLIGHTLY DARKER

BOOK MATCHES

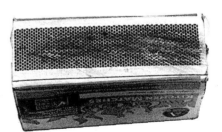

STRIKER PATCH ON SIDE OF BOX. DON'T GET THIS WET EVEN IF YOU USE WATERPROOF MATCHES

FIREPLACE MATCHES: THESE ARE UP TO 10 INCHES LONG

43. A MATCHLESS FIRE STARTER AND THREE MATCHING ONES

☞ *Water* … This common flame quencher may be used in several ways …

> *Faucets* … By installing hose threads on one bathroom faucet on each floor, you can connect a hose to this little hydrant and fight a fire wherever the hose will reach. You can also wash the family dog in a nearby bathtub. Most hardware stores carry these inexpensive connectors and they are easy to install. Three appear on the right.

44. A FAUCET WITH HOSE THREADS

> *Hoses* … Connect one to a spigot outdoors. To read how this can save a house, see page 61.
>
> *Buckets* … A joint compound bucket is a good size, but metal buckets won't melt or burn. Get one with a comfortable handle and keep it close to the flames.

☞ *Fire extinguishers* … These devices are typically fire-engine-red cylinders that contain pressurized expellants. When you squeeze a double handle on one's top, the expellent discharges through a nozzle to extinguish a small fire. The cylinders range from about 8 to 30 inches high and 2 to 6 inches in diameter. Each cylinder has a pressure gauge on top with a yellow needle that should rest on a pie-shaped "**FULL**" area between a "**RECHARGE**" area on the left and an "**OVERCHARGED**" area on the right, as appears in the circular dial below. Some units have hoses, but these are harder to operate because you need to squeeze the handles and hold the cylinder and aim the nozzle all at the same time. A fire extinguisher holds only 10 to 20 seconds of expellent, so use it wisely.

To use a fire extinguisher, step to its mount on the wall and undo the fasteners, grab the cylinder and aim it at the fire, and operate it according to the word **P A S S** as follows …

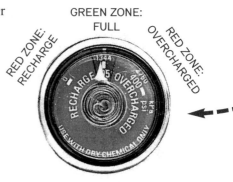

GREEN ZONE:
FULL

RED ZONE:
RECHARGE

RED ZONE:
OVERCHARGED

YELLOW INDICATOR
NEEDLE AT THE TOP

P *Pull out the safety pin* … Pull the safety pin on top while holding the extinguisher nearly upright.

A *Aim the nozzle* … Aim it at the fire's base, not the flames, while standing six to eight feet away.

S *Squeeze the handles* as you would a pair of pliers.

S *Sweep from side to side* across the base of the fire until it is out. Wait a few minutes to be sure, because a doused fire may reignite. Stir the burned area and any smoldering pieces with a shovel, or rake and break them apart, to make sure they are out.

Try to practice using a fire extinguisher in advance, because when the flames are leaping higher by the second is no time to learn how to use one. A good classroom is the turnaround outside your garage, attended

Classes of fire extinguishers ...

A ... extinguishes common combustibles such as cloth, wood, paper, rubber, foliage, and plastics.

B ... extinguishes flammable liquids as oils, tars, gasoline, lacquers, paints, solvents, and other oil-based products. Pouring water on these fires only makes them spread.

C ... extinguishes fires in electrical equipment such as computers, motors, appliances, lights, and wires. If you pour water on these fires the current can climb the water and electrocute you. But if you unplug the birning equipment or disconnect its circuit breaker you can often douse the flames with water.

BC ... extinguishes oil and electrical fires.

ABC ... extinguishes wood, paper, oils, and electrical fires; leaves a residue that's hard to remove.

CO₂ (carbon dioxide) ... extinguishes oil, gas, and electrical fires; leaves no harmful residue.

D ... extinguishes many chemicals and metals such as sodium, magnesium, and powdered aluminum.

K ... use on cooking oils, greasy cookware, and dirty range hoods. If small, suppress with baking soda.

45. HOW TO MOUNT AND USE A FIRE EXTINGUISHER

by every school-age member of your family. Buy three cylinders and let each student try using. If there's still some expellent left, let everyone use it again, until the cylinder is empty. Mount the second cylinder near the stove and the third in the garage, each low enough for a knowledgeable kid to reach. Get the empty cylinder refilled. This may be harder than you think, because one day I went to the local fire station to see how easy it is to refill a fire extinguisher. The dispatcher was the only person there. He said, "I don't know. Come back Saturday and ask the Chief." When you buy a fire extinguisher, ask the seller where it can be re-filled, but many may simply say go to the fire station when they don't really know —so check.

A fire extinguisher should be mounted on a wall at chest height where one can see it from twenty feet away, its operating label should face outward, and no furniture or other obstructions should be in front. Mounting is very important. You think this is easy? Guess again. First, the mount must be screwed or bolted (not nailed) into solid construction behind, and second, the belt fastener or other manner of holding the cylinder must be neither too tight or loose. If you buy an extinguisher that doesn't come with a functional mount (most don't), place the cylinder's base on a piece of cardboard, trace its circumference, cut out the disk, and use it to buy a snugly fitting mount.

First aid … When a disaster has laid you low, and you can't call 911 and you can't drive to a hospital, a first-aid kit is as essential to your health as water. In such times even a minor injury can be serious. Remember that one victim in our grim list died when "she cut her arm while shutting off the gas to her house and bled to death" —an accident that shouldn't have caused her to die.

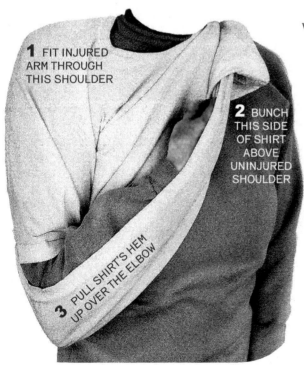

1 FIT INJURED ARM THROUGH THIS SHOULDER

2 BUNCH THIS SIDE OF SHIRT ABOVE UNINJURED SHOULDER

3 PULL SHIRT'S HEM UP OVER THE ELBOW

46. THE TEE-SHIRT SLING

Every home, apartment, vacation residence, workplace, car, and truck should have a versatile first-aid kit on board. Almost every item it should contain you can buy at a drug store. Fit the items into a plastic or metal box with a sealed lid, maybe tape a piece of styrofoam to its back so it won't sink in a flood, and keep it near a first-aid manual and a disaster preparation book.

One item in this kit is useful for making fires: alcohol prep pads. Open one, remove the alcohol-soaked gauze, and light it under some newspaper or similar tinder. Burns about a minute.

If you need a sling, you can make one from a tee-shirt as at left. Slip your head through its neck and slip the injured limb through its sleeve with the other sleeve bunched on your uninjured shoulder, then pull the shirt's hem outside the injured limb's elbow and up until the hem crosses your chest with the injured arm cradled inside the bottom of the shirt.

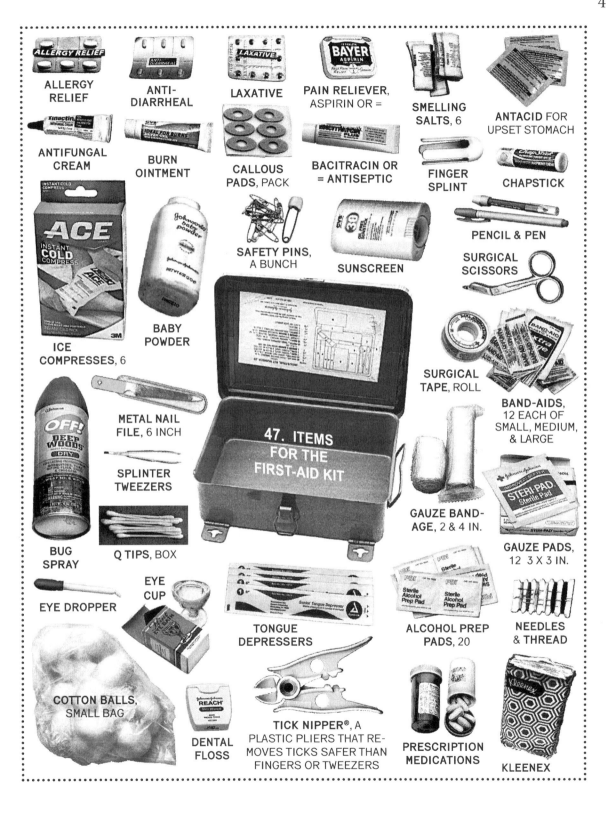

ALLERGY RELIEF

ANTI-DIARRHEAL

LAXATIVE

PAIN RELIEVER, ASPIRIN OR =

SMELLING SALTS, 6

ANTACID FOR UPSET STOMACH

ANTIFUNGAL CREAM

BURN OINTMENT

CALLOUS PADS, PACK

BACITRACIN OR = ANTISEPTIC

FINGER SPLINT

CHAPSTICK

ICE COMPRESSES, 6

BABY POWDER

SAFETY PINS, A BUNCH

SUNSCREEN

PENCIL & PEN

SURGICAL SCISSORS

SURGICAL TAPE, ROLL

BAND-AIDS, 12 EACH OF SMALL, MEDIUM, & LARGE

METAL NAIL FILE, 6 INCH

SPLINTER TWEEZERS

47. ITEMS FOR THE FIRST-AID KIT

GAUZE BAND-AGE, 2 & 4 IN.

GAUZE PADS, 12 3 X 3 IN.

BUG SPRAY

Q TIPS, BOX

EYE DROPPER

EYE CUP

TONGUE DEPRESSERS

ALCOHOL PREP PADS, 20

NEEDLES & THREAD

COTTON BALLS, SMALL BAG

DENTAL FLOSS

TICK NIPPER®, A PLASTIC PLIERS THAT RE-MOVES TICKS SAFER THAN FINGERS OR TWEEZERS

PRESCRIPTION MEDICATIONS

KLEENEX

Though not as urgent as administrating first aid, having plenty of ***writing materials*** in a disaster will help everyone in your party "administer communication". This includes paper, pencils and pens for writing notes, markers and crayons for kids to draw pictures, plus a waterproof container to hold them.

Sanitation ... In prolonged disasters two big killers are food poisoning and bacteria-caused illnesses; hence every cookware, utensil, and surface you use to prepare and eat food must be clean. This is done with the brawny team of equipment you see below. Spare no space as you stash plenty of each. The best germ killer is chlorinated bleach. This kills 99.9 percent of bacteria, viruses, and mildew, but is ineffective against Giardia (severe diarrhea spread by the feces of infected animals). A table on page 167 lists the effective

ISOPROPYL ALCOHOL

HYDROGEN PEROXIDE

LIQUID DISH DETERGENT

SCOURING POWDER

SOAPS, SEVERAL SIZES

CHLORINATED BLEACH, THE BEST DISINFECTOR

LOW-SUDSING DETERGENT, THIS IS KINDER TO THE ENVIRONMENT

BAKING SODA, A VERSATILE CLEANER

SCOURING PADS

BUCKET WITH SWING HANDLE & TIGHT LID

TOILET PLUNGER, ALSO USE AS AGITATOR FOR CLEANING CLOTHES WHEN YOU HAVE NO POWER

TOILET PAPER, PAPER TOWELS, NAPKINS, KLEENEX, KEEP IN MOISTURE-PROOF CONTAINERS

WASHCLOTHS, HAND TOWELS, BATH TOWELS, TWO SETS PER PERSON

NEWSPAPERS, A SMALL PILE FOR CLEANING BIG MESSES

PLASTIC GARBAGE BAGS & TIES, SEVERAL SIZES

48. SANITATION RATIONS FOR A DISASTER

RAGS A VARIETY OF TEXTURES FOR VARIOUS CLEANING CHORES

WASH TUB, FOR SOAKING OBJECTS SUCH AS DIRTY CLOTHES

WASHBOARD, GOOD FOR SCRUBBING CLOTHES BY HAND

bleach-to-water ratios for purifying water and preparing a number of cleaners. Wear high-cuffed rubber gloves and goggles over your eyes and a respirator over your nose when using this chemical because it can be caustic to your skin, lungs, and eyes. Bleach has a strong odor, it cleans better in cold water than warm, don't use it on wool or silk or water-repellant fabrics, don't use it in washing machine rinse cycles, and never mix chlorinated bleach with ammonia or any acid such as vinegar —because this produces chloramine which if inhaled can kill you. Windex and a few other cleaners contain ammonia. Never mix two cleaners together in an effort to create a "supercleaner". With any cleaner or disinfectant, read the label before buying and using it, and keep these dangerous chemicals from children and pets.

Lighting ... When darkness falls on Disasterville, you'll want some kind of illumination to see around and avoid stepping on nails, live wires, glass, snakes —you name it. Even during the day you'll need a light if you're hiding in a window-less shelter or must find something in a dark corner. A few light sources are detailed below.

WINDUP LIGHT

BATTERY

BALLCAP L.E.D. LIGHT

SWITCH LIGHTS

HEAD LAMP

MAG LIGHT

LED KEY LIGHT

WIDEFACE LIGHT

THE USUAL FLASH-LIGHT

POCKET LIGHT

49. A FEW FLASHY LIGHTS

☞ *Flashlights* ...
Everyone in your party, even three-year-olds, or maybe especially three-year-olds, should have a personal flash-light. A good first choice is a pocketsize *mag light*: they are lightweight and bright. A *headlamp* lets you see what you're doing while your hands are free, and you can mount one on a hardhat. Another hands-free brightener is a *baseball cap with a bill-mounted LED light*. Each has a tiny switch and a button battery built into the hat. Also useful is a *hanging light*, which can be mounted above a dining table or reading area. A *windup rechargeable flashlight* has a small hand-crank generator that charges a battery which brightens the light.

Except for wind-up lights, flashlights need batteries. Unfortunately these are fickle. Most likely you've put a couple batteries in a flashlight you may need someday, then a few months later you turn it on and ... no light! Sometimes the batteries have corroded, then you may lose the light too. Any battery loses its charge faster when old and cold. To minimize these problems, use batteries sparingly and keep them in their original packages at room temperature until you're ready to use them. For each flashlight have two sets of backup batteries, and it is best if all lights use one or two sizes to simplify inventory. Rechargeable batteries cost more, but they usually repay you over the long haul. Common batteries and what they are best used for appear below and in figure 50.

Alkaline … usually can't be re-charged, good for low-drain devices like clocks and radios.

Nickel-metal hydride (NiMH) … rechargeable, a good all-around battery.

Lithium … can't be recharged but powerful, good for high-drain devices like cameras and flash-lights.

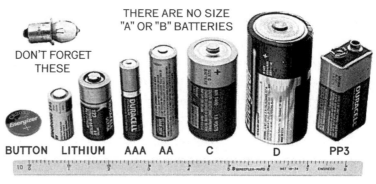

50. A BEVY OF BATTERIES

One way to re-energize a rechargeable battery is with a *solar battery charger*. If you have such a charger for your car, you can wire the charger to a vehicle's cigaret lighter receptacle bought at an auto parts store and plug your flashlight battery charger into the lighter receptacle. Ohm my! This could keep everything running day and night, ad infinitum. But a solar battery charger will work only during the day when the sun is shining well above the horizon.

☞ *Candles* … These thin wax cylinders with cloth wicks are nice for brightening the night. Among the best are birthday candles. They don't burn long —ten minutes or so— but their flame is bright and it takes only a layer of frosting to hold them upright. If you mount a birthday candle in a piece of bread you can eat the holder afterward. If you mount three candles several inches apart at differ-ent heights, the crisscrossing rays will create a fairly strong shadowless light. Or you could shape an

CANDLE WITH TIN FOIL REFLECTOR IN METAL HOLDER

THESE THREE FLAMES GIVE THE BEST LIGHT IF THEY ARE ABOUT 10 INCHES APART AND AT DIFFERENT HEIGHTS

BIRTHDAY CANDLE MOUNTED IN ENGLISH MUFFIN

THREE CANDLES ARRANGED TO CREATE A COMFORTABLE LIGHT

51. CANDLE MAGIC

CANDLE MOUNTED IN COFFEE MUG FILLED WITH MUD

aluminum foil reflector on one side of a candle to throw more light in the direction you need it, as appears in figure 51. This reflector is held by crumpling its base around the top of the candle, and as the candle burns down you slide the reflector down. If you're roughing it in the rubble and have no candleholder, fill a tin can or coffee mug with mud and mount the candle's base in the mud.

If the base of a normal candle is too large to fit into its holder, with a sharp knife shave some wax from its sides; if too small, wrap tin foil around its base. The holder should be metal (not glass or wood) that has a rim to catch the wax. Set the holder on a wide flat surface, not a pedestal where it could be easily knocked over, and locate it three feet from flammable objects. Failure to do this caused two victims in our grim list to die "in a fire started by a candle." Never mount a candle by dripping melted wax on a surface and setting its base in the soft wax. The candle could be easily knocked over, and if it burns down it could ignite the surface it is on and burn down the house.

☞ *Lanterns* … These cast light in every direction. Center one on or above a table so several eaters or readers can sit around it. With the advent of LED lights, why fuss with messy mantle models that can ignite flammable materials nearby? Kerosene lanterns aren't such a hot idea either: they are smelly, need plenty of ventilation, and their surfaces are dangerously hot —as evidenced by one victim in our grim list who "died after being burned by a kerosene lantern in his home."

Communication … When a disaster drives you into your safe room or similar sanctuary, you'll need to listen to the latest news broadcasts, updates, advisories, and weather forecasts as well as communicate with rescuers, relatives, and friends who may help you. Common methods are …

52. WIRELESS PHONE

☞ *Telephones* … Since phone lines are separate from electric lines, a corded phone will work if the power fails (cordless and speaker phones won't) unless the phone company's power line is also severed. Some companies provide customers with in-house batteries with up to eight hours of talk time. A good phone today is a wireless phone that rests in a cradle from where you can take the phone around the house.

☞ *Cellphones* … These allow wireless communication almost anywhere, but their coverage may be spotty in rugged terrain and rural areas, and during a power failure they won't work if too many people are using them or the tower has no backup power source. Cellphone batteries need a charger, which can be a wind-up recharger or a plug that fits into a standard electric outlet or a vehicle cigaret lighter.

☞ *Television* … You'll often see on-the-scene reporting of what is happening. The Weather Channel gives weather forecasts and reports disasters. The United States has a national warning system, the *Emergency Alert System (EAS)* that quickly informs the public of a national

53. CELLPHONE

emergency through local radio and TV stations. On TVs the message may be voiced or scrolled across the screen, and on radios it may begin with "We interrupt this program to…" Most TV sets won't operate during a power outage.

☞ **Battery-powered radio** … When the power fails, this device is often a disaster victim's prime source of information, since many radio stations announce local business closings, blocked roads, and other advisories. FEMA also has a radio network that announces the latest government response and recovery operations and where disaster victims can seek help, and the National Weather Service has a high-frequency FM weather band that repeats a taped message every four to six minutes from the nearest NWS office. Their broadcasts are updated every one to three hours, during severe weather they interrupt their broadcasts with special warnings, and during national disasters and nuclear attacks they announce warnings to schools, hospitals, and news media offices. This system operates about 380 stations nationwide and about 15 across southern Canada and most of them broadcast 24 hours a day and have a range of about 40 miles, which together reach about 90 percent of the nation's population. Coastal stations also provide weather information for boaters, fishers, and others engaged in maritime activities. These stations' broadcast frequencies are:

HAND CRANK
FOR CHARGING
BATTERIES

162.400 MHz (megahertz)   162.425 MHz   162.450 MHz
162.475 MHz   162.500 MHz   162.525 MHz   162.550 MHz

To learn more about this broadcast system, visit www.weather.gov or www.noaa.gov/.

SOLAR
CHARGER

**54.
WINDUP RADIO**

Some battery-powered radios today, known as *windup radios*, have a crank to recharge the batteries. Some also have a solar charger, an LED flashlight, and an outlet for charging smart phones (this can be connected to an AC wall outlet or a computer). Whatever radio you have, tape on a label with the most informative local stations on it, keep extra batteries nearby, and long before a disaster strikes test a few stations inside your safe room or other sanctuary to make sure reception is adequate. If not, you may need to install an antenna from inside the safe room to the outdoors.

☞ *Internet* … A plug-in computer won't work if the power fails. If the internet is still operating, you may be able to access it with a battery-powered laptop, smart phone, or tablet.

☞ **Send-for-help devices** … These electronic tracking transmitters are used to locate lost aircraft, sinking boats, and people in distress. When manually activated by a survivor or automatically activated by a crash or a sinking, the transmitter emits a beacon which is picked up by one or more satellites, which transmits the signal to its parent ground control station, which processes the signal and forwards the location to a national authority, which forwards the data to a rescuing authority, which initiates rescue or recovery operations —all within minutes.

BROAD-
CASTS A
DISTRESS
SIGNAL TO A
SATELLITE
THAT TELLS
RESCUERS
WHERE & WHO
YOU ARE

TRANSMITS UP
TO 30 HRS

BUILT-IN STROBE
LIGHT PROVIDES
VISIBILITY
DURING NIGHT
RESCUES

EASILY
CARRIED IN
A POCKET

IT FLOATS &
IS WATERPROOF

LETS YOU SEND
A PERIODIC
"CHECK IN"
MESSAGE
TO EMAIL
CONTACTS &
SHOWS YOUR
LOCATION ON
A MAP
APPEARING
ON A WEB
BROWSER

IN AN
EMERGENCY
YOU CAN SEND
A DISTRESS
SIGNAL THAT
NOTIFIES
LOCAL
SEARCH &
RESCUE
TEAMS
WHERE
YOU ARE

55. PERSONAL LOCATOR BEACON [24]   **56. SPOT SATELLITE MESSENGER** [25]

Chief of this tribe is the ***personal locator beacon*** (PLB). These vary in size generally from ciga-ret pack to paperback book and weigh from about $1/2$ to $2 1/2$ pounds. They can be purchased from marine suppliers, aircraft refitters, and outdoor stores. They last about 10 years, operate across a range of conditions −40 to +40 °C (−40 to +104 °F), and transmit for 24 to 48 hours.Their cost varies according to performance and specifications.

A similar device is the ***SPOT satellite messenger***, as in figure 56. Its satellite coverage area includes most of the western hemisphere except extreme northern and southern latitudes. With the purchase of an annual subscription, SPOT allows a victim in distress to send an up-to-41 character message via satellite to a ground control station. A variation called SPOT Connect allows a user to write a custom message using a smartphone.

☞ *Ham radio* … This network of amateur radio operators is known for providing useful information during disasters. To learn more about this communication, visit www.arrl.org/find-an-amateur-radio-license-class.

"HEY RED RYDER, THIS IS THE COTTONMOUTH ..."

REMOTE CONTROL MIKE

CONTROLLER WITH BACKLIT DISPLAY IS EASY TO OPERATE AT NIGHT

4X4 SPEAKER LETS YOU LISTEN WITH YOUR HANDS FREE

THIS LUXURY-MODEL TRANSCEIVER CARRIES 1355 CHANNELS & ACCESSES EMAIL FREQUENCIES

57. HAM RADIO TRANSMITTER [26]

Bedding … In a disaster a clean, dry, warm, soft berth is one of the quickest cures for bewildered brains, lost composure, frayed nerves, and exhausted muscles. Plan on three blankets, two changes of linens, a couple pillows, and a pair of mattress pads in a cool dry place for each person in your home. Keep the same for yourself in your workplace. Air them out every month or so. If a disaster deprives you of your normal berth, a few comforting alternatives are detailed on the next page …

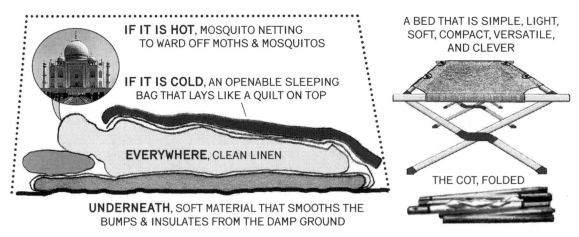

IF IT IS HOT, MOSQUITO NETTING TO WARD OFF MOTHS & MOSQUITOS

IF IT IS COLD, AN OPENABLE SLEEPING BAG THAT LAYS LIKE A QUILT ON TOP

EVERYWHERE, CLEAN LINEN

UNDERNEATH, SOFT MATERIAL THAT SMOOTHS THE BUMPS & INSULATES FROM THE DAMP GROUND

A BED THAT IS SIMPLE, LIGHT, SOFT, COMPACT, VERSATILE, AND CLEVER

THE COT, FOLDED

58. GETTING A GOOD NIGHT'S SLEEP IN DISASTERVILLE

If you must sleep on the ground … Have some kind of soft insulation underneath that smooths any bumps and keeps you insulated from the damp cold ground. A few possibilities, depending on the severity of the disaster, are (1) a mattress removed from a demolished house, (2) a row of rescued sofa cushions, (3) an air mattress, which can be stored in a small space, and (4) a *freight blanket* folded once over.

A freight blanket not only makes a nice bed mat in an emergency, it makes a warm overcoat if you need one quickly, and it can make kneeling on your knees a comfort instead of a pain. Between disasters it makes a fine pet bed, it will keep your car clean when you carry messy items, and it will protect fragile items when you move them. By placing a heavy object on a freight blanket spread on the floor and grabbing an edge, you can pull the object to where you want.

If it is cold … Consider sleeping bags. Buy ones that can be zipped open and laid like a quilt over each bed. Since this sleepwear is made in many sizes, shapes, thicknesses, and shell fabrics, don't risk a swing and a miss by buying this item online. Go where you can see and feel what you would buy. See how it zips open and closed. Look for hoods, draft collars, and inside pockets for wallets and other valuables. Buy or make an inner liner because this is easier to clean than the bag.

If it is hot … Shroud your berth with a layer of 7 x 10 foot fine-mesh mosquito netting to ward off annoying moths, mosquitoes, and other flying bugs. Fine-mesh cheesecloth works well too, and during the day it can be used for other things.

Everywhere … Have clean linen. You can make pillows by stuffing a pillowcase or large plastic bag with dirty clothes, stuffing from a damaged sofa, or anything that is soft and doesn't smell.

In many a disaster the king of beds is the *cot.* Each is portable (15 to 20 pounds), it makes a sociable sofa between sleeps, you can store plenty of gear underneath, and when you don't need it you can store it in little space. Opened, a cot is typically 78 inches long, 27 to 30 inches wide, and 14 to 18 inches high. Closed, these numbers shrink to about 36 x 7 x 5 inches. This is another item to buy for your workplace in case you get stranded there overnight.

Disaster equipment closet

This is the place to store everything you'll need after a disaster. Though the safe room is your sanctuary during a disaster, it is not where you should keep the tools you may need afterward. Better is a sizable closet near the garage door, which you would have a better chance of reaching if your house is severely damaged. Between disasters this room can serve as a utility closet with the garage nearby providing space to work in. This little vault needn't be more than 3 x 6 feet (interior dimensions); but as with safe rooms its floor, walls, and ceiling must be built so no tornado can lift it and no earthquake can level it. This construction can be added to most houses, and its cost would likely be less than the amount by which it would increase the value of the property. Figure 59 is an architectural drawing you can take to a professional designer or builder who will be able to read it like a book. As with safe rooms, if a nearby river rises above its banks, a levee fails, or a deluge floods your garage floor, this chamber could become inaccessible. Again, no one solution is perfect for every possibility.

Below are the items you should put in this vault in case a disaster comes knocking on your door. You may already have many of these items and may use them often.

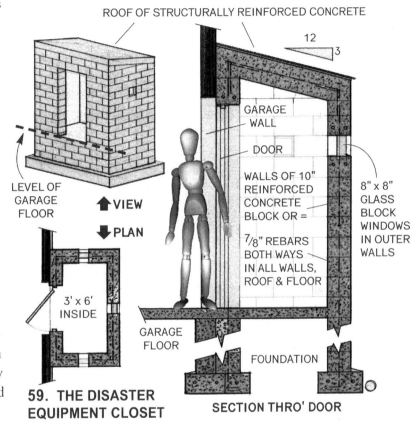

59. THE DISASTER EQUIPMENT CLOSET

☐ *Cheesecloth* … You can use this gauzy fabric to make teabags, fish and mosquito nets, face masks you can breathe through, curtains that will allow air to enter but which passing strangers can't see through, even summer clothes (sew the pieces together with dental floss). The soft nonscratchy fabric makes a good cleaning rag, and it can be washed and reused. It is sold in seven weaves from #10 (20 x 12 threads per square inch) to #90 (44 x 36 threads per square inch).[27] The higher the grade, the closer the threads and the heavier and sturdier the cloth. Have 100 square yards (only 30 x 30 feet).

☐ *Buckets* … You can't have too many of these. Nest a dozen inside each other so they take up little space. Best for the price are empty laundry detergent pails, joint compound buckets, and kitty litter buckets.

BOTTLE
STOPPER

DRINKING
CUP

POTATO BAKER

FILLER AND GUTTER
AROUND CANDLE'S BASE

SCOURING PAD

60. TIN FOIL: A TOOL WHOSE USE IS LIMITED ONLY BY YOUR IMAGINATION

☐ *Tin foil* … This versatile material has many uses: bottle stoppers, candle reflectors, drinking cups, food wrappers, curtains, shingles, even nuclear fallout protectors, as appears on page 138. Keep an 18-inch wide roll of heavy-duty foil in both the safe room and the disaster equipment closet.

☐ *Electric wire* … This is one of the unsung heroes of disaster preparedness. A 50-foot roll of the kind of cable electricians install in your house can be used for much more than conducting electricity. This cable has three wires each $1/16$ inch thick (two insulated wires conduct electricity and the third is a ground wire), and an outer jacket of insulation. The cable can be used as an emergency towing rope, each wire can be bent by hand into nearly any shape, and a bare wire makes a strong rope that won't burn (it can hold cooking pots over a fire). With this material the possibilities are endless. As a sample, when I tried to fry an egg in the earlier-described solar stove, I couldn't fit a regular frying pan into it so I made a frying pan out of a paint can top and three pieces of copper wire, as appears in figure 61. Another example of this wire's clever use appears in figure 164 on page 171.

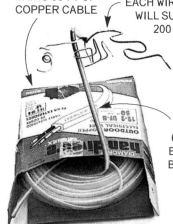

THIS BOX CONTAINS 50 FT OF COPPER CABLE

EACH WIRE WILL SUPPORT 200 POUNDS & WON'T BURN, YET YOU CAN BEND IT INTO ANY SHAPE WITH YOUR BARE HANDS

THE CABLE CONDUCTS 600 VOLTS & IS STRONG ENOUGH TO TOW A LARGE BRANCH OFF A DRIVEWAY

THE CABLE HAS 3 INSULATED COPPER WIRES, EACH $1/16$ INCH THICK

TWO CLEVER USES OF THIS VERSATILE MATERIAL

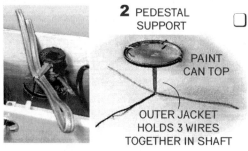

1 PROPPING A TOILET FLOAT SO IT WON'T FALL WHEN THE TOILET IS FLUSHED (SEE PAGE 171)

2 PEDESTAL SUPPORT

PAINT CAN TOP

OUTER JACKET HOLDS 3 WIRES TOGETHER IN SHAFT

61. THE OMNI-USEFUL COPPER WIRE

☐ *Plastic Sheet* … This filmy material is made in a variety of sizes and thinnesses: sandwich bags, zip-lok freezer bags, shopping bags, wastebasket liners, garbage bags, covers for dry-cleaned suits, polyethylene for construction jobs —the list goes on and on. In imaginative hands this material can be made into rain hats, raincoats, tablecloths, clothes (hold the pieces together with duct tape), windows, roofs, tarps, and dozens of other things. Stored in a dark dry place, this material will last for years. Buy a 20 x 50 foot roll at a lumber yard. Since this material rips easily, if you must anchor it to something, do so with a metal bottle top and a wide-headed nail as appears at right.

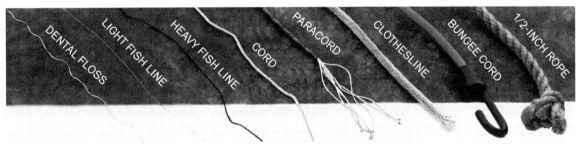

62. BOTTLE CAP SHEET TIE

ANCHOR IS UNDER THE SHEET

BLACK PLASTIC SHEET

CAP IS NAILED TO ANCHOR BELOW

☐ *Duct tape* … You may already know many ways to use this versatile and economical material.

☐ *Velcro* … This is better than duct tape in some cases.   Get a $^3/_4$ inch x 15 foot roll.

☐ *Rope* … Have several kinds, as appear below. A strong and economical rope made today is 550 pound paracord. Singe the ends of each strand and they won't unravel. A "nice to have" item is 100 feet of $^1/_2$ inch nylon rope for pulling heavy weights with a car or truck.

DENTAL FLOSS   LIGHT FISH LINE   HEAVY FISH LINE   CORD   PARACORD   CLOTHESLINE   BUNGEE CORD   1/2-INCH ROPE

63. A GALLERY OF STRINGS AND ROPES

☐ *Gloves* … Have several pair as appear below: leather for heavy work, cloth for light work, latex with high cuffs for washing, fur-lined ones for cold. Have extras in case they get worn or wet. Every person in your party should have several pair, as pictured below.

WORK GLOVES

GLOVES FOR COLD WEATHER

MITTENS FOR BITTER COLD

RUBBER GLOVES FOR WET WORK

64. SOME HANDY GLOVES

☐ *Wheelbarrow or cart* … Avoid inflatable tires that can go flat.
☐ *Trash cans* … Have several with tight lids.
☐ *Hunting knife* … One with at least a 6-inch blade plus a scabbard with a belt loop.

- *Hatchet* … This should also be sheathed in a scabbard with a belt loop.
- *Machete* … Great for clearing brush and branches; a good weapon too if you need it. Wrap its handle with friction tape to create a firm grip.
- *Whetstone* … For sharpening pointed and bladed tools from needles to axes.
- *Sling shot* … A quiet way to kill small game, especially rats and pigeons in urban environs. A bag of pea gravel or ball bearings from damaged machines offers cheap and plentiful ammunition. Some models shoot 30-inch arrows, which can bring down medium-size game. Check the Chief AJ QP-HFX Black with Black Super Powerband.

65.[28]

- *Flare gun* … This derringer is made for firing smoke flares in the day and incendiary flares at night by boats in distress on bodies of water, but you can use it on land as well. Wal-Mart and boating supply stores carry them, but if you order it online you'll pay a hefty shipping fee because the shells are explosives. If you buy one, buy another clip or two of the shells. But this shooter has a meaner use. If a stalker, burglar, or potential murderer tries to break into your house, if you shoot him in the face with this sidearm (it doesn't require a license to own) he might never stalk or steal again.

66. A SCARY PISTOL

- *Hand tools* … Many tools you would keep in the disaster equipment closet are small enough to fit into a toolbox, as listed below. You may already have many and enjoy using them.

67. TOOLS AND MATERIALS TO KEEP IN THE DISASTER EQUIPMENT TOOL KIT

- **Fluorescent tape:** good for roping areas & seeing people in the dark
- **Nails,** 50-60 of several types and lengths
- **Toothbrushes,** for cleaning in small spaces
- **Caulking gun,** plus tubes of caulk & adhesive
- **Friction tape,** to give tool handles a firm grip
- **Matches,** waterproof or in waterproof container
- **Push pins,** for holding thin things to thick things
- **Chalk box & chalk,** for making long straight lines
- **C-clamps,** also use as vices, handles, eyelets, & braces
- **Hammer,** a weight that feels comfortable in your hand
- **Screw drivers,** several sizes of both slot & Phillips heads
- **Pry bar,** also known as **wonderbar,** a big lever in little places
- **Carpenter's speed square,** helps you do accurate layout work
- **Bungee cords,** a hooked elastic cord that holds things in place
- **Dental floss,** can use as strong thread
- **Staple gun** (T50) plus box of staples
- **Hacksaw,** cuts metal, bones, etc.
- **Vise grip,** a few sizes & jaws
- **Wrenches,** from $1/4$ to $7/8$ in.
- **Pliers,** flat & needlenose
- **Office stapler,** staples
- **Files,** round, mill, rasp
- **Hand drill & bits**
- **Drinking straws**
- **Safety goggles**
- **Electric wire cutter & stripper**
- **WD-40,** a versatile lubricant
- **Spatulas,** 1 to 3 inch blades
- **Swiss army knife or equal**
- **Channel locks**
- **Electrical tape**
- **Tape measure**
- **Utility knife**
- **Keyhole saw**
- **Clothespins**
- **Hand saw**
- **Scissors**
- **Whistle**
- **lighter**
- **Awl**

❏ *Yard tools* … A lineup of these handy items and how they may be used appears below.

68. A LINEUP OF YARD TOOLS

CLIPPERS WITH LONG HANDLES FOR CLEARING BRUSH & CUTTING SMALL BRANCHES

BROOMS, PUSH BROOM, BRISTLE BROOM, & DUSTPAN

LEAF RAKE FOR GATHERING LIGHT DEBRIS

TINE RAKE FOR WORKING ROUGHER TURF

SLEDGE HAMMER, FOR NUDGING HEAVY OBJECTS. THE HEAD ACTS AS A SMALL ANVIL

PICK OR **MATTOCK,** FOR CHOPPING THRO' ROCKS, WALLS, DOORS, HARD CLAYS, & ROOTS

HOE, FOR CHOPPING THRO' ICE, AND PULLING OBJECTS & DEBRIS FROM HARD-TO-REACH PLACES

SQUAREPOINT SHOVEL HAS A RECTANGULAR BLADE. IT ALSO MAKES A GOOD DUSTPAN

SPADE HAS A HEART-SHAPED BLADE THAT DIGS MORE EASILY INTO SOIL

CROWBAR FOR LEVERING THINGS OR PRYING THEM APART

AXE, PLUS A SHEATH WITH A BELT LOOP

❏ *Siphon* … Besides emptying aquariums, swimming pools, and gas tanks, you can use this little hose to blow air onto a stubborn fire without singeing your eyebrows. The picture below shows how to siphon a liquid from a container. Insert one end of a $^1/_2$ inch diameter (outer dimension) clear (so you can see the liquid flowing inside) plastic tubing into the liquid to be drained until the tube's end is near the bottom, and hold the other end of the tube just above the container to be filled. The outer end must be lower than the inner end. Kneel with your mouth close to the tube and suck on it. If the tube is clear you'll see the liquid coming, then just before it reaches your mouth quickly

69. THE ANCIENT ART OF SIPHONING

CLEAR FLEXIBLE $^1/_2$ IN. DIA. PLASTIC TUBING

INNER END

OUTER END

OUTER END MUST BE LOWER THAN INNER END

drop the outer end into the container to be filled. To stop the flow, raise the outer end until it is higher than the inner end. This may not work on many newer vehicles because they have a siphoning obstruction above the tank.

- ☐ *Come-along* … To operate this hand winch, hook one end to something immovable and the other end to what you want to move, then pump the handle up and down.

- ☐ *Block and tackle* … This brute puller helps you move heavy items *laterally* or *away from* the direction you pull, as on the right. Add the come-along above, a trailer hitch, and some thick rope, and you can do all kinds of heavy work with the effort than it takes to steer a car.

- ☐ *Chain* … Get the kind that tow trucks carry, 20 feet long with a burly hook at each end.

- ☐ *Ventilating fan* … Use this during heat waves and when interiors need to be vented of moisture, chemical vapors, and the like.

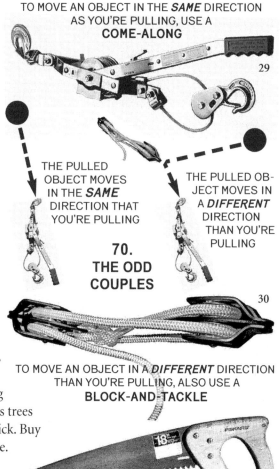

TO MOVE AN OBJECT IN THE *SAME* DIRECTION AS YOU'RE PULLING, USE A **COME-ALONG**

29

THE PULLED OBJECT MOVES IN THE *SAME* DIRECTION THAT YOU'RE PULLING

THE PULLED OBJECT MOVES IN A *DIFFERENT* DIRECTION THAN YOU'RE PULLING

70. THE ODD COUPLES

30

TO MOVE AN OBJECT IN A *DIFFERENT* DIRECTION THAN YOU'RE PULLING, ALSO USE A **BLOCK-AND-TACKLE**

- ☐ *Tree saw* … This "Armstrong Sawmill" with its lance teeth cuts trees and branches up to 5 inches thick. Buy one with an 18 to 30 inch blade.

- ☐ *Wire saw* … This flexible 27-inch saw fits in a shirt pocket and cuts wood, plastic, and ice.

72. WIRE SAW

71. TREE SAW

LANCE TEETH

- ☐ *Chainsaw* … This tool can extricate you from tons of fallen foliage, but it can cut a leg as well as a branch. First study the operating manual, or you could buy a few sutures at the local ER, or even suffer the fate of one victim in our grim list who "died of a chainsaw accident while clearing storm debris." Better yet, buy a book that describes how to use this tool safely and efficiently. Watch an arborist use one. Note all the other equipment he uses —wedges, ropes, axes, ladders, rags, rakes, brooms, digging bars, loppers, shovels, jugs of chainsaw oil. A chainsaw is not a lone tool but a member of a large team managed by a professionally skilled operator.

Gasoline chainsaws will work if the electric power fails, but they are fussier and heavier than electric models. With my electric chainsaw I have cut trees 450 feet from my house. Due to wire resistance through such a long cord (my first 100 feet is AWG 10 wire and the other lengths are AWG

12s) you may get only 7 amps at the trigger instead of 12. But if you cut gently and let the saw's weight do the work, you won't burn out the motor or trip the circuit breaker a long walk away. I also have a battery-operated chainsaw. After Hurricane Sandy knocked our power out and left a 9-inch tree across the edge of my turnaround, I removed it by toting the saw's charger and two battery packs to the local library which had power, where I charged the packs (an hour and twenty minutes each), then I sawed until the packs died. After three trips to the library I was done.

73. THIS CROSSCUT SAW IS 73 INCHES LONG AND COULD BE 100 YEARS OLD. ONE PERSON HOLDS EACH HANDLE. WHEN ONE PUSHES THE OTHER PULLS. THE PULLER PULLS A TINY BIT HARDER THAN THE PUSHER PUSHES.

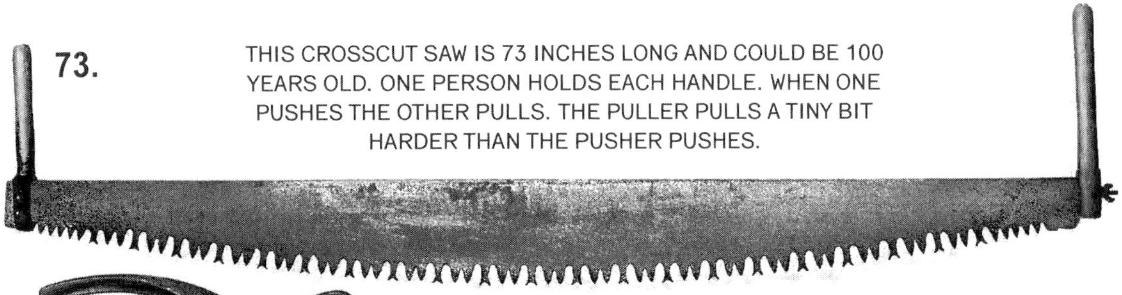

THIS SAW SET IS 10 INCHES LONG. THE GAP BETWEEN THE JAWS FITS OVER EACH TOOTH, WHICH IS BENT SLIGHTLY OUTWARD TO KEEP THE SAW FROM BINDING AS IT CUTS

☐ *Crosscut saw* … Though not everyone would need this tool, it was worth its weight in gold after the night of October 29, 2011, when winter storm Alfred unloaded 11 inches of wet snow on the deciduous trees laden with autumn foliage around my house. This cutter appears above and in this book's title page. The following après-disaster anecdote will help you appreciate its value.

During this storm twenty large branches fell across my turnaround and driveway —but the worst was a huge 21-inch-diameter trunk that lay across the driveway near the road out front. My wife and I had no power, no phone (the cellphone was dead), no way to get out, and no way for anyone to get in. We spent a day cutting and removing the twenty fallen branches with the Armstrong sawmill you see on the opposite page, then I snowplowed the driveway to the fallen tree. Next, I unearthed an old crosscut saw stored in a corner of the garage. I bought this cutlery at a flea market in 1975 with the idea that if I ever became trapped on my property and no other tool could free me, this might be my extrication. Now was the time to put this theory to the test. After setting the teeth with a saw set (a crucial tool that angles the blade's teeth slightly outward to keep the saw from binding as it cuts) I carefully filed each tooth. Then we soberly approached the fallen arbor.

Here I must emphasize that if you ever do this work, before touching a tool *carefully consider every possibility that could occur.* Imagine how the tree on each side of the cut will move when cut through. Will the crown end roll over? Will the trunk end flip back up? If the saw is still in the cut, could it be thrown outward across your face or body? What if the part you need to remove rests flat on the ground so that when your saw cuts through its teeth will scrape the ground and be dulled or ruined? (Here, either wedge the tree above the ground or dig away the earth under where the cut will be and slide a 2 x 4 or other lumber under the planned cut). If you are unable to envision these possibilities, please, hire a professional to do this work —and have a copy of his or her insurance certificate before giving the go-ahead. They might not come for months, but that's better than you taking up residence in a cemetery for even longer —as did five victims on our grim list who "died when storm-damaged trees fell on them while they were clearing debris."

Before Janis and I touched sawteeth to bark, we cleared the driveway of snow on each side of the tree and wedged twenty concrete blocks under parts of the trunk so when we cut through the tree it wouldn't twist or roll. Since the tree hovered a foot above the driveway, we looped a heavy chain around the trunk so that when we finished the cuts we could hook the chain to the truck and pull the cut log off the driveway. We cut the trunk end first, so if the trunk flipped up after the first cut it would take less wood with it. I angled the cuts on each side slightly outward toward the ground so when we cut the log it wouldn't bind between the trunk end and the crown end as it fell, and I angled the cuts slightly outward toward the truck so when I pulled the log away its ends wouldn't bind between the trunk and the crown. Then we started cutting. After two hours of gently, rhythmically pulling the handles back and forth (you would be amazed how easy it was once we started), with a final swish of the teeth the log fell with a THUNK on the driveway. A half hour later the power came on. I felt like I had been rewarded for good behavior.

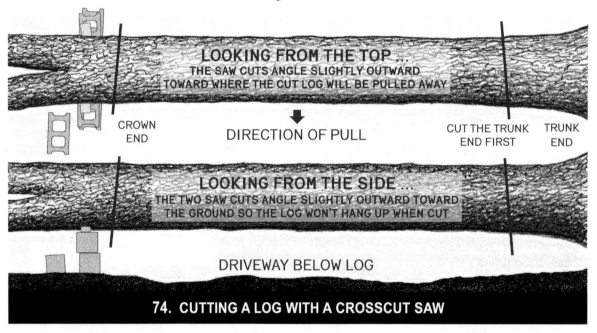

LOOKING FROM THE TOP ...
THE SAW CUTS ANGLE SLIGHTLY OUTWARD
TOWARD WHERE THE CUT LOG WILL BE PULLED AWAY

CROWN END — DIRECTION OF PULL — CUT THE TRUNK END FIRST — TRUNK END

LOOKING FROM THE SIDE ...
THE TWO SAW CUTS ANGLE SLIGHTLY OUTWARD TOWARD
THE GROUND SO THE LOG WON'T HANG UP WHEN CUT

DRIVEWAY BELOW LOG

74. CUTTING A LOG WITH A CROSSCUT SAW

☐ *Hose rack* ... Mounted on opposite sides of a house should be two *frostproof sill cocks* (spigots that won't freeze in cold weather) next to hose racks coiled with 75 feet of hose. The one you see in figure 75 is mounted just inside the garage, which makes it easy to use in inclement weather. The hose should be rubber, not vinyl which tends to kink, and the couplings should be metal, not plastic which can crack if a car rolls over them. Aside from watering foliage and washing windows and cars and driveways, this equipment is a useful firefighting tool. An anecdote will attest to this.

In 1986 a fire erupted in our house when my wife and I weren't home. A neighbor saw the flames, called the fire department, and ran over to a spigot and hose rack on the front of the house. With the hose's nozzle he smashed the window of the room the fire was in, then he swished the hose around inside the room until he thought the fire was out. Ten minutes later the fire re-erupted because it wasn't completely out —but by then the fire trucks were on the lawn. Without the hose on the front of the house, the fire and its smoke plus the water from the fire hoses would have destroyed much of the house.

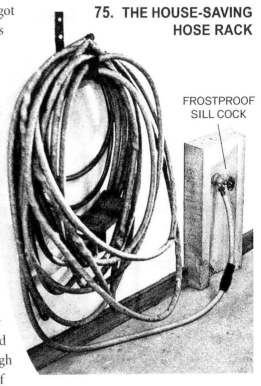

75. THE HOUSE-SAVING HOSE RACK

FROSTPROOF SILL COCK

Regarding the part of the house that was damaged, the standard advice is, "Contact your insurance agent." We quickly found there is more to this adage than meets the eye. Early the next morning we received a flurry of calls from several "insurance adjusters" who, for ten percent of our claim, said they would represent our best interests in dealing with the insurer. On the advice of a friend who had experienced a house fire, I skeptically tried one. We scoured though the charred remains, and he encouraged me to think of every scrap of paper that might have a penny of value. The list we made was a lot longer than I would have made myself. Then we set a replacement value for each item. For every price I said the item was worth, the adjuster wrote a much higher value! But he was clairvoyant beyond my poor power to add or detract. To explain what transpired *en toto*, one ruined item will suffice as example: a portable typewriter I had owned for ten years. The adjuster asked what I paid for it. "78 dollars," I hopefully replied. He said, "We'll put down 125 dollars." I remained calm. Later the adjuster said the insuror haggled him down to $80. So, discounting the adjuster's 10 percent commission, I received $72 for my used ruined $78 typewriter: *en toto*, an equitable settlement between owner and insuror as entered through one of our economy's back doors.

☐ *Respirator* ... This item is so important and so unfamiliar to most people that it merits a section all its own, which begins on page 75.

Personal needs

Now that you know what kind of shelter and tools you'll need if a disaster comes knocking on your door, let's home in on what you and everyone else in your party will need to survive and be reasonably comfortable until the worst is over. This includes what you will wear, what you'll need to keep clean and comfortable, emergency supplies, personal documents, and extra necessities that others may need which you can trade for necessities you don't have. All of these are detailed beginning on the next page.

☐ *Personal Relief Kit,* alias *Go Bag* or *Bug-out Bag* ... The idea behind this collection of necessities is that wherever you go it goes, then if you're suddenly trapped in a disaster you'll have what you'll need —for days if necessary— until rescuers arrive. It contains the items on the right, which you should keep in a fannypack, shoulder bag, or other container you can easily carry with your arms free. Select items that are small, narrow, flat, and shaped so they can knit together and nestle inside each other to create a compact kit of emergency items you can take anywhere. A good place to keep this kit is in your car, where it will be close by when you're driving and usually nearby when you're not, and store it out of view. If you commute to work, keep a second kit at work along with a pair of walking shoes. Tailor the list on the right to fit your own needs, rethink your needs every year or so, and update each kit as your needs change.

☐ *Toiletries* ... during disasters these can become precious possessions. Use for cleanliness more than appearance, though the latter can be psychologically important at times. Include a brush, comb, soap, shampoo, razor, shaving cream, lip balm, a dozen spare buttons with needle and thread, personal medicines, plus two washcloths and towels per person. Keep these items separate from the go-bag in a private area near a source of clean water.

☐ *Clothes* ... In a disaster this is your first shelter. In cold weather include a scarf, parka, gloves, socks, boots, maybe thermal underwear. In warm weather count on shorts, tee shirts, and flipflops. In any weather have rain gear and a change of work clothes. A few essential articles appear on the mannikin on

CHANGE OF CLOTHES

SUNGLASSES IN PLASTIC BAG

KLEENEX

TOILETRIES

TOILET PAPER

SOAP. WASH-CLOTH, TOWELS

PERSONAL

RAINWEAR, USE CELLOPHANE JACKET DRYCLEANER COVER

WORK GLOVES

DUST MASK

PENCILS & PENS

LABELS   OPERATIONAL

BILLFOLD WITH PERSONAL INFO & NOTEPAD

CASH & COINS, ESP. QUARTERS (KEEP THIS AT HOME)

COMMUNICATION

SIGNAL MIRROR

CELLPHONE & CHARGER

COMPASS, SMALL

LOCAL MAP

WHISTLE

ASPIRIN

PAIN RELIEVER

BURN OINTMENT

ALLERGY RELIEF

PRESCRIPTION DRUGS

PAPER CLIPS

WIRE

RUBBER BANDS

ANTACID

DENTAL FLOSS

SEWING KIT

STRONG THREAD, DUCT TAPE

SAFETY PINS

CHAP STICK

CHUNK OF BEESWAX TO STRENGTHEN THREAD

ANTI-DIARRHEAL

WATER PURIF. TABLETS

SMALL FIRST AID KIT

PIPE CLEANERS

MEDICAL

RAZOR, TOOTHPICKS

LAXATIVE

CALLOUS PADS

Q-TIPS

SUPPLIES

STRING FISH LINE

BIRTHDAY CANDLES

FISH HOOKS

LED KEYCHAIN LIGHT & EXTRA BATTERY

FIRE TINDER

TIN FOIL

HEAT & LIGHT

NAILS

76. YOUR PERSONAL KIT OR GO BAG

SMALL CANDLES

WATERPROOF MATCHES

TOOLS

SCISSORS

PARACORD

RASP

EATING

ROUND

UTENSILS

TEA BAGS

FLAT

CHURCH KEY

FILES, 6 IN.

CAN OPENER

ENERGY FOODS

SPONGE

COOKGEAR, POTS NESTLE INTO EACH OTHER

DISH DETERGENT, SMALL BOTTLE

BAGGIES

WATER

SWISS ARMY KNIFE OR = MULTI-TOOL

the opposite page. If a disaster is forecast, wash and dry your dirty clothes before the power fails.

You also may want to have a *beekeeper's suit*. This full-length suit of white fabric can protect you not only from stinging insects but dust, toxic chemicals, nuclear fallout, volcanic ash, and germs from dead bodies. If you decide to invest in a beekeeper's suit, buy one with a long heavy-duty zipper in front, an elastic waist, elastic wrist and ankle openings, a cloth helmet with a see-through veil that covers your face, forearm-length gloves, and several pockets. This garment should be a bit loose, not snug, so it is easy to slip on and off and move around in.

❑ *Personal documents* … Not everyone will need all the documents listed below, but you should protect the ones you should have from being destroyed in a disaster. Especially important are documents that would be difficult to replace or whose absence would delay an insurance claim or complicate other important matters. Keep them in a waterproof, fireproof, and portable container. Keep the originals in the safe room, put a copy (or flash drive) in a safe deposit box, put another copy in your roadside emergency kit in your car, send a copy to a trusted friend or out-of-town relative, and give one to the executor of your estate. Update them annually.

One document listed below merits further discussion: the inventory of household possessions. For this you could include lists, photos, and/or videos of important personal belongings (try to include the brand name, model, serial number, approximate date and place of purchase, original cost, purchase receipt, current worth, and replacement cost of each) plus less expensive items like clothes, linens, and furniture. Go from room to room, and include the closets, outdoor furniture,

---

77. PERSONAL DOCUMENTS YOU SHOULD KEEP IN A SAFE PLACE

❑ Inventory of **household possessions**, rooms, open drawers, closets, yard, etc.   ❑ **Houseplans**
❑ **Cash**, bills and coins, especially quarters. If local banks and ATMs close, the amount you need may vary widely depending on type and duration of disaster. In prolonged power outages $1,000 may be barely adequate.   ❑ **Will**   ❑ **Diplomas**   ❑ **Passports**   ❑ **Mortgages** ❑ **Land deeds**
❑ **Automobile titles & bills of sale** (make, model, license number, photo of each)   ❑ **Next of kin**
❑ **Driving directions** & GPS coordinates to your home or workplace   ❑ **Insurance policies**, cards
❑ **Family records** (birth, marriage, & death certificates) ❑ **Personal ID cards**   ❑ **Driver's license**
❑ **Photos**, yourself, family members, house, events   ❑ **Promissory notes**   ❑ **Medical records**
❑ **Employment information** (including resumés)   ❑ **Citizenship papers**   ❑ **Military records**
❑ **Income tax returns** & property tax records   ❑ **Business contracts**   ❑ **Adoption papers**
❑ **Important addresses** & phone numbers   ❑ **Credit card** copies   ❑ **Debts, obligations**
❑ **Bank accounts**, numbers, addresses   ❑ **Real estate** holdings   ❑ **Religious records**
❑ **Safe deposit box** number, address   ❑ **Computer passwords**   ❑ **Professional licenses**
❑ **Firearm photos** & serial numbers   ❑ **Marriage certificate**   ❑ **Investment portfolios**
❑ **Foreign residences**, related info   ❑ **Divorces, custodies**   ❑ **Immunization records**
❑ **Stock and bond certificates**   ❑ **Warranties, guaranties**   ❑ **Extra house & car keys**
❑ **Social Security number**   ❑ **Pet immunization records**   ❑ **Other**

HAT ... IN WARM WEATHER, ONE WITH A WIDE BRIM TO SHIELD YOU FROM SUN AND RAIN PLUS A CHIN STRAP TO KEEP IT ON IN WIND. IN COLD WEATHER, A FUR-LINED CAP WITH EARMUFFS.

SUNGLASSES ... ESSENTIAL IN SNOW OR BRIGHT SUN. SELECT ONES WITH LARGE LENSES AND SIDE SHIELDS.

BACK BRACE ... DURING A DISASTER YOU MAY PERFORM UNFAMILIAR PHYSICAL LABOR FOR LONG PERIODS. THIS IS NO TIME TO HAVE YOUR FIRST BACK INJURY.

WORK GLOVES

FOOTWEAR ... BEST ARE ANKLE-HIGH LIGHTWEIGHT BOOTS WITH WIDE LUGS THAT EASILY SHED MUD. HAVE HIGH RUBBER BOOTS FOR SLOG-GING THRO' MUD & WATER, IN-SULATED BOOTS FOR BITTER COLD, AND SANDALS OR FLIP-FLOPS FOR LOAFING AROUND THE SAFE ROOM. MAKE EXTRA LACES FROM STRING OR DEN-TAL FLOSS IF YOU HAVEN'T ANY SPARES.

PROTECTIVE HEADWEAR ... A FOOTBALL, MOTORCYCLE, OR LACROSSE HEL-MET IS STRONGER THAN A HARD HAT & WILL PROTECT YOUR HEAD MORE FROM THE SIDES. SHOUL-DER PADS ALSO ARMOR YOUR UPPER TORSO. BUT THIS GEAR IS COSTLY. SCOUT FOR IT AT GARAGE SALES & FLEA MARKETS.

KERCHIEF ... THERE ARE MANY REASONS WHY EVERY BOY SCOUT WEARS ONE: A SWEAT BAND, SLING, SIGNAL FLAG, EARMUFFS, NAPKIN, APRON, DUST CLOTH, WASH CLOTH, POT HOLDER, DUST MASK, ETC.

PONCHO ... THIS LIGHTWEIGHT RAINWEAR CAN DOUBLE AS A TENT, GROUNDCLOTH, & DEBRIS CARRIER.

WALKING STICK ... THIN, STRONG, CHEST HEIGHT. THIS CAN STEADY YOU WHEN YOU'RE TRAVELING THRO' ROUGH TER-RAIN —SUCH AS DESCENDING A SLIPPERY STAIRCASE AT NIGHT WHEN THE POWER IS OUT.

78. FASHIONABLE APPAREL IN A DISASTER

garage tools, and other areas that are important to you. Be thorough. If you have photos of a hun-dred lost or destroyed items whose current value is a dollar each, your insurance adjuster will write you a check for 100 dollars —but if you have no records you'll get nothing.

☐ *Bedding and sleepwear* ... Ideally two changes of linens, three blankets, pillows, mattress pads, or a sleeping bag with an inner liner per person.

☐ *Mosquito netting* ... In insect-infested areas this screenlike fabric can protect your face in the day and your body in bed at night. A 4 x 6 foot sheet sells for about 6 bucks, it weighs next to nothing,

66

you can fold it and stuff into a pocket, and you can sew two pieces together with fish line or dental floss. Anchor it to sturdy surfaces with staples, hooks, velcro, and the earlier-mentioned bottle cap and nail that appears on page 55. Add washers and other weights along the bottom to keep a curtain of mosquito netting or cheesecloth from blowing in a breeze. Coarser meshes will stop mosquitoes but not gnats or no-see-ums. This textile makes a fine fishnet, and can be fashioned into shrouds that fit over brimmed hats as well as jackets with hoods and long sleeves, and even full-length trousers.

◯ *Barter items* … If a disaster precipitates a monetary crisis, the value of a dollar may plunge. Then you may need to barter to obtain what you need until things return to normal. Tradeable items could be anything useful you can spare that others may need: food, tools, firewood, alcohol, ammunition, batteries, camping equipment, medical supplies, toothpaste, clothes, linens, your labor or knowledge, or a skilled service such as repairing autos and appliances, security services, deliveries, food preparation, pedicures, etc.

 # People with special needs

When people get older, their joints become stiffer and their muscles grow weaker, and even if they aren't labeled as disabled they may need help with such simple tasks as picking things off floors and getting in and out of cars and bathtubs. Also, young children and women who are pregnant or caring for infants have limited capabilities. Indeed, a better word for this sizable portion of our population is *encumbered*. As for the truly disabled, a little help from others can make their lives much simpler. As a sample, a few years ago I shared a hotel room with a blind person at a writer's conference. During an initial discussion he asked what was the shape of the room, so I guided him around the edge of the bedroom and bathroom until he had a mental idea of what the space was like. Later while he was sitting on his bed he asked me, "I can't find my suitcase, do you know where it is?" I replied, "It's on your bed a foot behind your back." With such people a tiny favor can go a long way.

To prepare people with special needs for disasters, first determine who in your family, workplace, or neighborhood will need special assistance and what their condition is. Since many may be embarrassed about their condition or worry about discrimination and such crimes as robbery, discuss their needs privately and gently. Emphasize how they will be more comfortable, and how others can help if they need to be rescued or evacuated.

Below are ways to prepare encumbered people for disasters…

☞ Learn what facilities your community has and what equipment local rescuers may have for aiding the disabled. If an elder lives in a nursing home, discuss with a staff member the building's evacuation procedures and other aspects of disaster preparedness. Discuss with special-care and food-service providers how to continue service during a disaster. Rely on public manpower and resources when you can. If you cannot provide for the person yourself, register for assistance with the local office of emergency services or the local fire department.

☞ Assemble a folder for each disabled person you are responsible for that (1) summarizes their condition, (2) includes insurance and medicare information and contacts, (3) lists medications (including pills, glasses, hearing aids, dentures, etc.) and special dietary needs, and (4) discloses what assistance the person may need with eating, bathing, shopping, and transportation. The disabled person should keep this folder nearby; and copies should be given to a family member, the local office of emergency services if any, and someone who lives outside the area.

☞ Stock up on critical items: physical equipment as walkers or wheelchairs (list each item's maker, model number, and seller), batteries for wheelchairs, medications and special dietary needs, food for service animals, medications requiring refrigeration, and the like. Particularly important are oxygen bottles, because if a person runs out of this s/he can die. Know how they can be refilled during a disaster; the seller/supplier of the tanks should have this information (some fire stations can do this). Failure to do this is why two victims in our grim list "died when their oxygen machines ran out of oxygen."

☞ Regarding the visually impaired: Can s/he read Braille? Does s/he use a cane? Does s/he have a radio? Can s/he type? Can s/he dial a phone? Does s/he have a guide dog who needs to be fed, watered, and bathroomed? There are many kinds of blindness (I once attended a national convention for the blind, and one evening during dinner I heard a blind person say to another across their table,

"I can tell your hair is brown, but nothing else." I also saw a person write a check after lowering his right eye to a half inch above the tip of his pen). So determine each blind person's capabilities and limitations, and provide them with the proper equipment. Make sure no sharp objects are nearby, and clear floors of items they could trip over.

☞ Regarding the hearing-impaired: Can s/he receive visual warnings? Does s/he have a notepad and pencil to communicate by writing? Does his/her home have visual alarms? If s/he has a TV, does crawl script or other printing appear across the screen? Telecommunication devices are available for the blind and the deaf, and some are portable.

☞ Regarding the mobily impaired: Does s/he have a wheelchair, walker, or crutches to get around? Discuss the person's needs with his or her employer. If a mobily impaired person lives or works on an upper floor, see that s/he has access to an *escape chair*. This wheeled seat allows its passenger to be evacuated down a stair more safely than in a wheelchair if an elevator is unusable. The chair can be quickly folded and stored near the top of the stairs, though each needs an attendant. Some models are unduly expensive, so shop around.

79.[31] **ESCAPE CHAIR**

☞ If the person lives in an apartment, ask the management to mark accessible exits that will be visible in a blackout, and arrange to aid the disabled from the building.

☞ Where a pregnant woman lives, see that her routines are simple and tension-free. Confine her activities to one floor, remove clutter from the floor, and make sure an ambulance can reach her if she goes into labor.

☞ See that non-English-speaking persons are safe and understand what is happening.

☞ Create a network of neighbors, relatives, friends, and coworkers who understand each person's needs, can aid him or her in an emergency, and know how to operate any needed equipment.

☞ When the danger is past, disabled persons may need extra help in returning home and resuming their normal routines.

Children also require special preparation before disasters, as detailed below. Whatever a child's age, have his/her doctor provide you with a copy of their medical and vaccination records.

Infants … Children from newborn to when they begin to walk. If a baby is in the neonatal intensive care unit of a hospital, find what the hospital's disaster plan is and where the baby would be sent during a disaster. A checklist of items for infants …

☞ Baby formula, bottles, baby food, powdered milk, diapers, medications, and related supplies. Mother's milk is especially desirable during disasters because it is naturally clean and requires no refrigeration, bottles, or water for preparing formula. The La Leche League (www.Lillian.org) provides information about breastfeeding for women affected by disasters.

☞ Diapers (8 to 12 a day) plus diaper wipes, a changing surface, and disinfectants for cleaning everything after each use. Dispose of used diapers in buckets with sealed lids.

☞ Small towels for drying after bathing, cleaning eating surfaces, and messes, plus baby laundry detergent. A laundry basket can serve as a baby bed.

☞ A portable crib or bassinet with bed sheets and soft sleeping surface, and a play pen.

☞ A basin for sponge baths, sponges, and gentle soap.

☞ A rectal thermometer and lubricant, non-aspirin liquid pain reliever, diaper rash ointment, pacifiers, teething rings, etc.

☞ Small blankets, pillows, extra clothes. Also a few dolls and baby toys.

80. DISASTER DIVERSIONS FOR YOUNG AND OLD

JIGSAW PUZZLES … CAN ENTERTAIN SEVERAL KIDS & GROWNUPS AT ONE TIME

LEGOS … ONE OF THE MOST "CONSTRUCTIVE" PASTIMES, ENJOYABLE TO TODDLERS AND GRANDPARENTS. ANOTHER IS BLOCKS: SEE WHO CAN BUILD THE HIGHEST SKYSCRAPER WITH THE FEWEST BLOCKS.

CARD GAMES … DEPENDING ON THE PLAYERS' AGES: WAR, FISH, GIN RUMMY, HEARTS, BRIDGE. ALSO SOLITAIRE (A BOOK OF THESE WOULD HELP). ANOTHER CARD GAME: GIVE TWO CONTESTANTS HALF A DECK AND SEE WHO CAN BUILD THE TALLEST HOUSE OF CARDS.

BOOKS … STORYTELLING IS GREAT (YOU MIGHT WANT TO SKIP THE GHOST STORIES). OLDER CHILDREN MAY BE HAPPIER CHOOSING THEIR OWN TEXTS.

Toddlers … Children who can walk but haven't yet started kindergarten. They need room to crawl and walk, and as they learn to talk they can discuss their feelings and tell what they need. Encourage simple, panic-free discussions about disasters, listen carefully, and give simple, clear answers to their questions. Stock up on …

☞ Soft bite-size foods (avoid small foods they could choke on).

☞ Toys like building blocks, pop-up books, coloring books, teddy bears and other cuddly animals, plus books that older people can read to them.

☞ Potty and diapers (6 to 10 a day).

☞ A safe area to play.

Older kids … Kindergarteners to junior high schoolers who haven't developed the muscles and judgement of grownups. They can eat with adults and usually can discuss their feelings and fears. Prepare them as follows …

☞ Show them how to dial the phone to reach the fire department, hospital, and police.

☞ Teach them how to look things up on a computer.

☞ Prepare a list of simple chores they could do, like setting the table and taking out the trash.

☞ When a disaster appears in the newspaper, read the article to them, then discuss their feelings about the incident. You could describe a potential situation and ask what they would do. Reward them with a "cookie badge" when they make cogent comments.

☞ Stock up on music, games, and art supplies.

Young teenagers … From junior high to driving age. These children are physically active and can usually communicate well with adults. They can read books and enjoy music on their own, many today can use computers, and most can help around the house and participate in family decision-making. A few ways to help them be ready …

PAPER GAMES … CONNECT-THE-DOTS, TIC-TAC-TOE, PAPER PLANES (COOKIE PRIZES TO THE FARTHEST FLIER), AND ORIGAMI (A BOOK WOULD BE HELPFUL). HAVE PENCILS AND PAPER FOR DRAWING, AND CRAYONS & COLORING BOOKS FOR PRESCHOOLERS.

BOARD GAMES … CHECKERS, PARCHESI, MONOPOLY, AND THAT GRAND MASTER OF ALL, CHESS. COOKIE PRIZES TO THE WINNAHS. A FEW NONBOARD GAMES ARE 20 QUESTIONS, CHARADES, AND SONGS WITH MANY VERSES.

☞ Read newspapers and magazines and watch TV with them. Discuss any disasters that occur: how they happen, the harm they do, and how to prevent or avoid them. Especially help them understand the harsher realities of disasters.

☞ If they are prone to have anger outbursts or engage in risk-taking behavior, discuss situations that could activate such behavior, and describe how calmer responses will create more effective results.

☞ Show them how to manage things at home if you are incapacitated.

Transportation

A car or truck is an important part of your efforts to prepare for, endure, and recover from disasters. This transportation will help you buy supplies, evacuate, clean up your property, and if you are ever stuck or stranded on the road it will provide you with shelter and a place to sleep. These vehicles are much more useful if each is equipped with an emergency roadside kit and a car pack as detailed below and appears in figures 82 and 85. One thing you should not carry in a car is a can of gasoline. To give you some perspective here, an explosion of one gallon of gasoline will create a fireball about four feet in diameter.

Roadside emergency kit ... This can be a small trunk (perhaps 14 inches high, 18 inches wide, and 30 inches long) that holds vehicle-related items. The best containers are made of translucent propylene (lets you partly see what's inside), have a hinged top with a watertight seal (keeps out moisture, dust, and pests), and have handles for carrying. It needn't be lockable (you might not have the key when you need to open it quickly), and it shouldn't have wheels (then it could roll around while you're driving). Some items in this container you'll also have in the disaster equipment closet, but each vehicle should carry duplicates in case you need them on the road. Some items such as tire chains aren't necessary in certain climates or geographic regions.

Three items in figure 82 whose names have the superscripts **A**, **B**, and **C** merit further comment ...

A. *Sidewalk chalk* ... These big colored chalks (about an inch thick and 4 inches long) are perfect for writing emergency messages on pavements, rocks, and other rough surfaces. Every driver should have at least one. These chalks are popular with artists who make beautiful drawings on city sidewalks.

B. *Help flag* ...When mounted on a car as appears on the right this distress signal can be seen a hundred yards away. It is made in Peru, Indiana that is, by Orion Products.

71

AUTO ESCAPE TOOL, BREAKS WINDOWS & CUTS SEATS (KEEP CLOSE TO DRIVER'S SEAT

SIDEWALK CHALK A

FRICTION TAPE

LOCK DE-ICER

AUTO FUSES

TIRE GAUGE

UTILITY KNIFE & EXTRA BLADES

HELP FLAG B

SNOW BRUSH, TO CLEAN WINDOWS & LIGHTS

ICE SCRAPER

SIPHON, 6 FT

MECHANICAL TOOLS

WINDSHIELD WIPER FLUID, 32 OZ BOTTLE

ROADSIDE REFLECTORS

L.E.D. PUCK LIGHT C

ELECTRIC WIRE, 25 FT

JACK & HANDLE

ANTIFREEZE

82. YOUR VEHICLE'S ROADSIDE EMERGENCY KIT

COME-ALONG

LUG WRENCH, HUBCAP LEVER, CROWBAR

3 POUND HAMMER, TO TURN LUG WRENCH & DO OTHER TOUGH CHORES

HAND-OPERATED TIRE PUMP (WORKS IF BATTERY IS DEAD)

MOTOR OIL

FIRE EXTINGUISHER, SMALL "ABC" TYPE

WATER, 2 GAL, FOR DRINKING, RADIATOR, & CLEANING

JUMPER CABLES, OR EQUAL CAR-TO-CAR STARTER

PICK & SHOVEL, TO DIG OUT TIRES, SHOVEL SNOW, ETC.

GAS CAN, 2 GAL (KEEP EMPTY)

TOW STRAP OR CHAIN

RESPIRATOR

SHEET & BLANKETS OR **SLEEPING BAG**

TIRE CHAINS, FOR DEEP SNOW

BUNGEE CORDS

PLASTIC SHEETING

RAGS

PAPER TOWELS

SAND, 40 POUND BAG

C. *LED puck light* … This is a hockey-puck-size flashing light that is visible a half mile away. Destined to replace the present candle-like roadside flares, these petite beacons float and are crushproof, corrosion-proof, waterproof, and they have a magnetic back for attaching to fenders and other metal surfaces on your car. They run 50 hours on a single charge and have several flashing patterns including Morse code **S O S**. They certainly have a bright future.

83. LED PUCK LIGHT

Car pack … Also known as a portable car kit, this is a small knapsack (see figure 85) that holds a number of items you may need outside the car if you work nearby or leave to seek help. This container should ride on your back so your arms are free, it should be waterproof in case it rains or snows, and it should have several easy-to-reach pockets outside. Some items in this pack and the emergency roadside kit you could carry in your pockets or around your neck, some you might not need in the area you drive in, and some are also in your go bag and first-aid kit. But it is a good idea to have the same good thing in two places, especially if it is small and cheap.

Weapons

Some abhor weapons while others embrace them. If you have a firearm, know how to carry, shoot and store it, be familiar with the ammunition it uses, and know your state and local laws. All this involves studying books, taking courses (the Civilian Marksmanship Program can help here), and constant practice. A .22 rifle can kill small game and scare away potential looters. If you are threatened by a mugger and have a flare gun in your pocket, shoot it in his face. Hatchets, knives, and machetes may be useful in close quarters if you are athletic and streetwise. Better may be a cannister of *pepper spray*. A 4-ounce container emits a cone-shaped fog 5 to 10 feet long for up to 30 seconds that will blind and choke the victim —if it isn't windy and the victim doesn't duck. Whatever you use, you will never kill anything that you miss; so practice constantly in advance, and use it sparingly if not well.

Practice in advance

Like a fire drill, the more you practice this book's advisories in advance, the better you will perform them when a disaster catches you unaware. It's also more fun to practice when you don't need to. Several weeks or months after you've packed your emergency kits, you may forget where each item is and be unable to find them when a disaster catches you unawares. One antidote for this is to open your emergency kits every few months and refresh your memory as to where it is and what it is for, and refresh its contents if necessary (the water bottles for example).

SMALL FIRST AID KIT

BUG SPRAY

TOOTHBRUSH. TOOTHPASTE

Q TIPS

ASPIRIN

CHAP STICK

MIRROR

DENTAL FLOSS

DUCT TAPE

TOILET PAPER

BLANKET IN PLASTIC BAG

CLOTHES, EXTRA CHANGE

GLOVES

WIDE-BRIM HAT

HATCHET IN SHEATH

PONCHO

SPARE SHOES

CAMERA, TO DOCUMENT ACCIDENTS, LANDMARKS, ETC.

LOCAL MAPS

HUNTING KNIFE IN SHEATH

TIN FOIL, SMALL ROLL

THERMOMETER

NOTE PAD

WHISTLE

SMALL COMPASS

BINOCULARS

PARACORD, 200 FT

85. THE PORTABLE CAR KIT

RUBBER BANDS

PENCIL, PEN, ERASER

FLASHLIGHT & EXTRA BATTERIES

SWISS ARMY KNIFE OR =

DUST MASKS, 3 IF AIR CONTAINS DUST, TOXINS, ETC.

FISH HOOKS

STRING & FISH LINE

FIRE TINDER

WATER-PROOF MATCHES

RAZOR, TOOTHPICKS

PIPE CLEANERS

NAILS

CANDLES, SMALL

SPONGE

WIRE

FREEZER BAGS, SEVERAL TAKE UP LITTLE SPACE

PAPER CLIPS

SAFETY PINS

NEEDLES &THREAD

FILES

KLEENEX

ENERGY FOOD

TEABAGS

CAN OPENER

PLASTIC UTENSILS

CHURCH KEY

DYE MARKER

DISH DETERGENT

LIFESTRAW WATER FILTER

WATER PURIF. TABLETS

WATER

74

Often harder than occasional practicing is ***periodic testing.*** The local fire department does this every Monday night. If I want to see the show, I can watch the station doors open and the fire engines roll onto the tarmac, and while some of the crew sweeps the floors in the cavernous interior behind, others put on their fire hats and galoshes and open the cabinets all around and check the equipment. Especially fun to watch is the hook-and-ladder truck whose outriggers extend from the vehicle's four corners to stabilize it as the long ladder rises from the engine's top and its sections telescope high above the station's roof, then the ladder slowly rotates in a full circle. Then all these mechanisms are reversed, until the long red truck rolls back into the garage, hopefully not to move an inch until next Monday night.

You should check your equipment like this too. It is the number one way to make sure everything will work the way you want when a disaster comes sneaking into your yard, your house, your life.

Generators, anyone?

Why pay a thousand dollars or more for a cubic yard of material that ravaged the environment in its making, costs several hundred dollars more for an electrician to install safely, and needs monthly testing? Improperly installed or used, onsite generators can kill in minutes —which is why five people on our grim list "died of carbon monoxide poisoning while operating a gasoline generator in their home." For every person who dies, possibly hundreds more are sickened with headaches, speech disabilities, partial blindness, seizures, fibrillation, permanent memory loss, and neurological damage. For these reasons never locate these units within 20 feet of a building. During hurricane Sandy, a standby generator installed beside an apartment complex three miles from my home was found to be sending carbon monoxide into one of the apartments.

An onsite generator must also be protected by a weatherproof enclosure with a strong foundation that can withstand high winds —which kicks the cost up another few thousand dollars. They also cost money to run: a 3-kilowatt unit (which produces up to 3,000 watts of electricity) consumes about 3 gallons of gas every 5 hours (that's nearly three dollars an hour), so if the power fails the owner may have to drive to a service station every day or so, which wastes more gas, then wait in a long line at the pump which wastes time and still more gas, and all of this imposes even greater demands on local supplies —and if everybody tries to do it, soon nobody can do it. In fact, all the dollars that many would spend to run an onsite generator would likely exceed the dollars they would lose if all the food in their freezer spoiled.

Onsite generators also are inefficient: a 3-kilowatt genset produces 3,000 watts of power even if you use only a 40-watt light bulb (with utility power you consume only what you use). Sometimes they won't start. They break down. Their wires can overheat and burn. They need tuneups and valve jobs like any internal combustion engine. Before refilling they should be shut off and allowed to cool because gasoline spilled on a hot surface can explode. And running one makes you a noisy neighbor.

Finally, generators rob you of the opportunity to be resourceful. Though disasters are no fun, when you know you can overcome them with your mind and eyes and hands you'll be more confident and clever in everything else you do — and the dollars you would spend will be returned to you as dividends of dominance, strength, and self-reliance. Your neighbors will like you more, and you'll have more money in your pocket for better days.

86. A DEBRIS CLOUD FROM TWO FALLEN BUILDINGS [33]

Respirators

What would you do if you suddenly found yourself choking on the very air you breathe? What would you reach for? Where would you go? Where could you find or buy what you needed? How would you even *know* what you needed, weeks or months or years in advance?

Generally you can live for three weeks without food and three days without water, but only three minutes without air. Such deprivation could occur in several ways. You could be inside a burning building whose thick smoke you could not escape like the Happy Land nightclub fire near New York City in 1990, in which 87 trapped people breathed their last. You could be near a factory that spews an airborne poison into the air like the one in Bhopal, India, in 1984, which killed 18,000 people and injured 558,000 more.[34] Or you could be near a tall building that collapses like the World Trade Center in September 2001, which created a huge debris cloud whose vapors contained more than 30 respirable toxins: particles of pulverized cement and glass, smoke from burning plastics and other combustibles, fumes of disintegrated copper and a dozen other metals, vapors from volatile organic compounds and PCBs, and disease pathogens from plumbing fixtures used just before the collapse. The chances are slim that you would ever experience such disasters —yet these events do occur. Particularly vulnerable are densely populated areas that have a number of tall buildings which could collapse not only due to terrorist attacks but hurricanes, fires, explosions, construction failures, and other calamities. Such areas include every urban environment in America, indeed the world. Furthermore, airborne hazards spread by terrorists may carry disease pathogens, some that are deadly smell sweet, and some are so potent they can kill you before your nose detects them. Most people haven't a clue what they would do during those dreadful moments when their nose warns their brain that the air entering their lungs is unsafe. Sadly, the solution is not as simple as going to the nearest hardware store and buying a one-size-fits-all respirator that removes every airborne hazard and is simple and comfortable to wear.

The truth?

There are many kinds of respirators —but none will remove every toxin you could inhale. Worse, few retailers carry any at all. You can buy them online, but this is one product you should try on before you buy it; because it could be useless if it doesn't fit properly, or you don't know how to use it correctly, or you don't know how to replace its filters when they need changing, or you don't know how to store it correctly when not using it. And instructors who can explain these things are hard to find. As a result, trying to save your life in a respiratory disaster is a minefield of misconceptions and misapplications.

What is a respirator?

... A respirator is a facepiece which contains a filter that protects the wearer against hazards in the air prior to inhalation. The facepiece fits over the wearer's nose and mouth, and is held in place with straps, harnesses, or other methods. Some protect the wearer from particles floating in the air, while others keep the wearer from inhaling biological agents, airborne chemicals, and air containing little or no oxygen. Each may protect against one hazard quite well but offer little or no protection against another. Most respirators have one filter, mounted in front of the nose and mouth, or two, mounted on each side of the nose in front of the cheeks, while a few have a hose whose upper end is mounted in front of the lower face and whose lower end is connected to the filter mounted on the chest or behind the waist. Each may cover the bottom half of the wearer's face including the nose and mouth, it may cover the entire face, or it may enclose the head. A half-face respirator is typically worn where the contaminants are not toxic to the wearer's eyes or facial area (example, a person who is spray-painting an object), but a person working with chlorine gas would need a full-face respirator. Knowing what you would use a respirator for is an important criteria for buying one. This is easy for specific occupational or health hazards, but difficult for a homeowner who wants to protect ones' family against any airborne disaster that could occur.

Respirators are made in many different styles and sizes to accommodate all types of face shapes. But some won't fit on faces wearing glasses, some will leak around the edges if the wearer has facial hair, some prevent the user from talking, and most won't fit small children and infants due to their small faces. These possibilities are why you should try a respirator before buying it. Be especially sure it will fit snugly against your face. You should also know how and when to put it on and take it off, how to replace its filters, how to store and keep it in working order, and how to dispose of it properly when necessary. Also, breathing through most respirators is slightly more difficult than breathing in open air, so people with asthma or emphysema may have trouble using them. Most do not supply oxygen (if you use them near a fire you could suffocate due to lack of oxygen or succumb to carbon monoxide), and most have parts that will melt if exposed to hot temperatures.

Filters

... This is a respirator's most important part: all other components are made to facilitate its function. Most common filters fit into a canister about the size of a tunafish can that contains a porous material that removes particulate matter and/or a sorbent or catalyst that removes vapors and gases from inhaled air. Though a dozen or so filters are available, each will remove some toxins but none will remove everything. Particularly troublesome is carbon monoxide. This product of combustion snatches up all the oxygen in the air that you need to stay alive —so it deprives you of the very molecules you may believe the filter will deliver. This problem confronted the rescuers after the World Trade Center towers collapsed, one of whom said: "You couldn't begin to move into an area safe from carbon monoxide, we couldn't find one."[35] A method has been tentatively developed that converts carbon monoxide to carbon dioxide, which would at least allow the wearer a few extra minutes to escape to a safe area. Some respirators have a small motor that can push air through them plus a battery or other portable source of energy to run the motor. These devices usually remove a greater number of agents and have a greater capacity before the filter needs replacing, but they are expensive. Most filter cartridges have a limited shelf life, they must remain in airtight packages until they are used, and when used they don't last forever: they slowly fill with the removed hazard until they become clogged, then must be replaced. A little hunting on the internet will uncover a number of instruction manuals and product listings regarding the purchase and use of respirators and filters. Particularly informative are OSHA, 3M, and the U.S. Department of Defense.

Extra equipment … A respirator may require extra equipment if it is to protect your lungs safely. If the airborne hazard could damage your eyes or skin, you must wear goggles, a face mask, or a full-face model, and possibly gloves and protective clothing. If the disaster site experiences drilling, blasting, breaking up concrete, heavy vehicles loading rubble, or other loud noises, you will need to protect your ears. If the airborne hazard is accompanied by scattered debris, downed power lines, and slick, tilted, or oily floors, you may need to wear rugged water-resistant work clothes, heavy work gloves, and thick-soled rubber boots, and even carry a walking stick. To eliminate any onsite surprises, make sure the devices on and around your head as well as the rest of your apparel all fit comfortably together. Thus you should try everything together before buying anything.

Use factors … Several onsite factors influence the use of respirators and filters. Whatever the situation, the second thing you should do (the first being to flee the area if you can) is, if you can, *find what the hazardous agent is.* Then you can more capably consider the following …

117

Suddenness of onset … Some agents initially endanger an area at very low concentrations and slowly increase, while others quickly envelop you with dangerous or lethal concentrations. Fortunately the great majority arrive slowly, first invading your nostrils with a noxious whiff, so you usually have time to seek protection before you are incapacitated. Only if you linger with your nose and mouth uncovered may you suddenly lose consciousness. If the vapor should suddenly envelop you, you need the proper equipment close by. In the World Trade Center collapse, people enveloped by the debris cloud could breathe through a shirt sleeve or other fabric for a short while until they reached safe air.

Concentration … If the agent is smoky or misty, you can gauge its concentration by how much it reduces visibility. If this is less than 30 feet, most filters clog rapidly, and you may need several cannisters to protect yourself.

Density … This is the airborne hazard's weight compared to air. If lighter than air, the agent will float upward and you should flee downward —into basements, tunnels, and the like. If heavier than air, the agent will settle downward and you should flee upward —into the upper floors of multistory buildings and similar elevations. In the Bhopal disaster, the gas cloud was slightly heavier than air and hovered close to the ground as it spread through communities of mostly one-story dwellings. If these areas had multistory buildings, people could have fled to the upper floors and survived.[36] As for carbon monoxide, it is 97 percent as dense as air, which is so slight it will take many minutes for this gas to settle below the air you breathe —but it can take only four minutes to kill you.

Length of exposure ... Will you need a respirator only until you can escape the agent, or will you need it for such lengthy activities as rescuing victims, retrieving valued belongings from the affected area, or because you must remain where you are? If any of the latter or you will engage in strenuous exercise, your apparatus must be more robust or you should carry extra cannisters.

87. DUST MASK

The weather ... Is it cold? Hot? Windy? Rainy? Snowy? In hot weather many airborne toxins become more volatile and dissolve more easily in water. In windy weather they are blown away —good if you're upwind, bad if downwind. In rainy weather the air is washed of toxic particles, but some can become so heavy they can collapse roofs: a common occurrence with volcanic ash. As for snow, it is slippery and dangerous and hides everything, which makes it more dangerous to perform needed operations.

The major respirators ... These are detailed below ...

Your clothes ... By unbuttoning a shirt sleeve or burying your nose and mouth in the crook of your bent elbow, you may buy enough time to reach safe air. You can also grab a paper towel, tissues, piece of newspaper, or a cloth or paper napkin and ball it up, wet it, and shove it in your mouth and hold your nose so you breathe only through your mouth. If you are wearing a bandana, fit it around your face masked-bandit style. If you have on a tee shirt or turtleneck sweater, fit it over your head so the shirt's neck rests on the bridge of your nose and the fabric below falls about your neck and shoulders.

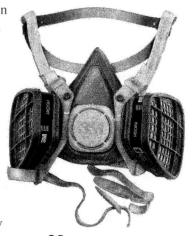

88. CHEMICAL CARTRIDGE RESPIRATOR

Dust mask (figure 87) ... This is a cup-shaped porous material that fits over your nose and mouth. It has a metal strip over the bridge of your nose that you can pinch to close any openings around the mask below your eyes, and it has elastic side bands that you slip over your head or fit over your ears. These respirators filter only particles of dust. They are widely available in hardware stores.

Chemical cartridge respirator (figure 88) ... This fits over your lower face and has one or two cartridges that filter chemicals, gases, and vapors from the air you breathe. Except for common dust and smoke particles you must know what the airborne particle is and select a filter that will remove it. Some hardware stores sell these units also.

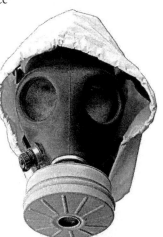

89. GAS MASK

Gas mask (figure 89)… This rubberized mask protects your face and eyes and has a cartridge at your chin. The best models have an NBC (nuclear, biological, chemical) filter that absorbs nuclear fallout, most biological agents, paint sprays, and the like. Another full-face mask is a *powered air-purifying (PAPR) respirator*. This has a visor that offers wide visibility and a battery-powered fan that pulls hazardous air through the filter, making it easy to breathe.

Escape hood (figure 90) … This shrouds your head and has a transparent face, neck seal, and motorized cannister filter mounted on the front or back. This will protect you from most chemical and biological agents in terrorist attacks, toxic fumes from hazardous material accidents, nuclear fallout, disease germs in epidemics, and smoke or dust from explosions. But they are expensive.

Self-contained breathing apparatus (SCBA) … This is used by firefighters and scuba divers (note the acronym) to provide a constant supply of oxygen. It has a snugly fitting facepiece that instead of containing a filter draws pure air from a pressurized tank mounted on the wearer's back. It weighs 30 pounds or more, lasts about an hour, and requires training to operate.[38]

90.[37] **ESCAPE HOOD**

Up to now we have discussed disasters in general. The next 28 pages describe how to prepare for a number of specific disasters well before they may arrive.

To prepare for a blackout

These advisories apply for heat waves, storms, and other disasters that cause the power to fail.

☞ Keep your vehicle's tank at least two-thirds full. Gas station pumps run on electricity and many stations have no generators.

☞ Place bricks or large plastic containers of water or other liquids in your refrigerator or freezer if it isn't full. Leave an inch of space at the container's top since water expands as it freezes. The bricks or water will absorb heat that otherwise would thaw the food. For more about this see page 110.

☞ If you regularly use the garage to enter your house, carry a key with you or hide one just outside (but not in an area that could be flooded) in case the garage door won't open. Know where the manual lever of your electric garage door opener is and how to operate it.

☞ Some cities have a law that says in high-rise buildings one escape exit door on every three floors must be openable from the stairwell to allow a person fleeing from an emergency on one floor to descend a few floors and re-enter the building without having to go down to the first floor. Also, many high-rise buildings can remotely unlock all exit doors during an emergency. However, for security reasons, in many buildings no emergency door can be opened from the stairwell, and if you pass through such a door you must descend to the first floor to re-enter the building unless someone inside on an upper floor will re-open a door for you. If you live or work in a high-rise building, find what the local law or building policy is regarding its emergency doors and which floors near yours may always be unlocked.

To prepare for a hurricane

A hurricane is a large area of moisture-laden winds moving from 74 to 180 miles per hour that rotate counterclockwise around a calm central eye. These storms originate in the tropical Atlantic, and they occur along U. S. coasts from eastern Maine to Southern Texas from June 1 to November 1 but mostly from late August through September. An average of two hurricanes per year strike the U.S. Today the National Weather Service can fairly accurately predict hurricane paths for five days in advance and it issues three kinds of hurricane alerts …

Hurricane Advisory … This gives the name of the storm, its present and forecasted direction, its forward velocity, maximum velocity of its rotating winds, and location of the eye. These messages are issued at six-hour intervals at midnight, 6:00 a.m., noon, and 6:00 p.m., Eastern Daylight Time.

Hurricane Watch … This alert occurs within 72 hours of a hurricane's potential arrival in an area. It indicates the storm is a real possibility but not imminent. This message is meant to warn residents in the area to listen to further advisories and act quickly if hurricane warnings are issued.

Hurricane Warning … This indicates that the hurricane is expected to reach a particular coastal area within 24 hours and its residents can expect high winds, dangerously high water, and/or very high waves. Residents should gather survival materials and either protect their homes or evacuate.

Hurricanes can damage large areas with *rains*, *surges*, and *winds*, as follows …

Rains … Normally 5 to 10 inches but 20 inches or more if the storm moves slowly. As the storm moves inland, its heavy rainfall combined with local topography can cause widespread flooding in lowland areas and devastating landslides in hilly terrain.

Surges … As a hurricane moves over the ocean, its high winds push the water before it into a dome that may be 20 feet high and 100 miles wide. This volume is highest where the winds are strongest, it is higher when it occurs at the local surf's high tide, and is higher still when the high tide occurs during a full or new moon. As the storm approaches landfall the dome of water rises slowly, but as the storm's eye reaches land the water may rise 3 or 4 feet in an hour —then wind-whipped waves packing a wallop as much as 1,700 pounds per cubic yard hammer any buildings and elevated terrain in its path. After the eye passes the water recedes — then as the surge rakes back into the sea it may wash away buildings weakened by the initial surge. Ninety percent of hurricane fatalities are due to surges. The worst in America struck Galveston, Texas, in September 1900 and left several square miles of the city under 15 feet of water and washed more than three miles inland. Here is an eyewitness account: "Houses near the beach began falling first. The storm lifted debris from one row of buildings and hurled it against the next row until eventually two-thirds of the city had been destroyed."[39] You wouldn't want to get in the way of a force like this, which killed 8,000 people in a small city.

Winds … These masses of moist air move in a certain direction and rotate counter-clockwise around a central eye. Their windspeed at any one place is the sum of the storm's forward speed (which averages 15 to 40 mph) and its rotational speed (which may be as high as 180 mph). Hence as the storm moves, its windspeed and wind direction vary, as sketched in figure 91. The strongest winds typically occur 20 to 30 miles to the right of the eye, and they dissipate as the storm travels over land.

To give you an idea how dangerous hurricane winds are, here is a formula that converts wind power from miles per hour to pounds per square foot …

$$V^2 = 384\,P$$

wherein V = velocity (mph)
and P = air pressure (psf)

According to this formula, a 50 mile-an-hour wind exerts a pressure of 6.5 pounds against a square foot of vertical area. If you're $5^{1}/_{2}$ feet tall and of medium build, your body's front is about 7 square feet in area; so a wind blowing at you at 50 mph will push against you with a force of about 39 pounds. You could resist this if you lean into the wind and the ground isn't slippery. However, a wind's pushing power increases according to the *square* of its speed (note the exponent ^{2} in the formula above) —so if a 50 mph hurricane will push against you with a force of 39 pounds, a 100 mph

91.

30 MPH FORWARD

145 MPH ACTUAL VELOCITY

120 MPH ROTATIONAL VELOCITY

IF YOU ARE HERE

ACTUAL VELOCITY AT ANY POINT IS VECTOR SUM OF FORWARD & ROTATIONAL VELOCITIES

EYE

HURRICANE ROTATES COUNTER-CLOCKWISE USUALLY BETWEEN 80 & 150 MPH

HURRICANE MOVES FORWARD USUALLY BETWEEN 20 & 30 MPH

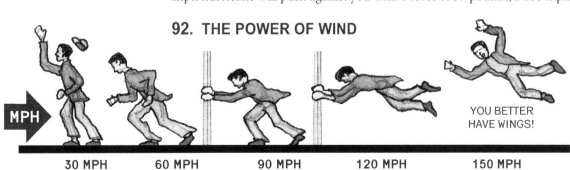

92. THE POWER OF WIND

MPH

YOU BETTER HAVE WINGS!

30 MPH 60 MPH 90 MPH 120 MPH 150 MPH

hurricane will push against you with a force of 175 pounds, and a 150 mph hurricane will push with 410 pounds! If this force gets under you, it will send you flying through the air like a feather in a pillowfight. It certainly is not a nice way to meet your neighbors. Similarly, if a hurricane blows against a two-car garage door (typically 18 feet wide x 6 feet 8 inches high) at 50 mph it will push against the door at a pressure of about 670 pounds, at 100 mph it will push against the door at 3,000 pounds, and at 150 mph it will push at more than 7,000 pounds! As further proof, see what a Florida hurricane did to a sheet of plywood in figure 93 on the right.

Now let's rev these numbers up to the force of an EF5 tornado, whose winds may exceed 250 mph. A 250 mph wind will press against the above garage door with a force of more than 19,500 pounds. That's nearly ten tons! This force will flatten the garage door and when it enters the garage behind will either blow down the far wall or deflect upward, then —since the connectors between a wall and roof are usually weak— this force will usually lift the roof off the garage and scatter it into the sky. A 250 mph wind will also

93. [40]

bludgeon your body with a force of nearly 1,150 pounds, which is a quick way to earn a one-way ticket to a funeral parlor. Now you know why you should get away from high winds fast, far, and deep.

To prepare for a hurricane well before it arrives, know your community's warning systems, disaster plans, and evacuation routes so you can reach them quickly. Also…

F
FROM
114

☞ Know your property's elevation above sea level and any nearby rivers and lakes. Know how far it is from any sea or lake shores and higher elevations inland. Know if you live in a flood-prone area and the location of any levees and dams whose failure could flood you.

☞ Know an escape route you can follow at night, and practice it with your family. Be able to reach high ground in 15 minutes by car, bike, or foot. If any multistory concrete structure is nearby and you can reach the third floor, you will likely be safe.

☞ Trim the trees and shrubs around the building so winds won't easily damage it.

☞ Repair loose and clogged rain gutters and downspouts.

☞ If you have a garage door, have a professional installer strengthen the door by adding girts across its back and bracing the glider wheel tracks.

☞ Anchor playhouses, sheds, and other outbuildings to permanent concrete foundations. Straps, cables, chains, posts, and auger anchors will not secure these structures in high winds.

☞ Mount easily operable storm shutters on each window or cut pieces of $3/4$ inch exterior-grade plywood to fit over your windows as described on page 16. As this earlier text indicates, this seemingly simple "Sunday chore" for laymen is typically a time-consuming job for professionals.

☞ Reinforce any banks or ramparts below your house with rip-rap or other large rocks to keep floods from eroding them. Locate building materials, sandbags, tools, and other items on high ground so they will be above flood waters when you need them.

☞ Check your insurance coverage.

To read how to prepare for a hurricane days before it arrives, turn to page 114.

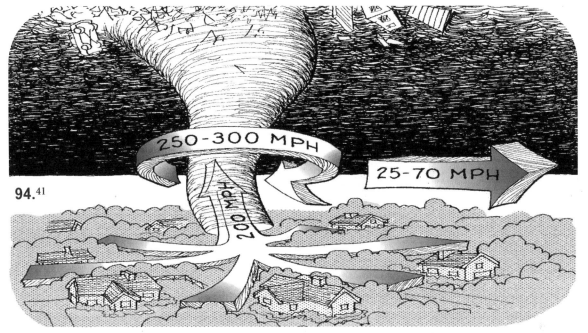

94.⁴¹

To prepare for a tornado

A tornado is a writhing serpentine funnel that usually travels east to northeast at speeds of 25 to 70 miles an hour and often takes an erratic skipping path, its tapered tip hopping randomly over one area then descending furiously on another. The funnel's walls of rain, dust, and debris whirling counterclockwise at speeds exceeding 250 miles an hour can send facades and roofs flying through the air like frisbies, exposing floors to high-velocity debris and heavy rain; and the funnel's whirling creates a vacuum inside which draws the surrounding ground air toward its base that sucks up everything it passes over like a huge vacuum cleaner and spouts clouds of fragments into the sky. Such winds can peel bark off trees and pavement off streets. In flat open country the funnel can be seen from afar, but in wooded areas it may descend on its victims before they have a chance to seek shelter, the only warning being a dark sky and a characteristic roar that makes you wonder, "What's a freight train doing around here?"

Compared to a hurricane, a tornado's winds are much stronger but they pass over a much smaller area. As a comparison, the damage path of the tornado that struck Joplin, Missouri, in May 2011 was less than a mile wide and thirty miles long, while the damage path of hurricane Katrina that struck New Orleans, Louisiana, in August 2005 was hundreds of miles wide and thousands of miles long.

Here is the best you can do to prepare for these violent forces...

☞ Near the beginning of tornado season (March to May in southern states and summer in northern states, though they can occur anytime), make sure your safe room or similar sanctuary is stocked with food and other necessities. Store mattresses, sofa cushions, thick blankets, and other protective coverings close by, since being struck by flying debris is the greatest danger in tornadoes.

☞ Make a list of local emergency weather radio stations and paste the list on your radio.

☞ Know how to turn off your building's electricity, gas, and water.

☞ Practice a tornado drill in your home or workplace once a year.

☞ At public buildings you regularly visit, know where their emergency shelters and bathrooms are. Every director of a school, shopping center, nursing home, hospital, sports arena, stadium, mobile home community, and place of business should have a tornado safety plan in place, with signs posted to direct occupants to safe shelters. These directors should regularly run drills.

☞ If you build a house east of the Rockies, include an underground tornado shelter or safe room.

To read how to prepare for a tornado just before it occurs, turn to page 124.

To prepare for a tsunami

When an undersea earthquake, mountain landslide, volcanic eruption, major explosion, glacier calving, or similar force sends massive volumes of earth into a body of water, the earth's impact creates one or more huge waves, known as tsunamis (soo-nä´-mes), that ripple outward. As a tsunami rolls across open water it may move at 500 miles an hour but be only three or four feet high, hardly noticeable by large ships. As the wave reaches shallow water it compresses from front to back, which causes its speed to decrease and its crest to rise. Near the shore the surf may recede for several minutes with an ominous low sucking sound and expose the ocean floor for hundreds of feet from shore. Unwitting observers may gaze in wonder and pick fish from the exposed sand —but they have little time to flee to high ground. For the next few minutes the sea fills in, then builds to a mountainous crest as much as 100 feet high that moves forward at 50 miles an hour. As the crest advances ashore, its momentum smashes any flimsy buildings in its path and may flood coastal areas several miles inland. Then the flooding recedes and rakes inundated areas and damaged buildings with a ferocious undertow that erodes building foundations, pulls down weakened buildings, and carries away masses of debris into the sea. Several tsunamis may arrive 20 to 30 minutes apart, and the first may not be the largest. [42]

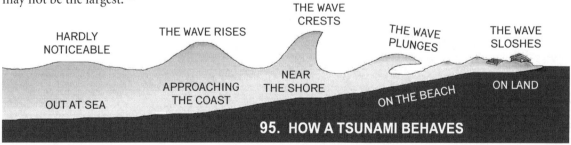

THE WAVE
CRESTS

HARDLY
NOTICEABLE

THE WAVE RISES

THE WAVE
PLUNGES

THE WAVE
SLOSHES

APPROACHING
THE COAST

NEAR
THE SHORE

ON LAND

OUT AT SEA

ON THE BEACH

95. HOW A TSUNAMI BEHAVES

To give you an idea how destructive this wall of water is, when you were young did you ever jump off a high diving board into a swimming pool and land on your face? Remember how it *hurt*? When you hit the water you were moving at 18 miles an hour. Imagine hitting the water at *fifty* miles an hour. It would knock you unconscious, then you drown. If a tsunami moving at fifty miles an hour hit a two-car garage door it would clobber this construction with a force of more than 300 tons! Fortunately —if such a word can be used for such devastation— after a tsunami's wave breaks, it mostly sloshes forward and rises around any object it encounters. To see a tsunami in action, visit http://www.youtube.com/watch?v=RDOu wMj7Xzo.

Tsunamis can spawn further disasters. In March 2011, the tsunamis caused by an earthquake off the coast of Japan not only killed 18,000 people and destroyed crops and livestock over many square miles [43], it seriously damaged three nuclear reactors.

Most people associate tsunamis with oceans, but they can occur in any large body of water. A huge one occurred in the harbor of Halifax, Nova Scotia, in December 1917 when a French cargo ship loaded with wartime explosives collided with a Norwegian freighter. The resulting explosion sent a 60-foot tsunami across the water that tore ships from their moorings, lifted the Norwegian freighter and threw it ashore, flooded surrounding dockyards, and swept three blocks up the surrounding hills. The blast alone created a fireball of hot gases and a shock wave that traveled 5,000 feet per second, flattened 400 acres, deposited a 1,140 pound chunk of the French ship's anchor two miles away, broke windows 50 miles away, and killed 2,000 people and injured 9,000 more. [44]

And consider this eyebrow-riser that occurred centuries ago on Lake Geneva in Switzerland. A mountainside slid into the upper end of the lake and created a huge wave that rolled down the 40-mile long lake and was 26 feet high when it drowned the town at its mouth. You can create a wave like this in your kitchen sink: fill it with water, drop a coffee mug in one side, and watch the tiny tsunamis that roll across the water to the far side. It's scary to think such a disaster could occur anywhere a mountain rises near a lake. [45]

If you live or work near any large body of water, you may want to take these precautions …

☞ Know what sirens and other tsunami warning systems are installed in your community. Automated systems have been installed in Pacific Rim nations that detect oceanic earthquakes and similar disturbances and warn coastal populations to flee before any giant waves reach land.

☞ Know your community's evacuation routes to safe areas.

☞ Be observant when you are at the beach, near a river mouth or bay or bayou, or in lowland terrain near an ocean or large lake.

☞ Have some water purification tablets and a Lifestraw personal water filter. If a tsunami floods possibly square miles of countryside, pure water may be scarce —a case of "Water, water everywhere but not a drop to drink."

☞ Have an engineer inspect your house or place of work for structural defects that would make the building more vulnerable to damage by a tsunami. Have a contractor correct them.

☞ If you are vacationing near a body of water, ask the manager of where you are staying how guests would be alerted if a tsunami approaches. Also ask …

  ● Does the place have well-marked emergency exits?

- Does it have an evacuation plan? If so, ask for a copy and read it in the lobby, where you can look around at what the plan describes and ask the manager further questions.
- Is there a map of evacuation routes from the building to safe ground?
- Is the building built of concrete? If so, good.
- Is it well-maintained? In a poorly maintained building there is an increased possibility of undetected or ignored structural defects decreasing the strength of the building.
- In your room, look out your window and note how high you are above the ground, and what you might do if a tsunami arrived.

To read how to prepare for a tsunami just before it arrives, turn to page 121.

To prepare for a landslide or mudslide

A landslide is a downward movement of a fairly dry mass of earth that is triggered by such terrestrial agitations as an earthquake, erosion, volcanic eruption, blasting, or vibration of machinery and traffic. A mudslide typically originates in steep clayey soil that has become saturated by heavy rains and/or melting snowpack, especially where wildfires or human land mismanagement have removed the ground cover that normally would have absorbed much of the water above the clay. These massive movements typically occur with no warning, the earth moves with the consistency of pancake batter down mountains and through valleys at speeds approaching 200 miles an hour; and they dislodge further masses of earth,

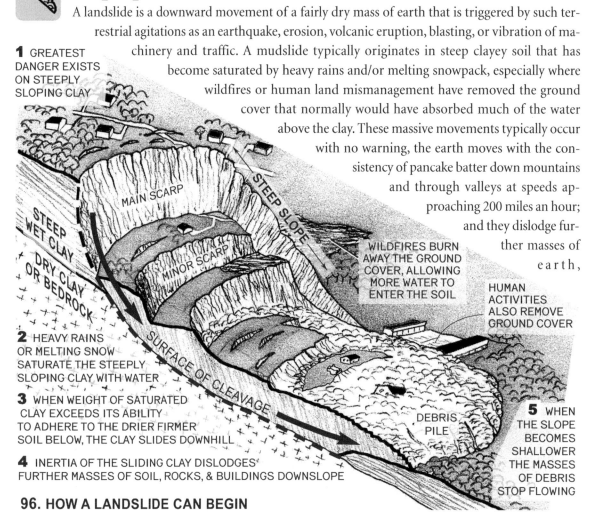

1 GREATEST DANGER EXISTS ON STEEPLY SLOPING CLAY

MAIN SCARP

MINOR SCARP

STEEP WET CLAY

DRY CLAY OR BEDROCK

STEEP SLOPE

SURFACE OF CLEAVAGE

WILDFIRES BURN AWAY THE GROUND COVER, ALLOWING MORE WATER TO ENTER THE SOIL

HUMAN ACTIVITIES ALSO REMOVE GROUND COVER

2 HEAVY RAINS OR MELTING SNOW SATURATE THE STEEPLY SLOPING CLAY WITH WATER

3 WHEN WEIGHT OF SATURATED CLAY EXCEEDS ITS ABILITY TO ADHERE TO THE DRIER FIRMER SOIL BELOW, THE CLAY SLIDES DOWNHILL

4 INERTIA OF THE SLIDING CLAY DISLODGES FURTHER MASSES OF SOIL, ROCKS, & BUILDINGS DOWNSLOPE

DEBRIS PILE

5 WHEN THE SLOPE BECOMES SHALLOWER THE MASSES OF DEBRIS STOP FLOWING

96. HOW A LANDSLIDE CAN BEGIN

97. HOW A LANDSLIDE CAN END [46]

rock, trees, and buildings downhill. As the slide reaches shallower slopes it spreads and thins to form a debris pile at the slide's base that is often impenetrable and dangerous for rescuers to enter. Tons are a trifling yardstick for describing the immensity of these forces.

Witness this landslide that occurred on a long mountainside 10 miles east of Jackson, Wyoming, in June 1925. Following the melting of heavy winter snowpack and several weeks of heavy rain, a mile-wide swath of earth and rock hurled down the mountain to the Gros Ventre River at the mountain's base. But the earth didn't stop there. Having acquired the consistency of liquid it sloshed 300 feet up the opposite slope! The slide formed a 200-foot-high dam across the Gros Ventre River that created a five-mile-long body of water which local residents aptly named Lower Slide Lake. Two years later, part of the dam failed and a six-foot wall of water raced 25 miles downstream and killed six people and hundreds of farm animals. A gripping account of this tragedy reveals that "a local resident predicted the slide in advance," that "engineers determined the dam was permanent and safe," that some residents "refused to believe the water was coming." [47] Sometimes you don't know who to trust.

Here's an even bigger example. In May 1970, an undersea earthquake off the coast of Peru dislodged part of the summit of Mount Huscarán, Peru's highest peak, 22,204 feet tall and 60 miles inland. Then a mile-long, 3,000-feet-wide mass of rock, glacial ice, and snow cascaded downhill at speeds up to 180 miles an hour for 11 miles and buried 20,000 people who never had a clue what was coming. [48] It is hard to come to grips with the idea that a mountain 11 miles away from your home in the valley could wipe you and your loved ones off the face of the earth.

From 1967 to 1972 I lived in Big Sur, California, a mountainous region that often experiences landslides. The worst occurred after several days of heavy winter rain on a mountainside that had experienced a forest fire the previous summer, and for six weeks the slide blocked the only highway through the area. We coped as follows. Anyone living south of the slide who wanted to go north drove to its south edge, walked 500 feet across the slide, and caught a ride north; and vice-versa. Rarely did anyone have to wait more than half an hour, and the scenery was beautiful.

If you think your house and land could be damaged by landslides, take these precautions…

☞ Study the topography of your property and neighboring acres. Does the land slope? Do you live in a canyon or river valley? If so, look at it closely. When I lived in Big Sur we didn't worry about landslides until it began to rain. After days of rain we often found reasons to visit a friend in the more planar regions of Carmel or Monterey forty miles north. This is cogent counsel for those who feel that at any time they could be entombed by a landslide.

☞ Learn if your area has a history of landslides. Level land with no hills nearby is not immune, since something could happen miles away that could bury you —as occurred 25 miles downstream from Lower Slide Lake.

☞ Obtain from an engineer a *geomorphometry analysis* that quantifies your property's morphological, hydrological, and ecological characteristics.

☞ Build retaining walls and plant deep-rooted native plants on sloping terrain around your house.

☞ Form a community emergency plan in which each person contributes time and resources until life returns to nearly normal.

When I lived in Big Sur we had an expression regarding landslides: Keep your knapsack under your bed. That pretty well says it all. To read how to prepare for a landslide days before it may happen and if it suddenly happens, turn to pages 120 and 141.

 # To prepare for an avalanche

Imagine a landslide of snow. That's what an avalanche is. It can be the size of a badminton court and so shallow it hardly has the force to break a skier's leg; or it can be half a square mile in area and dozens of feet deep, and once it starts sliding its tons of snow, ice, rock, trees, and other debris can dislodge further areas below and pulverize everything in its path.

If ever there was an instructive avalanche, it's hard to beat the one that buried the village of Wellington, Washington, in March 1910. After the town received 11 feet of snow in one day, a lightning strike caused a slab of snow to break loose from a nearby mountainside whose ground cover had been removed by a forest fire the summer before. A mass of snowpack a quarter mile wide, half a mile long, and ten feet deep cascaded toward two snowbound trains at a railroad depot where the snow crushed the depot and swept the trains over a 150 foot cliff, killing 96 people. Three days later a similar avalanche killed 63 railroad workers in nearby British Columbia.[49] In the photo in figure 98 on the right, taken the summer after the Wellington avalanche, note the two-foot-thick trees that were snapped like matchsticks by the sliding flakes of snow.

Another instructive avalanche occurred in January 1954 in the village of Blons, Austria. The snow buried the village and as rescue workers were digging people out a second avalanche buried the first, killing a total of 200.[50] In the winter of 1820 an avalanche descended on the village of Obergesteln, Switzerland, and destroyed only one building, an oven-filled bakery —but it caught fire and burned down the town.[51] This is an example of how one disaster can spawn another.

If you ever visit a mountainous region that has received a lot of snow, take these precautions …

☞ Learn what weather and snow conditions cause avalanches in the area: time of year, time of day, snowpack stability, steepness of slope, wind and temperature changes, etc. Take an avalanche safety course. The National Avalanche Center

98. APRÉS AVALANCHE [52]

offers an online tutorial at www.fsavalanche.org.

☞ Read and obey all signs, and look for bulletins posted by rangers and information at resorts and government offices. Colorado has seven hot lines that cover avalanche-prone areas in the state, and mountainous regions often issue updated radio forecasts during avalanche season.

☞ If you will drive, hike, ski, snowboard, or snowmobile in avalanche country, carry a lightweight shovel and an avalanche probe (a collapsible metal pole you can insert in the snow where someone may be buried).

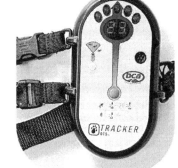

☞ Consider buying an *avalanche transceiver*. This emits a beacon that should you be buried in an avalanche signals your location to rescuers. With some devices you can send and receive messages. Wear this device on your top layer of clothing beneath your coat.

99. AVALANCHE TRANSCEIVER [53]

☞ To read a good article on how to survive an avalanche, visit http://www.artofmanliness.com/2011/12/14/how-to-survive-an-avalanche.

To read how to prepare for an avalanche days before it may happen, turn to page 115.

To prepare for a volcanic eruption

If you think a landslide or avalanche is terrifying, imagine increasing the cascading debris' temperature until it can soften steel. Volcanoes can also spout flying rocks in ballistic arcs that land miles away; they can pulverize cubic miles of solid rock into clouds of ash as fine as dust that smother hundreds of square miles of terrain; they can issue rivers of molten lava that can flow for miles and ignite a house the way a match ignites paper; they can create blast waves traveling at nearly the speed of sound that flatten everything they pass; and they can send pyroclastic waves of hot gases downslope that incinerate everything in their path. The ash alone can damage lungs, clog vehicular carburetors and radiators, ruin electronic equipment, and collapse roofs. If the volcano's cone is clad in snow or glaciers, they may melt and mix with the earth below to form mudslides that race down the slopes faster than a car can drive, demolishing everything in their paths and creating vast floods at lower elevations.

And volcanoes can spawn further disasters. When Mount Pinatubo erupted in the Philippines in June 1991, it did so as a typhoon struck the islands. The typhoon's heavy rainfall mixed with the clouds of ash and made them so heavy that they buried roads, caved in roofs and killed the inhabitants inside, buried acres of crops about to be harvested, and destroyed medical clinics and hospitals which prevented the injured from seeking medical aid.[79] When Mount St. Helens erupted in 1980, the collapse of its north flank created a massive debris slide that four miles north of the summit still had enough momentum to flow over a ridge more than 1,150 feet high, then it flowed another 13 miles down the North Fork of the Toutle River and filled this valley an average depth of 150 feet. Part of the landslide flowed into Spirit Lake, raising its bottom 295 feet and its surface 200 feet.[54] Note in the map below that mudflows extended more than 20 miles from the summit.

Often a volcano will rumble, puff smoke, and trickle magma days before it erupts. Seismic devices can detect such activity and give surrounding populations enough warning to evacuate. During the eruption of Mount Mayon in the Philippines in September 1984, though clouds of volcanic ash smothered areas 30 miles away and several pyroclastic flows swept down the slopes, no casualties occurred because 73,000 people had left the area as advised by local scientists.[80]

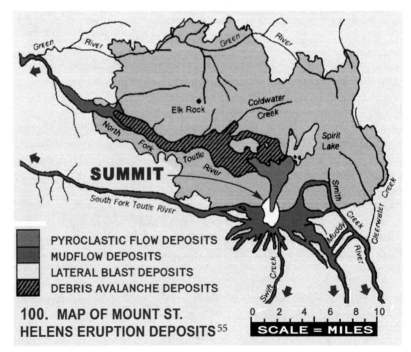

PYROCLASTIC FLOW DEPOSITS
MUDFLOW DEPOSITS
LATERAL BLAST DEPOSITS
DEBRIS AVALANCHE DEPOSITS

100. MAP OF MOUNT ST. HELENS ERUPTION DEPOSITS[55]

0 2 4 6 8 10
SCALE = MILES

The only preparation you can make well before such immense forces arrive is to depart early. Have the usual calamity commodities on hand so you can put them in your car or truck when you leave.

To read how to prepare for a volcano days before it may erupt and if it suddenly erupts, turn to pages 120 and 141.

To prepare for an earthquake

When the tectonic plates that form the earth's crust slip, tremors radiate through the earth's mantle. The primary tremor, moving at perhaps 13,000 miles per hour, causes the earth to shake parallel to its advance. Then a secondary wave, moving perhaps half as fast, makes the ground shake perpendicular to the first tremor's advance, either horizontally or vertically depending on the direction the plates originally moved against each other. Witnesses have reported that these forces feel like the bottoms of their feet are being hit by a sledgehammer. Next, surface waves may arrive, moving as waves do across water, causing the ground to rock to and fro in a direction parallel to the waves' advance. Thus the earth quakes back and forth one way, then back and forth either sideways to the first movement or up and down, then in a slow rocking-chair motion. During the next few days the ground may experience aftershocks caused by the terrestrial plates settling into their new positions; then the above motions may be repeated but less intensely. [56]

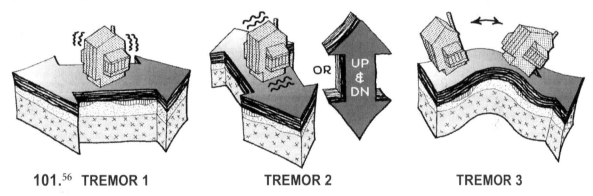

101.[56] **TREMOR 1**   **TREMOR 2**   **TREMOR 3**

Buildings cannot possibly remain undamaged by such huge forces, but architects try to design them to keep from collapsing at least until occupants have time to escape. Still, much damage is often done. A filled cabinet can snap its usual screw fasteners like toothpicks and sail across the room and smash things on the far side. Mirrors and pictures can hop off their hooks and scatter the room with shattered glass. Tall furniture can slide across floors and plow through walls and end up in your yard.

You can minimize this damage by securing cabinets, mirrors, and pictures to walls and tall furniture in place with connectors as appear in figures 102 and 103 on the next page. You can take these architectural drawings to a designer or contractor and say, "This is what I want," knowing that these professionals will understand these drawings and secure your furnishings with strong connectors that will help keep them where they belong. The directives written below will further assist you in seeing that this work is performed correctly.

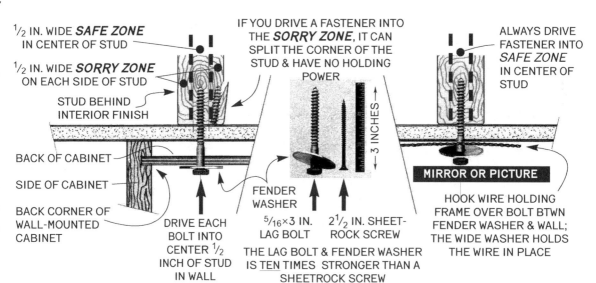

½ IN. WIDE **SAFE ZONE** IN CENTER OF STUD

½ IN. WIDE **SORRY ZONE** ON EACH SIDE OF STUD

STUD BEHIND INTERIOR FINISH

BACK OF CABINET

SIDE OF CABINET

BACK CORNER OF WALL-MOUNTED CABINET

DRIVE EACH BOLT INTO CENTER ½ INCH OF STUD IN WALL

IF YOU DRIVE A FASTENER INTO THE **SORRY ZONE**, IT CAN SPLIT THE CORNER OF THE STUD & HAVE NO HOLDING POWER

FENDER WASHER

3 INCHES

$5/16 \times 3$ IN. LAG BOLT

$2½$ IN. SHEET-ROCK SCREW

THE LAG BOLT & FENDER WASHER IS TEN TIMES STRONGER THAN A SHEETROCK SCREW

ALWAYS DRIVE FASTENER INTO SAFE ZONE IN CENTER OF STUD

MIRROR OR PICTURE

HOOK WIRE HOLDING FRAME OVER BOLT BTWN FENDER WASHER & WALL; THE WIDE WASHER HOLDS THE WIRE IN PLACE

102. FASTENING CABINETS AND MIRRORS TO WALLS: LOOKING FROM THE TOP

To fasten a cabinet to a wall …

1. Locate the studs' edges within $1/16$ inch, even if you have to cut open the finished surface to be sure. Later you can cover the hole. Then subtract $1/2$ inch from the stud's sides (not enough "meat" in this area to hold the connector), which leaves only $1/2$ inch down the center of each $1½$ inch-thick stud to make a strong connection.

2. When fastening a heavy object to the wall, do not use a $2½$ inch sheetrock screw but a 3 inch long by $5/16$ inch diameter *lag bolt* inserted through a *fender washer*, a big washer with a tiny hole, as in figure 102 above. This bolt and washer is ten times stronger than a sheetrock screw.

3. Drill a $7/32$ inch pilot hole

103. FASTENING REFRIGERATORS TO WALLS: LOOKING FROM THE SIDE

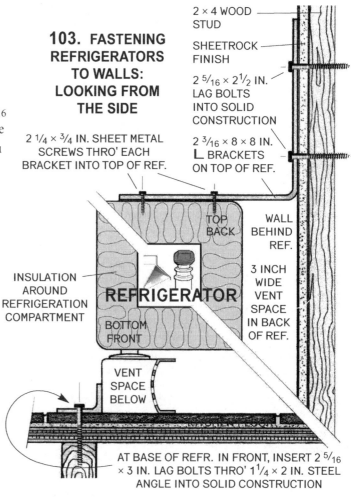

$2¼ \times ¾$ IN. SHEET METAL SCREWS THRO' EACH BRACKET INTO TOP OF REF.

2 × 4 WOOD STUD

SHEETROCK FINISH

$2 5/16 \times 2½$ IN. LAG BOLTS INTO SOLID CONSTRUCTION

$2 3/16 \times 8 \times 8$ IN. **L** BRACKETS ON TOP OF REF.

TOP BACK

WALL BEHIND REF.

INSULATION AROUND REFRIGERATION COMPARTMENT

REFRIGERATOR

3 INCH WIDE VENT SPACE IN BACK OF REF.

BOTTOM FRONT

VENT SPACE BELOW

AT BASE OF REFR. IN FRONT, INSERT 2 $5/16$ × 3 IN. LAG BOLTS THRO' $1¼ \times 2$ IN. STEEL ANGLE INTO SOLID CONSTRUCTION through the back of the cabinet and the wall finish into the center of the stud. After you've drilled the hole, look at the sawdust that comes out of the hole. Is it light yellow, like wood? Or reddish-brown —like a knot? If it's a knot, back up and drill again, an inch or so higher or lower.

To fasten a mirror or large picture to a wall …

1. Screw a $5/_{16}$ inch x 3 inch lag bolt and fender washer into a stud, again as in figure 102.
2. Fit the wire holding the frame behind the big washer.

To keep a refrigerator and tall heavy furniture from dancing around …

1. Strap its top to the wall behind with hefty metal brackets.
2. Hold its base in place with a steel angle bolt to the floor across the front, as in figure 103.
3. Do the same with your water heater, and attach a flexible connection between it and the pipes it connects to as appears in figure 104.

To keep a large table from rollerskating about …

☞ Fasten two opposite legs to the floor with 6 x 6 inch **L** brackets.

To keep water and gas pipes from breaking in a quake …

104. FLEXIBLE CONNECTION[57]

☞ Have a plumber install *flexible connections* as in figure 104.
☞ If you have propane or other fuel gas, have the gas company install an *auto gas shut-off valve* (see figure 105) that will automatically turn off when triggered by strong vibrations.
☞ Have a plumber install an *auto water shutoff valve* (see figure 106) on your supply water main that shuts off the water and sounds an alarm if its flow exceeds a preset limit.

105. AUTO GAS SHUTOFF VALVE[58]

Other tips …

☞ In cabinets, securely fastened or not, place large, heavy, or breakable objects on lower shelves, and install latches on the doors. Put books in cabinets with shelves inside and clear plexiglass doors on the front so you can see them from outside, and install latches on the doors.
☞ Hang mirrors, pictures, and other heavy objects away from beds, couches and anywhere that people sit.
☞ Brace chandeliers and other overhead light fixtures.

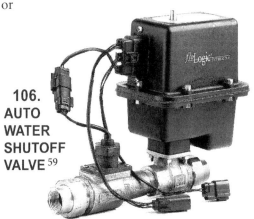

106. AUTO WATER SHUTOFF VALVE[59]

To read how to deal with an earthquake when it suddenly occurs, turn to page 140.

To prepare for a blizzard or ice storm

In this disaster deep accumulations of snow and/or thick coats of ice often combine with high winds to snap trees, bring down power lines, collapse buildings, and immobilize whole regions. If the power fails and your heating won't work, you can freeze to death in your home. Even after the storm passes, melting snow and ice can cause floods. People usually don't die from the snow and cold as much as from fires erupting in improperly tended heat sources, carbon monoxide poisoning in closed rooms, falls on ice, and accidents on treacherous roads.

If severe winter weather is expected where you live, the local National Weather Service office may issue one of the following advisories …

☞ *Winter Storm Watch* … Severe winter weather (heavy snow, sleet, freezing rain, or a combination thereof) is likely to occur in the next 12 to 36 hours. Listen for further advisories and be prepared to act quickly if warnings are issued. Freezing rain is rain that freezes when it hits the ground, coating the surface with ice. Sleet is rain that turns into ice pellets before reaching the ground; it bounces when hitting a surface and does not stick to objects. Accumulations of freezing rain and sleet can make roads slick and dangerous.

☞ *Winter Storm Warning* … A significant winter storm or hazardous winter weather is imminent and may be a threat to life and property. Take protective action. Go to a safe place, listen for further instructions. A Winter Storm Warning may include one or more of the following …

- *Heavy Snow Warning* … Snowfall of six inches or more.
- *Ice Storm Warning* … Heavy accumulations of ice will make travel extremely dangerous and will damage trees and power lines.
- *Blizzard Warning* … Heavy snow and strong winds will create dangerous wind chills and frequently reduce visibility to $1/4$ mile or less for at least three hours. Seek refuge immediately, stay indoors, and don't drive.

☞ *Winter Weather Advisory* … Significant winter weather (snow, freezing rain, or sleet) is expected to cause significant inconveniences and may be hazardous, especially to motorists. A Winter Weather Advisory usually indicates the time it will remain in effect (i.e. SNOW ADVISORY REMAINS IN EFFECT FROM 4 AM TO 5 PM MST MONDAY FOR ELEVATIONS ABOVE 4500 FEET) and it may include one or more of the following …

- *Snow Advisory* … The criteria for this advisory varies from area to area. Any measurable snow constitutes an advisory in Florida, while 3 to 5 inches does the same in New England.
- *Wind Chill Advisory* … Combined low temperatures and high winds are dangerous and can cause humans to suffer hypothermia and frostbite. Dress warmly and do not go outdoors unless absolutely necessary. Wind chill, or wind chill index, is the perceived temperature based on its actual temperature and wind speed: the faster the wind blows the colder the temperature feels. It is not the actual air temperature but what the air feels like to the average person. Wind chill has nothing to do with the temperature at which water freezes. If

the temperature is 35°F and the wind chill is 20°F, water-filled radiators and pipes will cool only to 35°F and not freeze.

- *Freezing Rain/Sleet Advisory* … Light accumulations of ice will create hazardous travel conditions and may damage plants, crops, or fruit trees.
- *Blowing/Drifting Snow Advisory* … Accumulations of blowing or drifting will create poor visibility and hazardous driving conditions.[60]

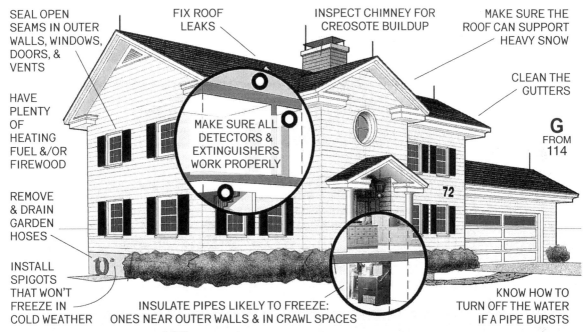

SEAL OPEN SEAMS IN OUTER WALLS, WINDOWS, DOORS, & VENTS

HAVE PLENTY OF HEATING FUEL &/OR FIREWOOD

REMOVE & DRAIN GARDEN HOSES

INSTALL SPIGOTS THAT WON'T FREEZE IN COLD WEATHER

FIX ROOF LEAKS

MAKE SURE ALL DETECTORS & EXTINGUISHERS WORK PROPERLY

INSPECT CHIMNEY FOR CREOSOTE BUILDUP

MAKE SURE THE ROOF CAN SUPPORT HEAVY SNOW

CLEAN THE GUTTERS

G FROM 114

72

KNOW HOW TO TURN OFF THE WATER IF A PIPE BURSTS

INSULATE PIPES LIKELY TO FREEZE: ONES NEAR OUTER WALLS & IN CRAWL SPACES

107. PREPARING FOR WINTER STORMS

Here are ways to winterize your home or workplace well before cold weather arrives…

☞ In the fall, cut trees or branches that could fall on buildings or driving lanes during winter storms.
☞ Know safe evacuation routes from your home or work to local shelters.
☞ Know how to contact other family members if you must evacuate and are separated, as detailed on page 11.
☞ Teach children how to call 911 and use the radio to listen for emergency advisories.
☞ Install Class ABC fire extinguishers near each heat source and smoke/CO alarms outside sleeping areas. If you already have them, make sure they work properly.
☞ If you have a fireplace or woodstove, store plenty of seasoned firewood outside well in advance of cold weather. Fit each hearth with a fire screen large enough to catch sparks or embers that could pop out. If the damper doesn't open fully due to moisture crustation or soot buildup around them, clean them until they work. Make sure the flue is clear of bird nests and other obstructions, as in summer birds may nest there, then install chimney caps with meshed openings. The fireplace

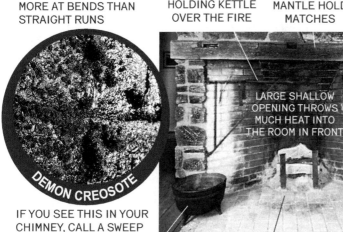

CREOSOTE COLLECTS MORE AT BENDS THAN STRAIGHT RUNS

CRANE FOR HOLDING KETTLE OVER THE FIRE

NICHES IN MANTLE HOLD MATCHES

FIREPLACE TOOLS: POKER, TONGS, SHOVEL, BROOM

ACCESSORIES: POPCORN POPPER, AROMATIC HERBS, BELLOWS

LARGE SHALLOW OPENING THROWS MUCH HEAT INTO THE ROOM IN FRONT

PLACE FOR STORING FIREWOOD CLOSE BY

DEMON CREOSOTE

SITZ BATH FOR BATHING IN FRONT OF THE FLAMES WHEN THE POWER FAILS

IF YOU SEE THIS IN YOUR CHIMNEY, CALL A SWEEP

KETTLE FOR BOILING WATER WHEN THE POWER FAILS

ANDIRONS KEEP LOGS FROM ROLLING OUT

HEARTH IS LARGE & STRONG ENOUGH TO SPLIT FIREWOOD ON

KEEP A FIRESCREEN OVER THE FIRE WHEN NO ONE IS NEARBY

108. A FIREPLACE FOR ALL STORMS AND SEASONS

in figure 108 above has all these features, and more. Though you may not want to tear down the heart of your house to build a likeness of this hearth, it's nice to know the ideal, in case you ever have the chance to fashion it into reality.

☞ Have the chimney cleaned regularly. The biggest danger is *creosote*, a crumbly substance resembling black popcorn that clings to the walls of fireplaces and flues. Shine a light into these areas. If you see any, scrape it off as best you can with a wire brush or square-point shovel and call a chimney sweep. It is also a myth that you should clean a chimney once a year. This varies depending on how often you use it, how green is the wood you burn (green wood creates more creosote than dry wood), the species you burn (softwoods create more creosote than hardwoods), and how straight is the flue (creosote collects more at bends). If you rarely use a fireplace you may need to clean its flue only once every few years; but if you heat your house all winter by burning unseasoned pine in a woodstove whose flue has two 90-degree bends in it, you may need to clean the flue once a month. It is better to clean a chimney in the spring than the fall, because over the summer any creosote buildup during the previous winter will slightly corrode the masonry.

☞ Make sure your home and workplace is well-stocked with all the calamity commodities described from pages 35 to 61 in this book, and that all are stored in a strong place where you can reach them easily in the dark.

☞ Make sure each person has a warm coat, gloves or mittens, hat, scarf, boots, and other winter clothing in case the power fails or they must go outside. Equip sleeping areas with extra blankets, quilts, and sleeping bags that can open and cover the bed.

☞ Keep plywood, plastic sheeting, lumber, sandbags, and tools handy in case you need them.

☞ Make sure you have snow shovels, ice chippers, bags of sand, a pushbroom, and other snow tools. In my forty years of living on my property, based on local snow averages I have scraped more than 1,500 inches of snow from my driveway and I have never used a snow blower. I've never liked them because they cost hundreds of dollars, use gasoline, sometimes they won't start, and the rotating auger blades are dangerous. Through the years I have managed well with the blizzard busters that appear on the right.

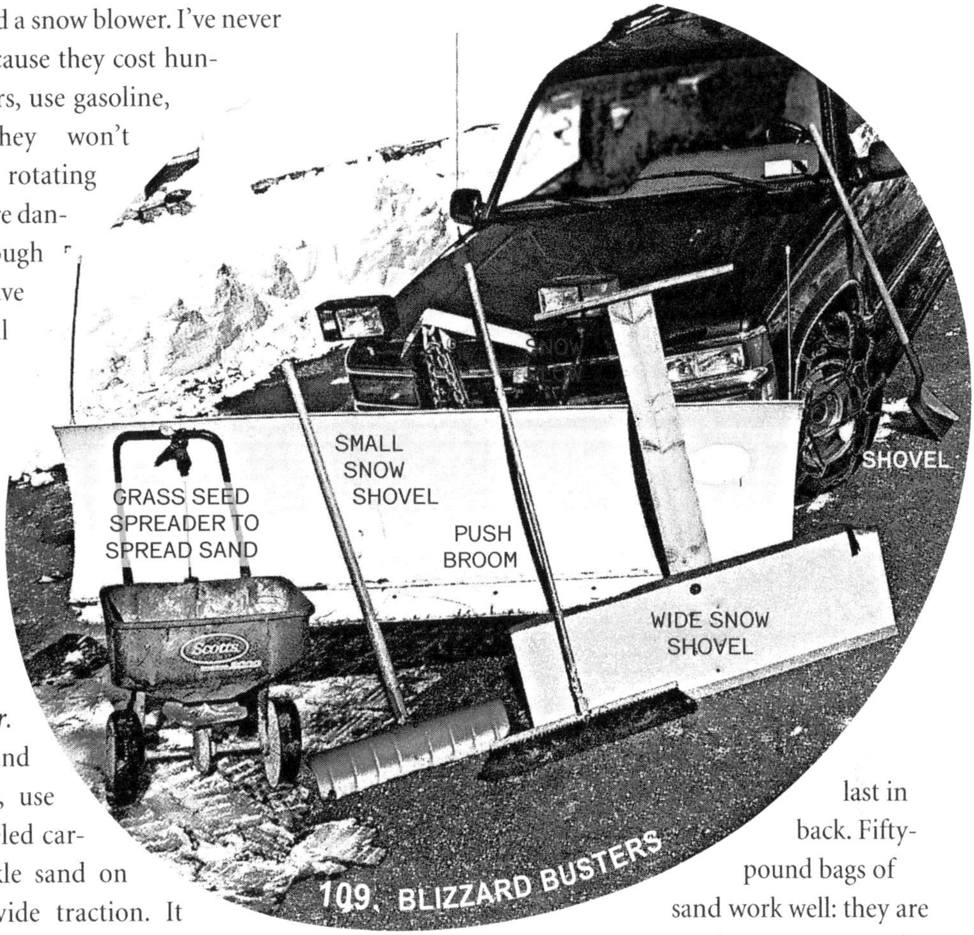

☞ One item on the right deserves further explanation: the **grass seed spreader**. If drives and walks are icy, use this two-wheeled carrier to sprinkle sand on them to provide traction. It spreads the sand evenly and is easy to load, and is superior to slinging sand with a shovel which leaves lumps in some places and nothing in others. Don't use rock salt; it costs more than sand, doesn't provide as much traction, injures plants, and seeps into the water table. Also don't use ashes as they are slippery.

☞ If you use a snowplow, you'll need a four-wheel-drive vehicle that is large enough to mount the plow on, plus you must counteract the weight in front with an equally heavy bal-

GRASS SEED SPREADER TO SPREAD SAND

SMALL SNOW SHOVEL

PUSH BROOM

WIDE SNOW SHOVEL

SHOVEL

109. BLIZZARD BUSTERS

last in back. Fifty-pound bags of sand work well: they are inexpensive, light enough to load, and afterward the sand is useful in other ways. Keep the plow in the garage so it will stay dry, mount it before the flakes fly, and face it toward the door so you won't back out over the snow and pack some down, making it harder to scrape up. The luggier your tires are the easier your labor will be, but if more than eight inches is forecast, perhaps you should wrap four tirechains around the tires.

☞ If your driveway receives snow that is too little to justify plowing it, you still must remove the snow before it turns to ice. I do this with a giant

98

110.   STEP   TURN   TILT

snow shovel I made of a 48-inch-wide piece of sheet metal mounted on a 2 x 6 shaft with a 1 x 4 crosspiece on top. I walk down one side of the driveway with the crosspiece against my stomach until the snow on the blade is so high (about a foot) that I can't push it anymore, then I turn the blade to the side and tilt it up to dump the snow by the driveway. I never lift the blade; I only push, turn, and tilt it. This work is about as hard as hiking with a 20 pound knapsack on your back, and I can clear two turnarounds and 300 feet of driveway in an hour. This shovel appears in figures 109 and 110. The blade, good as it is, works only on paved surfaces and a few inches of snow, and every few years the bottom edge of the blade wears out and I have to replace it.

☞ Winterize vehicles as follows …

N
FROM
112

- Have the maintenance schedule in the owner's manual checked by a dealer or mechanic.
- Make sure the ignition system and battery work perfectly and the battery terminals are clean; that the radiator has enough antifreeze; that the windshield wipers work and the washer fluid reservoir is full; that the exhaust pipes have no leaks or crimps; that the brakes, power steering, heater, defroster, headlights, taillights, and hazard lights all work properly.
- Make sure the tires have plenty of tread.
- Put in the trunk a 40-pound bag of sand, kitty litter, or equally granular material for spreading on icy areas.
- Lubricate the door and trunk locks with lock lubricant to keep them from freezing.
- If necessary, replace existing oil with winter-grade or SAE 10W/30 oil.
- Make sure each car has a roadside emergency kit and car pack as described on pages 70 to 73 of this book.

☞ If you would like to volunteer to serve in a disaster, let local organizations or emergency services know you are interested well in advance of winter weather.

To read how to prepare for deep snow or ice days before it arrives, turn to page 114.

To prepare for a flood

Floods are devastating not only because they may inundate many square miles of land, but also because of two ingredients they contain.

One is silt. Floodwater can weigh up to twice as much per cubic foot (up to 125 versus 62 pounds) than clear water due to the silt it contains. While the water is moving, these gritty particles scrape like rough sandpaper and erode creek banks, wash away yards, tear away porches, shred machinery, abrade building foundations, carry away basement walls and collapse everything above. The abraded particles accumulate in the moving water, making it even more abrasive, and when the water slows down the silt falls out of the water and deposits on the areas below. If floodwater enters your house, you may end up with a few inches of mud on your floors and a few shoals of mud in your yard.

The other ingredient floodwater contains is debris. This includes lighter-than-water objects like fallen trees that float like battering rams and heavier objects like boulders and stoves that roll along the bottom of the current. Large floating trees may smash any buildings and bridges in their path, and pieces of glass and metal may settle in the silt in your house and yard. Add a few cars and trucks bobbing like corks in the current along with greases from streets, feces from barnyards, fertilizers from croplands, and trash from storm drains —and you know why floodwater not only is the result of a disaster but is itself a disaster.

Floodwaters may rise gradually or suddenly. Though gradual flooding is more common, sudden or *flash floods* are far more dangerous because they can arrive without warning, sometimes on a perfectly sunny day with not a cloud in the sky. Then a dry creek can become a raging torrent in minutes due to heavy rains, melting snow, and/or a breached dam miles upstream. If the liquid won't kill you the solids will. To see a flash flood in action, take a look at http://www.youtube.com/watch?v=Dniren.

Floods are usually worst when two conditions coincide: i.e. heavy rains during a spring thaw, or a hurricane surge during a full moon. These calamities can wreck havoc in three ways …

1. The rising waters can ruin every manmade object they encounter —houses, machines, everything. When a flood inundates the lower regions of a house, you can't just wait for the waters to recede and move back in —you have a major reclamation project on your hands, one that could take months. Sometimes the only practical solution is to tear the building down and start over —hopefully on higher ground.

2. Flowing floodwater carries an amazing amount of power. Flowing water 15 inches deep can sweep away a car, and as little as 6 inches deep can sweep you off your feet. Such surges claimed the lives of three more victims in our grim list: two children "after being swept away from their mother by a surge of water," and another "when a surge of water swept him off a sidewalk."

3. Surprisingly, floods can cause fires. When moving water meets live power, sparks can fly. During Hurricane Sandy a surge on Breezy Point flooded a utility transformer, causing it to explode, which started a fire that burned 126 homes to their soggy foundations.[61]

All this adds up to floodwater being one of the nastiest disasters you could encounter. Even if your property has never flooded, it might be at risk due to recent developments upstream —then record rain accompanied by excessive runoff and undersize storm drains could submerge areas that never saw the underside of a flood. Even if water never enters your property you may be affected by local street closures, power outages, and curtailment of public services.

One local document may help you determine how safe you might be: a *Flood Hazard Boundary Map*. These are land maps usually with contour elevations on them that show lowland areas susceptible to flooding. Most municipal public works departments have them, as do many mortgage lenders and insurance companies. If you live in a valley or other lowland area, or near a river, stream, swamp, bog, or bayou, this document may hold your interest for most of an afternoon.

Many authorities today advise homeowners to buy flood insurance. But due to recent disastrous floods in several states and the threat of rising sea levels damaging coastlines everywhere, some flood insurors are raising their premiums as much as ten times what they were a few years ago. They are no dummies, and their risk-sharing charts will always show how they can make more money than they spend. This book can only suggest that you look into this, not what your decision should be. As an alternative, you might raise your house one floor and build in the space below a livable basement with solid concrete walls whose flooding would cause minimal damage; or you could set the house on piles that would let floodwaters surge beneath the structure. While these alternatives are costly, if done well they'll cost less than replacing a lost house.

If a flood could threaten your house and land…

☞ Have all the usual calamity commodities on board as described on pages 35 to 66 of this book.

☞ Know what evacuation routes to take if you leave your property. Don't just look at a local map and pick the quickest main road, because part of this route could be submerged in a flood. Instead, contact your local town hall or rescue center and ask for this information.

☞ Consider building berms, diverting walls, or retaining walls between your house and any creek, topographical depression, or any other floodable terrain nearby. Have this construction designed by an engineer and built by a contractor. The cost of this work might be partly offset by increased property values and decreased insurance premiums, not to mention less flood damage.

☞ Anchor any fuel tanks on your property so they won't float away in a flood. To see a way to do this, go to **B** on page 21.

☞ Seal basement and foundation walls with waterproofing materials to minimize seepage.

☞ Make sure your electrical panel board is located at least 12 inches above your dwelling's maximum possible flood level.

☞ Place your furnace, water heater, washer, and dryer on cement blocks at least eight inches above the floor. Even if they still won't be above maximum flood level, the less damage they may incur could make the difference between cleaning it and replacing it.

☞ Consider installing a sump pump in the lowest part of your basement, crawlspace, or similar depression that can remove accumulating floodwater. This is usually a good solution for small amounts of flooding. Have an electrician install the wiring, and make sure the drain hose extends to a lower elevation somewhere outside the house. You could install a battery-operated backup in case the power fails.

☞ Consider mounting a rowboat close to your porch if you

have one or near your back door. Put a pair of oars in it, and mount it up-side-down on a pair of sawhorses or similar pedestal. Select and locate this craft so you can easily reach down and flip it right-side-up if you have to.

☞ Know a way to reach high ground if floodwaters suddenly rise and you can't use your car.

☞ Fasten heavy furniture firmly to the floor as detailed on pages 92 and 93.

☞ Store above maximum flood levels, either indoors or outdoors, whatever lumber, boxes, garbage bags, plastic sheeting, tarps, duct tape, rope, bungee cords, and other sup-plies you will need to protect your belongings as detailed beginning at **H** on page 117.

To read how to prepare for a flood days before it occurs, turn to page 116.

To prepare for a heat wave or drought

In these disasters the biggest threats are heat exhaustion and dehydration due to high temperatures. To minimize these dangerous discomforts well before they could occur in your area …

☞ Before warm or dry weather begins, make sure any window-mounted air conditioners fit snugly and op-erate efficiently. Close any floor heating registers close by. If your air conditioning system has ducts, have a professional insulate them. Once a week, remove accu-mulated dust from intake grilles with a vacuum cleaner.

☞ Weatherstrip doors and windows to keep out hot air.

☞ Keep storm windows up during hot or dry seasons, as they increase the insulation over the glass behind.

☞ Where the sun will shine several hours on a window,

block the sun in one of the following ways …

- Mount behind the pane a reflector such as foil-covered cardboard.
- Duct-tape aluminum foil to the pane.
- Cover the pane with drapes, shades, or louvers.
- Install awnings outside the windows.

☞ Place rain barrels under gutter downspouts and install other cisterns where they are practical.

☞ Outdoors, plant native and drought-tolerant trees, ground covers, and shrubs. Lay mulch at the base of trees and plants to reduce evapora-tion and keep the soil cool.

☞ Remove weeds, as they consume water and steal water from desirable plants.

☞ If you have a lawn, raise your mower blade to its highest level (at least 3 inches) so the grass will grow deeper roots and hold more moisture. If you use sprinklers, locate them so the whirling water lands on the lawn and not paved areas.

☞ Water only early in the morning or after sunset when temperatures are lower and water evaporates less, and do so no more than two hours a week. Water for one or two long periods (known as deep wa-tering) rather than several short peri-ods. Deep watering promotes deeper and more extensive root systems which improves drought resistance. Watering should penetrate six to twelve inches deep for turf and bed-ding plants, and twelve inches for perennials, shrubs, and trees. Wa-tering an area with a one-inch depth of water moistens sandy soil to a depth of about 12 inches.

To prepare for a wildfire

First dismiss the idea that wildfires occur only in large forests. As proof, witness this account that occurred in Oakland, California, in October 1991. "In a vacant lot a brush fire driven by winds up to 65 miles per hour became a crown fire that rapidly spread southwest, tossing embers from burning houses and vegetation into the air as it went. The winds swept embers across an eight-lane freeway and a four-lane freeway where they floated back to earth and ignited hundreds more houses. The now-huge fire's expanding gases generated its own wind which, combined with the ambient wind, created a cyclonic firestorm that threw more embers in all directions until the blaze had literally vaporized 3,800 homes in a 1,520 acre area and killed 26 people." This is no time to flee to a safe room, because if the flames don't get you the heat or fumes will. Here are a few more chilling facts about this conflagration …

☞ Many narrow winding roads were crowded with parked cars, many in front of fire hydrants, which kept fire trucks and ambulances from reaching certain areas and connecting fire hoses.

☞ The flames destroyed power lines to 17 pumping stations in the Oakland water system which caused firefighters to run out of water.

☞ Fire teams from neighboring communities found that the hydrants at the fire site had different-size outlets for their hoses and couldn't use them.

☞ The City of Oakland couldn't communicate with neighboring districts due to antiquated equipment and limited statewide radio frequencies created by budget restraints in preceding years. [62]

Although the Oakland Hills Fire has modern lessons to teach, this book would be remiss if it didn't mention the granddaddy of all American urban wildfires, the Chicago fire of 1871. Here is an account …

The fire's spread was aided by the use of wood as the predominant building material, a prior drought, and strong southwest winds that carried flying embers toward the heart of the city. At the time more than two-thirds of the city's structures were made entirely of wood, most houses and buildings were roofed with flammable tar or shingles, and all the city's sidewalks were built of wood. When the fire broke out, at first residents were unconcerned, unaware of the risk. Firefighters were also tired from having fought a fire the day before, and after fighting the flames through the first day they became exhausted. For two days the fire raged out of control through neighborhood after neighborhood of houses, apartments, and mansions, most built of wood and dried from the drought. On the third day, as the fire's eastern advance was halted by the shores of Lake Michigan and its western advance was checked by winds blowing east, rain helped douse the flames. More than 300 people died, more than 100,000 people lost their homes, and 3.3 square miles of the city were burned to a crisp. [63]

Until we have societies that function perfectly we will always have to worry about this kind of disaster happening in our neighborhoods. To understand how to best deal with these fiery forces, whether in a forest of trees or a forest of buildings, first one must know their anatomy, as follows …

A wildfire may be a *surface fire* (the flames spread along the ground), or a *crown fire* (the flames race through the treetops). Advancing fires can also kill a house with *firebrands* or *flamefronts*. Firebrands are pieces of burning debris lofted into the sky by strong convection currents that can be carried far ahead of advancing flames and ignite any flammable material they fall on. Flamefronts are walls of fire that usually pass a given area in one to five minutes. Since it normally takes two to three minutes of exposure to flames to ignite wood, a passing flame front may leave one house undamaged while the house next door burns to the ground. Plastic gutters and vinyl siding are unsafe as they can melt; and though metal roofing or siding won't burn, these thin materials can become so hot that the wood sheathing beneath them ignites. Masonry facades and clay tile roofs are not perfect foils either: a spark or ember can enter an attic vent, plumbing vent, broken window, or other opening in these materials and gut the construction from inside.

There are three essential strategies for dealing with wildfires: *impedance*, *evacuation*, and *coping*, as detailed below …

Impedance … This involves covering the ground around your house and cladding its facades and roof with materials that will slow the spread of fire. These are detailed in this section. Also useful are a number of advisories from *Prepping your house and property* beginning on page 13.

Evacuation … This involves knowing how to leave your property when a wildfire approaches, particularly how to prepare the house before you leave and what to take with you. This is covered in the *Just Before* section on pages 123 to 124.

Coping … What to do if you find yourself trapped in a building that is on fire. This is covered in the *Suddenly* section on pages 130 to 133.

INSTALL CLAY TILE OR METAL ROOFS

COVER VENTS WITH ¼ INCH WIRE MESH

CAP FLUES WITH ½ INCH MESH SPARK ARRESTERS

CLEAN ROOFS & GUTTERS

INSTALL FROSTPROOF SPIGOT & HOSE RACK ON OPPOSITE SIDES OF HOUSE

FIT SHUTTERS ON OUTSIDES OF WINDOWS & FIRE-RESISTANT DRAPES ON INSIDES

PRUNE BRANCHES TO 10 FEET ABOVE GROUND

AVOID WOOD DECKS & SHEDS

CLEAN TRASH & JUNK FROM AROUND HOUSE

KEEP WEEDS DOWN

SURROUND HOUSE WITH STONE WALLS, MASONRY TERRACES, PAVED TURN-AROUNDS, SWIMMING POOLS, ETC.

LANDSCAPE WITH PLANTS THAT RESIST FIRE

111. PROTECTING YOUR HOUSE AND GROUNDS FROM APPROACHING WILDFIRES

In addition to the tips pictured on the left, here are other things to do well before a wildfire could occur …

☞ Know your nearby water sources: hydrants, ponds, creeks, swimming pools, etc.

☞ Install incoming power lines underground if you can.

☞ Landscape your yards with fire-resistant plants. To learn the best for your area, google *Firewise Plants for Front and Backyards.*

☞ When it turns warm and dry, remove wood

furniture, debris, and other burnables from around the house.

☞ On opposite sides of the house install frostproof spigots and hose racks with 75 feet of hose.

☞ Enroll in a fire prevention workshop. Many localities offer them for free. Check www.firewise.org.

☞ Soak oily rags with water and hang them outside to dry, then soak them with water again and place them, still wet, in a sealed plastic bag in your normal trash.

☞ About once a month conduct a fire drill. Someone sounds the alarm in the night then monitors the other family members' exits. Practice evacuating the building blindfolded, because the smoke generated by many fires often makes it impossible to see. Also practice staying low to the ground when escaping, because floor-level temperatures may average 90°F but at eye level they may be 600°F and be more toxic.

☞ If your house has windows whose sills are more than six feet above the ground, buy a ladder of the right height and have everyone practice using it. This is a good idea for second-story windows because you have to be somewhat athletic to use an escape ladder. Ladders are also useful around the house between disasters.

To prepare for a wildfire just before it arrives, turn to page 123.

To prepare for a chemical or biological agent

In the United States some five million facilities make, use, or store hazardous (HAZMAT) materials. Even greater is the number of pipes, ships, trucks, and trains that transport these materials. If something goes wrong they can cause death, serious injury, and long-lasting health problems plus damage to buildings and property. Though some HAZMAT accidents cause explosions, they kill and injure most people by releasing toxic or poisonous gases into the air. Witness the tragedy at Bhopal, India, in December 1984, when 16 tons of a poisonous gas escaped from a Union Carbide pesticide factory and spread over an area exceeding 30 square miles, killing 18,000 people and injuring 558,000. This calamity began when water leaked into a storage tank filled with 45 tons of a potent pesticide and caused a runaway chemical reaction that opened the tank's valves while a nearby refrigeration system was shut down, a flare tower designed to burn off the gas was disconnected, and a scrubber that could have detoxified the gas was turned off. [64]

Equally horrifying is a chemical or biological attack by terrorists. Though these acts were outlawed by the Geneva Convention due to the horrors of mustard gas, phosgene, and chlorine in World War I, they still pose a threat today. We need look no further than August 2013 to know this —when the Syrian government launched rockets that spread a blanket of suffocating gas over several neighborhoods, killing nearly 1,500 civilians.

Whether these disasters are caused by industries accidentally or terrorists on purpose, to their victims they are often bewildering because it typically takes time for authorities to determine what happened. Well in advance of these insidious occurrences, be informed of their possibilities and be prepared for their eventualities by doing the following …

☞ Find out if your community has a Local Emergency Planning Committee (LEPC). These organizations collect information about explosives, flammable substances, toxins, poisons, biological agents, and radioactive materials made in their jurisdiction, any local facilities or industries that store or use them, and any local highways, railroads, waterways and pipelines that convey them to and from other locations. In addition to pinpointing foreseeable hazards they try to minimize the materials' risk to the community and its people, and they develop emergency plans in the event of a serious accident in the area. Their information is publicly available on request. To find if there is a LEPC in your area, google Local Emergency Planning Committees and follow the prompts.

☞ If you believe you could be exposed to hazardous chemical or biological agents, try to learn where the likely sources of exposure are and what evacuation routes lie in opposite directions. Have a radio or other transmitter that will immediately notify you of any danger in your area, and have a snugly fitting gas mask with a proper filter for each person in your party.

☞ If you live or work in a place where hazardous materials are made, used, or stored, do the following …

- Make sure they are properly contained and stored, and inspect them periodically for deterioration. If any containers become brittle due to chemical attack, freezing temperatures, and/or exposure to ultraviolet light, they may crack or break, especially when moved.

- Do not let hazardous liquids remain in pipes or containers when production has stopped. Drain them to prevent future breakage due to freezing temperatures, collisions with other objects, and other accidents.

- See that all check valves, dump valves, and relief valves work properly and are insulated from freezing with heat blankets, heat tape, frost boxes, or similar devices.

- Inspect all antifreeze loop valves to make sure they are open. Chain and lock them in open position if possible.

To read what to do if a chemical or biological attack suddenly occurs, turn to page 139.

To prepare for a nuclear emergency

During a nuclear reactor meltdown, particles exposed to neutrons from the explosion become radioactive. This matter radiates from "ground zero" and is absorbed by rain and carried by prevailing winds miles away, subjecting everything in its path to radiation. The particles emit three rays: *alpha*, *beta*, and *gamma.*

Alpha rays are the weakest. Most cannot penetrate human skin, but are hazardous if they enter your body though your mouth or lungs. *Beta* rays are a hundred times stronger. They can burn your skin and penetrate $1/_8$ inch into your flesh, and if you breathe them or eat food exposed to them they will damage your lungs and digestive tract. When beta particles land on foliage and pavement, they take three days to decay to harmless levels unless washed away by rainfall or hosed down. After the nuclear meltdown at Chernobyl, Russia, in April 1986, the city of Kiev 60 miles away hosed down its streets to clean them of fallout and reservoired the runoff in gutters and sewers until it had decayed. *Gamma* rays are the strongest. They can pass through most materials including your body. Prolonged exposure can damage your body's cell structure, but brief exposure is virtually harmless. [65]

As destructive as they are, radioactive rays are indetectable by sight, smell, touch, or taste. Only your brain can protect your body by employing the strategies below …

Distance … The farther you are from the radiation's source, the better. If a nuclear reactor accident occurs, authorities order the public to evacuate to increase the distance between them and the radiation.

Shielding … The heavier and denser the material between you and the radiation, the better. Alpha rays can be blocked by paper and light clothing, beta rays by thick clothing, plastic, glass, and aluminum, and gamma rays by thick heavy materials such as concrete, brick, earth, and lead (the best). If your house has a basement surrounded by concrete walls and solid earth, this area will usually protect you against nuclear fallout, though radioactivity can enter windows and seams in the construction.

Time … The longer you avoid exposure to radioactive rays the better. Alpha rays reduce quickly to harmless levels, beta rays usually decay to safe levels in three days, and gamma rays typically decay to one percent of initial levels in two weeks. If a nuclear reactor fails, authorities will monitor any release of radiation and determine its danger to local populations.

ALPHA RAYS CAN'T PENETRATE YOUR SKIN, BUT ARE HARMFUL IF THEY ENTER YOUR BODY BY BREATHING OR EATING

BETA RAYS CAN BURN YOUR SKIN AND DAMAGE YOUR LUNGS & DIGESTIVE TRACT

GAMMA RAYS CAN PASS THRO' YOUR BODY, BUT BRIEF EXPOSURE IS VIRTUALLY HARMLESS

112. HOW NUCLEAR FALLOUT CAN HURT YOU

Local governments and public utilities have *emergency response plans* if a nuclear reactor fails. The plans typically define two *nuclear emergency planning zones*: Zone 1, an area within 10 miles of the reactor site; and zone 2, an area within 50 miles, as in figure 113. If a nuclear accident releases radiation in your area, warning sirens or other alerts will activate, and TV and radio stations will report local fallout patterns and advise how to protect yourself. Nuclear power plants also announce a possible nuclear emergency as follows …

Notification of unusual event … A small problem has occurred at the plant. No radiation leak is expected. Officials will notify federal, state and county governments.

Alert … Small amounts of radiation could leak inside the plant. Federal, state and county governments will be on standby in case they are needed.

Site area emergency … Small amounts of radiation could leak from the plant but not beyond the site. Area sirens may activate. Residents living near the plant should listen to their radio or television for information. If necessary, state and county officials will act to ensure public safety.

General emergency … Radiation could leak beyond the plant site. Sirens will sound. State officials will act to ensure public safety. Residents who live near the plant should listen for public information and follow official instructions. [66]

In April 1986 at the nuclear reactor at Chernobyl, Russia, a power surge led to a reactor vessel rupture and a series of steam explosions which caused the reactor to ignite and explode, then radioactive fallout drifted over much of western Soviet Union and Europe.[67] The worst nuclear accident in America occurred at the Three Mile Island nuclear reactor near Harrisburg, Pennsylvania in March 1979. A minor mechanical failure compounded by human error damaged the nuclear reactor core. A serious release of radioactive materials was avoided, though small amounts of radiation were detected 20 miles from the site.[68]

If you live within 50 miles of a nuclear reactor…

113. INDIAN POINT NUCLEAR EMERGENCY ZONE MAP [69]

☞ Know your community's warning systems, disaster plans, and evacuation routes for your home, workplace, schools, day care centers, and other buildings your family frequents. Obtain emergency information from the public utility that operates your nuclear power plant.

☞ Keep your safe room or similar sanctuary well-stocked with nonperishable food and water, a battery-powered or hand-crank radio, extra flashlights and batteries, important documents, clothing and bedding, and a snugly fitting gas mask with an NBC filter for each person in your party.

☞ Plan to feed and care for any pets. A cat needs a litter box indoors. Dogs may be tethered briefly outdoors on the side of the building away from ground zero and washed thoroughly afterwards; or cordon an area in the basement where the dog can relieve itself. More about pets on page 173.

☞ In case you may need to go outdoors, store gloves, thick clothes, tin foil to wrap around your head, and ski goggles to protect your eyes that comprise the "fallout suit" described on page 138.

To read how to prepare for a nuclear emergency just before it occurs and if one suddenly occurs, turn to page 122 and ▌ on page 138.

Days Before

The primary source of information for reporting a disaster a few days before it may arrive is the National Weather Service (NWS). This organization, headquartered in Silver Spring, Maryland, oversees 122 weather forecast offices located in all 50 states, U.S. territories, and adjacent coastal waters. These facilities continually record temperature, precipitation, and a dozen other climatic factors and they track major disturbances such as hurricanes, blizzards, wildfires, and HAZMAT (hazardous materials) incidents. These stations send their data to a central office that has access to satellite imagery and comprehensive forecast models. The central office prepares detailed weather forecasts for the nation and issues notices a few days in advance of any weather event it believes could pose a significant threat to citizens or property lying in its path. These notices are usually *watches*, or *warnings*, and *advisories*, as follows …

Watches … These are issued when a developing weather event is possible but not imminent. Listen for further information and be prepared to act quickly if warnings are issued.

Warnings … These are issued when a hurricane is expected to strike your area within twenty-four hours, when a strong thunderstorm may reach your area within a few hours, and when a tornado has been sighted in your area or indicated by radar. The danger is serious and everyone should go to a safe shelter, turn on a battery-operated radio, and wait for further instructions.

Advisories … These are issued at six-hour intervals at midnight, 6:00 a.m., noon, and 6:00 p.m., Eastern Daylight Time; they describe the present position, forecasted movement, and intensity of a developing weather event. A special advisory is issued if a significant change occurs, and an intermediate advisory updates significant information at two- or three-hour intervals.

Virtually every radio and TV station uses this data to forecast the weather for its broadcast area.[70]

Days before a disaster could arrive is when your brain's gearbox shifts from "neutral" to "forward". Here begins the countdown toward the moment of truth, when you must make the most critical decision regarding an approaching disaster: Should you *leave* your home, or should you *stay*? You may not need to, or be able to, make this decision until minutes before the disaster strikes or even until it passes. As such, this urgent decision exists on a continuum of time that could extend from days before a disaster strikes until after it has occurred.

However, this decision is only the first of a series of decisions you may need to make depending on how the disaster unfolds. For example, if you leave, where will you go? If you stay, how will you cope? These decisions also depend on such combined factors as is your house demolished and you *can* leave, or is it demolished and you *can't* leave? The agony of all this is that usually you must pass through this gauntlet of decisions *when you don't have adequate advance information to make the best choice.* Make all the right decisions, and you're safe. Make one wrong decision, and you could die. For these reasons, this vital *leave* or *stay* decision and its subsequent choices, plus the information you may need to make each best choice along the way, appear several times during the next 70 pages of this book.

Now let's describe a few general preparations to make a few days before a disaster arrives …

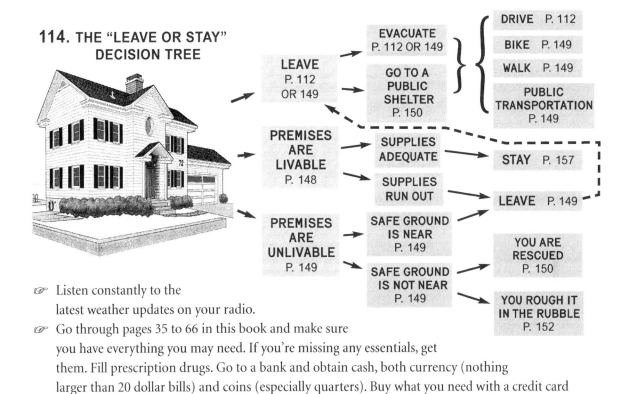

114. THE "LEAVE OR STAY" DECISION TREE

☞ Listen constantly to the latest weather updates on your radio.

☞ Go through pages 35 to 66 in this book and make sure you have everything you may need. If you're missing any essentials, get them. Fill prescription drugs. Go to a bank and obtain cash, both currency (nothing larger than 20 dollar bills) and coins (especially quarters). Buy what you need with a credit card or check to preserve your cash.

☞ Fill your car's tank with gas, because if the power fails gas pumps won't work unless the station has a generator. Check the oil, radiator, wiper fluid reservoir, antifreeze, and the battery. Be sure the lights, hazard lights, wipers, ignition, heater, and defroster work. Repair any that don't work.

☞ Pack precious possessions in waterproof containers if they could be damaged by water.

☞ Do the laundry, including linens and towels, if you anticipate a power failure.

☞ If you have cisterns or rain barrels, make sure they are clean and capped, their openings aren't clogged, and any filters and related devices work properly.

☞ If you have a swimming pool and heavy rains could fill it, drain the water to a foot below the top. Don't empty it; you may need the water for cleaning, flushing toilets, and other things; and an empty pool can cave in or pop out of the ground. Turn off the system's electric power —pumps, lights, chlorinator, everything. If the pump and motor aren't solidly sheltered, wrap them to keep sand and water out. Think twice before throwing the patio furniture into the pool: you might damage the furniture or the pool. Add extra chlorine to kill contamination.

☞ If your house has a fuel gas or oil tank, check the fuel levels. If they're low, fill them.

☞ Clear tables and work surfaces; in a disaster you will perform different tasks that require more space. Remove clutter from floors and circulation areas that may be hard to see in the dark.

☞ Store pure water in capped containers: at least two gallons per person per day for at least three days.

☞ The day before the disaster may strike, fill the washing machine and fill and cover any containers you have with water. Close each bathtub drain as appears at right (or it may slowly leak) and fill the tub with water. You can drink this water the first day and afterward use it for washing, cleaning work surfaces, and flushing toilets.

1 CLOSE THE DRAIN   **2** SEAL RIM WITH DUCT TAPE

115. SEALING A BATHTUB DRAIN

☞ Set the refrigerator and freezer temps to their lowest settings to preserve food as long as possible. During a power failure most full freezers will keep foods frozen for about three days if the room temperature is 70 degrees (longer if the temp is lower, shorter if higher). For half-full freezers cut the numbers

116. KEEPING YOUR FOOD COLD WHEN THE POWER FAILS

by 40 percent. The thawing rate of the food inside depends on the freezer's size (the larger it is the more it will keep things frozen), amount of food in it (full is best), kind of food (meat stays colder than baked goods), and enclosing insulation (the thicker the better). Here are three ways to double the time a refrigerator will keep food cold without using dry ice:

1. Cover its top and sides with blankets, quilts, cushions, styrofoam, and other insulating materials you have. In figure 116 note the sofa cushion, wool blanket, and quilt draped over the refrigerator's top.
2. Stuff every cubic inch of the food compartment with bricks and containers of liquids. A cubic foot of brick holds 1,300 times more coldness than a cubic foot of air and a cubic foot of water holds 3,400 times more. The food compartment of the refrigerator at left contains eight bricks, a bucket filled with three gallons of water, used orange juice cartons filled with water, and three gallons each of antifreeze, water seal, and paint remover —and that's only what you see from the front. Stocking your fridge with thermal reservoirs like this the day before a possible power failure can keep your food as cold as several chunks of dry ice, and you may need to go only as far as your garage to get them.
3. If you have snow, pack some four inches deep in a bucket, remove this "cake" and put it in a plastic bag, and place it in the top of the fridge or freezer (set it on a pan to collect the meltwater).

If you try to chill your food with dry ice, the time and money you spend driving —if you can— may be more costly than losing your food. But if you are desperate to get dry ice for your fridge, here are some specifications. 50 pounds of dry ice (about 9 x 10 x 10 inches) should keep a full 18 cubic-foot freezer below freezing for two days at room temperature and 25 pounds should do the same for a 10-foot freezer. If you put dry ice in the refrigerator compartment, set it at the top on heavy cardboard or plywood and keep food 10 inches away so it won't freeze; also as dry ice warms it emits carbon dioxide which should be vented outdoors. There last two factors reduce the effectiveness of using dry ice to keep your food frozen. When handling dry ice, wear gloves to minimize the risk of frostbite.

After making the above preparations, as the disaster draws near you must decide whether to *leave* or *stay*. If local authorities order you to evacuate, your choice is made for you. Otherwise your decision will largely depend on how severe the disaster will be, how well equipped you are, and how strong your safe room or similar sanctuary is. One way to determine this is with the *disaster safety assessor* on the left. The top corner represents a disaster's SEVERITY, the lower left corner represents how well EQUIPPED you are, and the lower right corner represents your shelter's STRENGTH. Now put a dot in this triangle where it best describes your situation. If the disaster may be severe, you are well equipped, but your shelter isn't strong, put a dot near **A**. (i.e. close to SEVERE, close to EQUIPPED, far from STRENGTH). If the disaster may be weak, you are well equipped, and your shelter is strong, put a dot near **B**. The higher the dot, the more you should leave, and the lower the dot, the more you should stay.

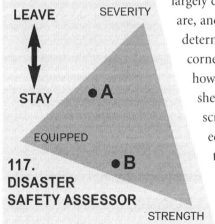

If you decide to leave…

D A Y S   B E F O R E

☞ Know where you will go before you leave. Make reservations or contact the person or place you will possibly drive to. Know the primary and alternate routes, and when you may arrive. If authorities advise a route, take it. Inform your family and friends of your plans, while traveling listen to traffic reports on the radio, and when you reach your destination, call to say you arrived.

☞ Try not to travel alone. Three adults make a good team (if one gets hurt the second tends the victim while the third seeks help). Travel with other cars if you can. Make sure everyone has the same plan.

☞ Listen to weather forecasts on the radio.

☞ If you have pets, know which lodgers along the way will take them. Include places outside your area in case local facilities are closed or full. Except service animals, pets are not usually permitted in public shelters. More about pets on page 173.

☞ Check your car and make sure everything is working as described at **N** on page 98.

☞ Bring your purse or billfold, cell phone if you have one, portable radio, water, food, clothes including an overcoat, spare shoes, flashlights, batteries, blankets, tools, and your personal relief kit. If much business and per-

K FROM 121

sonal information is on your computer, bring it or put your data on a thumb drive. Add other important items until the car is full. Wear comfortable work clothes that will protect you against the weather plus lightweight hiking boots, dark glasses, cap, and a bandana.

☞ Write a police note saying where you will go so they can contact you if necessary. Put the note in an envelope, label it POLICE, and place it between the door and its frame (this should keep the note from blowing away in high winds).

☞ Close and lock all windows, the garage door, and exterior doors unless flooding is a threat (then leave the doors open so the water will create equal pressure on both sides of the exterior walls and not cave them in).

☞ Do not leave a message on your answering machine that says you are not at home, as this could attract burglars.

☞ If you can, leave early in the morning so you'll be on the road during the day when stores are open, and so you'll have more daylight to reach a safe haven if something goes wrong or congestion slows you to a crawl.

☞ Just before you leave, do the following …

- Close fireplace dampers and heating or cooling vents.
- Unplug all electrical devices, and lower any antennas if you can.
- Turn off the electrical system's master circuit breaker, the plumbing's supply main valve, and the gas system's shutoff valve if you have one.
- If floods threaten, open basement or lower-floor windows a few inches to let water enter indoors in order to equalize pressure on both sides of the walls.

1 COVER PANES WITH BIG **X**s OF DUCT TAPE

2 CLOSE DRAPES TIGHTLY

119.
DISASTER WINDOW DRESSING

- If winds threaten, duct-tape big **X**s on the windows and draw any drapes, blinds, or curtains over the windows to help contain any flying glass,. Insert wedges around the bases of sliding patio doors to keep them from lifting off their tracks.

☞ Fill your gas tank soon and always keep it at least two-thirds full. If possible stay on main roads, as the police patrol them more often. Don't expect any luck in shopping for needed supplies along the way. Steer clear of downed power lines, and be alert for fallen trees, landslides, fallen rocks on the road as well as washed-out roads and bridges. In rainy weather avoid coastal and low-lying roads, and do not drive over flooded roads.

☞ Listen to the radio for the latest updates and advisories. Also see **L** on page 133.

☞ In cold weather do the following …

- Clear car windows of snow and ice. Don't drive until your windshield is defrosted.
- Watch for slick ice under bridges, on overpasses, and in shaded areas. Road conditions can vary due to changing sun and shade patterns as well as temperatures.
- If the pavement is snowy or icy, drive slowly, brake gently, and begin braking well before coming to an intersection. If you start to skid, pump the brakes, steer in the direction of the skid until you regain traction, then straighten your vehicle.
- If a snow plow is coming towards you, give it plenty of room to pass; its plow blade may extend over the center line which might not be visible. If you approach a snow plow from behind, resist the urge to pass it because a plowed road is safer to drive on than an unplowed one.

☞ If the air is foggy, dim your headlights or use foglights if you have them. Do not exceed ten miles per hour, and stay well behind any vehicles in front. If the fog is dense, pull well off the road and stop.

☞ If conditions suddenly worsen, turn back or seek shelter in a strong building on high ground. The second floor in a steel or concrete parking garage is usually a good choice.

☞ If you don't have a car, consider a bike. Carry a waterproof knapsack on your back, saddlebags over the rear wheel, and a trailer behind, like the one below. If you flee on foot, pile your belongings on a wagon or sled if you have one.

120. BIKE TRAILER [107]

**D
A
Y
S

B
E
F
O
R
E**

If a hurricane is forecast

If a hurricane may strike your area in a few days, planned appointments, meetings, and entertainment may quickly be cancelled or postponed; and vgue ideas of visiting supermarkets, pharmacies, and hardware stores to stock up on what you would need suddenly become essential errands. A few tasks to perform at home are (some of these are detailed on pages 82 and 83) …

☞ Trim threatening foliage around the house.
☞ Cover windows with shutters or measured and stored panels of plywood.
☞ Make sure any outbuildings are anchored, and clear the yard of lawn furniture and other objects that could blow around.
☞ Strenghten garage doors to withstand the impact of high winds.
☞ Turn fridges and freezers to their coldest settings.
☞ Do the laundry. Set aside the clothes you'll need plus rainwear, rubber boots, and sturdy shoes.
☞ If a surge could flood you, every time you go upstairs carry another armload of belongings to an upper level.
☞ If you have pets, care for them as detailed at **M** on pages 173–74.
☞ Know how to evacuate. Trace your route on a roadmap. Know where the nearest emergency shelter is.
☞ Check your insurance coverage.
☞ If you will evacuate, do as detailed on pages 112, 149, and 150.

To read how to prepare for a hurricane well before and just before it may arrive, turn to page 80.

If deep snow or ice may arrive

If the power fails and you stay home, you'll need to cook food and keep warm with no electricity. If the heat source has a flame it will need ventilation, or the room could fill with carbon monoxide. This is why three victims in our grim list "died of carbon monoxide poisoning in their home or apartment." If the air feels stuffy or you feel sleepy, quickly open two windows a quarter inch on opposite sides of the building.

Isolate a small area that includes the kitchen and a bathroom by closing any doors to the rest of the house or blocking them with drapes, blankets, plywood, or large pieces of cardboard. Part of a basement may suffice because the surrounding earth minimizes heat loss. Avoid rooms with large windows and uninsulated exterior walls. Also …

☞ Make sure you have protected your home or workplace as detailed at **G** on page 95.
☞ Make sure you have all the calamity commodities described in pages 35 to 61 of this book.
☞ Winterize your vehicles and keep the gas tank full (in addition to having enough gas this will keep the fuel line from freezing).
☞ Make sure all cellphones and other battery-powered devices operate properly.
☞ Make sure everyone has warm clothes.
☞ If you remove ashes from a fireplace, shovel them into a metal garbage can with a tight lid. Never use plastic or cardboard because the coals can remain hot for days. Since the coals generate carbon monoxide, take the contained ashes quickly outdoors and let it sit for a week to cool. Then dump the ashes on bare ground well away from the house.

To read how to prepare for a blizzard or ice storm well before it may arrive, turn to page 94.

If an avalanche could occur

Avalanches occur in mountainous areas that accumulate deep snow, during heavy snow or rain, and when the snow is melting on sunny days. These slides may rush downhill at speeds faster than a car can drive, and if they don't crush you they can encase you in snow that is as solid as concrete —then you can't move or breathe and you die. They often occur repeatedly in chute-like depressions on steep slopes between trees on both sides that end at jumbles of rock, earth, and broken trees. They usually occur in remote regions, but they can pose a threat to ski resorts, mountain villages, roads, and railways.

Avalanche forecasting is difficult. Forecasters use local snowpack observation and detailed weather reports to publicize the optimal possibilities of a slide occurring in certain areas.[41] Obey any signs, bulletins, or other announcements that warn that local avalanche hazards are high. Listen to the radio for this information, ask about local conditions at resorts and government offices, and heed the following advisories …

121. ANATOMY OF AN AVALANCHE

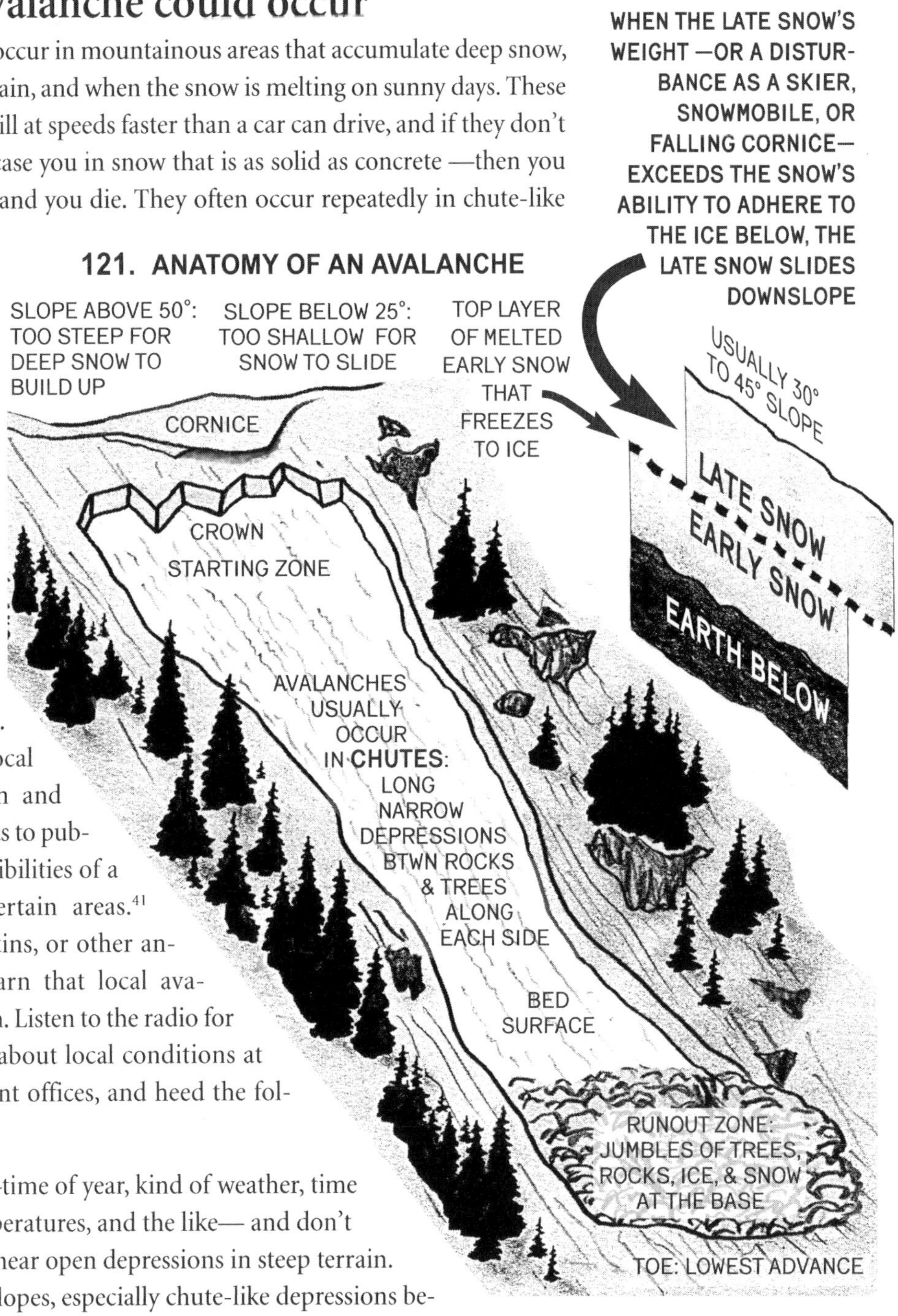

WHEN THE LATE SNOW'S WEIGHT —OR A DISTURBANCE AS A SKIER, SNOWMOBILE, OR FALLING CORNICE— EXCEEDS THE SNOW'S ABILITY TO ADHERE TO THE ICE BELOW, THE LATE SNOW SLIDES DOWNSLOPE

SLOPE ABOVE 50°: TOO STEEP FOR DEEP SNOW TO BUILD UP

SLOPE BELOW 25°: TOO SHALLOW FOR SNOW TO SLIDE

TOP LAYER OF MELTED EARLY SNOW THAT FREEZES TO ICE

USUALLY 30° TO 45° SLOPE

LATE SNOW
EARLY SNOW
EARTH BELOW

CORNICE

CROWN

STARTING ZONE

AVALANCHES USUALLY OCCUR IN CHUTES: LONG NARROW DEPRESSIONS BTWN ROCKS & TREES ALONG EACH SIDE

BED SURFACE

RUNOUT ZONE: JUMBLES OF TREES, ROCKS, ICE, & SNOW AT THE BASE

TOE: LOWEST ADVANCE

☞ Know the signs —time of year, kind of weather, time of day, rising temperatures, and the like— and don't drive, hike, or ski near open depressions in steep terrain.

☞ Be wary of steep slopes, especially chute-like depressions between 30 and 45 degrees that have no trees rising above the snow. The absence of trees tell you that avalanches have slid here before and will slide here again. Another sign of danger is a *runout zone*: a mound of broken trees and rocks at the base of a chute.

D
A
Y
S

B
E
F
O
R
E

☞ Be aware of shadows creeping across a snowcovered slope. A sunny area will be 12 degrees warmer than a shaded area a few feet away; so if the shaded area is 30 degrees it will be frozen while the sunny area will be 42 degrees and will melt and could slide. As shadows creep across snowy slopes these conditions constantly change, especially during late sunny mornings.

☞ Know when it most recently snowed, since 95 percent of avalanches occur during or within 24 hours of heavy rain or snow. If large snowballs as much as two feet in diameter are rolling downhill, this indicates the temperature is increasing upslope.

☞ If you are hiking where avalanches are a danger, walk with another or in a small group, stay fifty feet apart, and have each person tie a 30 foot "rope tail" to the back of his/her waist, all of which increase the chance of one person locating another who is buried in the snow. If the area looks like an area around a recent avalanche, turn and go back.

☞ If you drive in avalanche country, your vehicle should have four-wheel drive, winter tires, chains, a full tank, and survival supplies. Listen to the radio for local highway advisories. If you see a sign that says **Avalanche Area**, do not stop and get out of your car and look around — keep driving, or better yet back up to where you can turn around. If an avalanche blocks the road, back up to a safe area if you can. Where one avalanche occurs others may do so nearby. If you can't back up, stay in your vehicle with your seat belt on; rescuers can find a car in the snow more easily than a person outside a car. Call 911 if you can. Don't drive through small avalanches.

☞ Whether you're driving or on foot, If it's near dark, turn back.

To read how to prepare for an avalanche well before it may occur, turn to page 88.

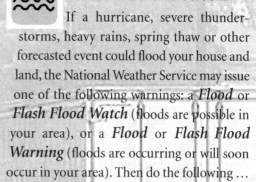

If floods threaten [118]

If a hurricane, severe thunderstorms, heavy rains, spring thaw or other forecasted event could flood your house and land, the National Weather Service may issue one of the following warnings: a *Flood* or *Flash Flood Watch* (floods are possible in your area), or a *Flood* or *Flash Flood Warning* (floods are occurring or will soon occur in your area). Then do the following …

☞ Prepare to evacuate if necessary. If so, consider what supplies you will need when you return to clean up and repair any damages as detailed beginning on page 178. If the walls are wood framing, permanent structural damage will likely occur if floodwaters rise more than two feet above the first floor.

☞ Move any trailers or emergency building materials such as plywood, plastic sheeting, lumber, nails, sandbags, shovels and other tools to high ground where you can reach them if necessary.

☞ Tie down any heavy equipment and materials. You'd be surprised how easily some heavy objects bob like corks in a flood (cars and trucks come to mind). Even if they don't float, flood currents can push them along the bottom of the water which not only destroys them but also anything they may bump into —like your house.

☞ Bring inside any lawn furniture, mowers, garbage cans, signs, potted plants, and any other objects that could be swept away; or tie them down securely.

☞ If you have a drilled well, seal its cap with heavy plastic and duct tape.

Indoors, twenty-four hours before floods may arrive,

do the following ...

☞ Remove doors from doorframes and cabinets, or they may warp.

☞ Remove from the walls all pictures, mirrors, plaques, and decor. Clear desks, tables, and shelves of books and small loose objects. Empty cabinets and drawers. Strip beds of linens and blankets. Empty closets of clothes and shoes. Remove curtains and drapes from windows, and take up rugs and carpets from floors if you can. Remove plants, perishable foods, electronic equipment, furniture, and appliances.

☞ Store small items in sturdy containers lined with garbage bags, wrap large items in large plastic bags sealed with tape, and place everything on counters, tables, cheap furniture, or doors laid on sawhorses; or carry upstairs to the second floor. After storing everything at higher levels, cover with tarps or plastic sheeting secured with ropes, bungee cords, or duct tape.

☞ Empty wastebaskets and clean fireplaces and woodstoves so that floodwaters won't spread their contents through the house.

☞ On floors where flooding may be shallow, move furniture, computers, and the like at least 12 feet from windows and skylights to avoid damage from rain and shattering glass.

☞ Locate all chemicals (lye, pesticides, etc.) above potential floodwater levels.

☞ Leave exterior doors open to equalize pressure indoors and out; this will help keep buildings from shifting and collapsing.

☞ Turn off all plumbing and gas lines and disconnect the electric power.

One way to keep a flood out of a house is to surround it with a *foundation wrap*. This involves wrapping the building's base with plastic sheeting as described below and in figure 122 on the next page. This is a cantankerous construction, and after thinking it through you might decide the result isn't worth the effort. Then again, in some circumstances it may be less vexing and expensive than erecting a new house ...

1. Clear any shrubbery or other obstacles around the foundation until a five-foot aisle of fairly flat earth exists completely around it. Remove any stubs of cut shrubbery that could puncture the plastic sheathing you'll lay on this area (you could dig the shrubs out by the boles and save them for replanting later).

2. Cover basement windows and other openings in the foundation with sheets of $3/4$ inch exterior-grade plywood nailed to 2 x 4s and 2 x 6s fitted into the openings. A carpenter will know how to do this and the other steps below.

3. Dig a trench 12 inches wide and 6 inches deep with its inner edge 3 feet from the foundation wall and deposit the dirt 5 feet from the wall. Leave no sharp rocks in the trench.

4. Lay the plastic sheeting, 6 mil thick and 8 to 10 feet wide, against the foundation wall so its inner top edge aligns with the first floor's rim joists above the wall. Along this line fasten the sheeting to the framing with furring strips. Go up a couple feet if the flood might rise higher, but above this the water's lateral pressure will likely cave in the house.

5. Place the lower part of the sheeting across the ground, into and out of the trench, and onto the ground a foot beyond. Where two sheets overlap, the lap should be 3 feet wide. On the lower sheet apply two bead of panel adhesive 12 inches apart and press the upper sheet into the beads to create a watertight lateral seal. Plastic sheeting can be pierced

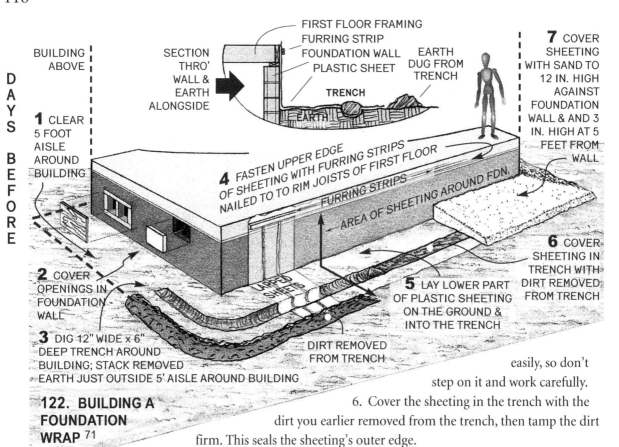

DAYS BEFORE

BUILDING ABOVE

1 CLEAR 5 FOOT AISLE AROUND BUILDING

SECTION THRO' WALL & EARTH ALONGSIDE

FIRST FLOOR FRAMING
FURRING STRIP
FOUNDATION WALL
PLASTIC SHEET

EARTH DUG FROM TRENCH

TRENCH

EARTH

7 COVER SHEETING WITH SAND TO 12 IN. HIGH AGAINST FOUNDATION WALL & AND 3 IN. HIGH AT 5 FEET FROM WALL

4 FASTEN UPPER EDGE OF SHEETING WITH FURRING STRIPS NAILED TO TO RIM JOISTS OF FIRST FLOOR

FURRING STRIPS

AREA OF SHEETING AROUND FDN.

2 COVER OPENINGS IN FOUNDATION WALL

3 DIG 12" WIDE x 6" DEEP TRENCH AROUND BUILDING; STACK REMOVED EARTH JUST OUTSIDE 5' AISLE AROUND BUILDING

LAPPED SHEETS

DIRT REMOVED FROM TRENCH

5 LAY LOWER PART OF PLASTIC SHEETING ON THE GROUND & INTO THE TRENCH

6 COVER SHEETING IN TRENCH WITH DIRT REMOVED FROM TRENCH

122. BUILDING A FOUNDATION WRAP [71]

easily, so don't step on it and work carefully.

6. Cover the sheeting in the trench with the dirt you earlier removed from the trench, then tamp the dirt firm. This seals the sheeting's outer edge.

7. Cover the sheeting with sand 12 inches high against the foundation wall and taper the sand to 3 inches high at a distance of 5 feet from the wall. This will hold the sheeting in place if the flood has little or no current. [71]

If you need to protect a building from flooding with *a sandbag dike*, build one as follows …

1. Locate the dike on solid terrain, fit it into natural contours, shape it short and low, and include large rocks and other heavy impermeable objects. Avoid trees and other objects that could weaken this barrier, and leave eight feet of space between the dike and any buildings it protects.
2. Strip the sod and remove any ice and snow from the area the dike will rest on.
3. Dig a 6 x 18 inch bonding trench down the center of the area where the dike will be built.
4. Fill each bag (usually made of plastic or rough fabric) half full of sand, silt, or clay, and don't tie its top (if the top isn't tied, any air in the bag can escape when other bags are laid on it, which creates a firmer dike). For 100 linear feet of dike you'll need about 800 bags if one foot high, 2,000 bags if two feet high, and 3,400 bags if three feet high. Estimate how much sand you will need as follows. If a sandbag contains about $^2/_5$ cubic foot of sand and the dike will be 3 feet high, you'll need about 3,400 bags. If it takes two people about a minute to fill each bag, a little math says you'll need about

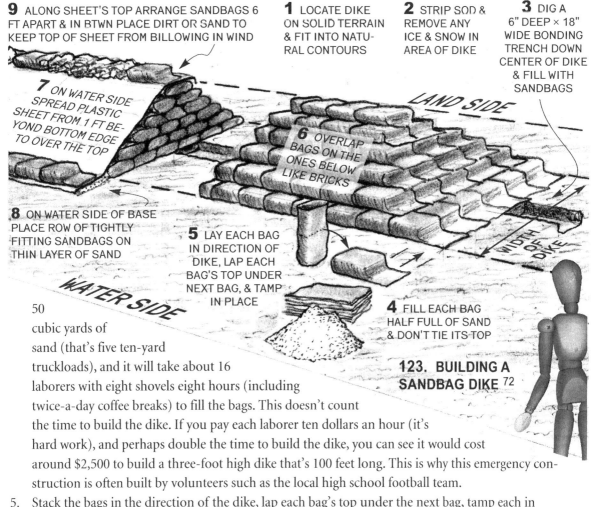

9 ALONG SHEET'S TOP ARRANGE SANDBAGS 6 FT APART & IN BTWN PLACE DIRT OR SAND TO KEEP TOP OF SHEET FROM BILLOWING IN WIND

1 LOCATE DIKE ON SOLID TERRAIN & FIT INTO NATURAL CONTOURS

2 STRIP SOD & REMOVE ANY ICE & SNOW IN AREA OF DIKE

3 DIG A 6" DEEP × 18" WIDE BONDING TRENCH DOWN CENTER OF DIKE & FILL WITH SANDBAGS

LAND SIDE

7 ON WATER SIDE SPREAD PLASTIC SHEET FROM 1 FT BEYOND BOTTOM EDGE TO OVER THE TOP

6 OVERLAP BAGS ON THE ONES BELOW LIKE BRICKS

8 ON WATER SIDE OF BASE PLACE ROW OF TIGHTLY FITTING SANDBAGS ON THIN LAYER OF SAND

5 LAY EACH BAG IN DIRECTION OF DIKE, LAP EACH BAG'S TOP UNDER NEXT BAG, & TAMP IN PLACE

WIDTH OF DIKE

WATER SIDE

4 FILL EACH BAG HALF FULL OF SAND & DON'T TIE ITS TOP

123. BUILDING A SANDBAG DIKE [72]

50 cubic yards of sand (that's five ten-yard truckloads), and it will take about 16 laborers with eight shovels eight hours (including twice-a-day coffee breaks) to fill the bags. This doesn't count the time to build the dike. If you pay each laborer ten dollars an hour (it's hard work), and perhaps double the time to build the dike, you can see it would cost around $2,500 to build a three-foot high dike that's 100 feet long. This is why this emergency construction is often built by volunteers such as the local high school football team.

5. Stack the bags in the direction of the dike, lap each bag's top under the next bag, tamp each in place, and overlap the next layer on the one below width-wise and length-wise like bricks.

6. When the dike is built, along the water side of its base spread a layer of earth or sand one inch deep and one foot wide.

7. Spread 6-mil plastic sheet against the dike so the sheet's bottom edge extends one foot beyond the layer of earth and the sheet's upper edge extends over the dike's top. Lay the sheet loosely so it can conform to the sandbags behind as the rising water presses against the bags.

8. Along the sheet's base place a row of tightly fitting sandbags or rocks to form a watertight seal along the dike's base.

9. Along the sheet's top place sandbags six feet apart and in between place dirt or rocks to keep wind from billowing the plastic.

10. As you work, avoid walking on the plastic or puncturing it with sharp objects. [72]

To read how to prepare for a flood well before it may occur, turn to page 99.

If a volcano may erupt

If you have read on page 90 how devastating a volcanic eruption can be, you'll know that the best way to cope with a volcano that could erupt near you is to evacuate fast and far. If you do so…

☞ Keep your gas tank full and know your route. Avoid valleys and other low-lying regions as this is where lava and mud tend to flow.

☞ Load your car with buckets, shovels, hoes, hatchets, and other tools in case you need them along the way. Wear long-sleeved shirts, trousers, and goggles or eyeglasses, but not contact lenses as airborne ash can make them grate in your eyes.

☞ Bring water, flashlight, battery-operated radio, goggles, and a gas or dust mask. If you have no mask, fit a tee-shirt or turtleneck over your head until its neck rests on your nose.

☞ If you stay, keep the ash outdoors by closing windows and doors, covering chimneys, and sealing vents. If the ash becomes deep, rake or shovel it off the roof, especially if rain is forecast, because the ash will absorb rain and become very heavy. Wear a respirator at all times. Several are described on page 78.

To read how to prepare for a volcanic eruption well before and if one suddenly occurs, turn to page 90 and 141.

If a landslide may occur

Although a landslide usually occurs suddenly, it often results from accumulated winter snow, heavy rain, and spring thaws. If these occur in nearby mountains or hills and you live in a lowland area, seriously think of evacuating. If you live on sloping terrain and its base begins to bulge, or your dwelling's doors or windows begin to stick in their frames, or cracks appear in the walls, or steps start inching away from the facades, or fences and trees begin to tilt downhill, abandon serious thinking and quickly leave the building in a direction lateral to the slope. If the terrain you vacate remains still and you hear no rumbling, trees cracking, or boulders banging upslope, you could risk tiptoeing back indoors and grabbing a few possessions. Otherwise, the more footprints you make the safer you'll be. Other precautions…

124.⁷³

☞ Stay away from steep slopes during heavy rains, especially if they are covered with snow or have experienced a fire the past year.

☞ If you are driving and see any collapsed pavement, piles of mud, or fallen rocks ahead (roadside embankments are particularly susceptible), back up as fast as you can carefully do so.

To read how to prepare for a landslide or mudflow well before it occurs and if one suddenly occurs, turn to pages 86 and 141.

Just Before

In some disasters you may have only minutes or at most hours to take cover. These include tornadoes, tsunamis, wildfires, nuclear meltdowns, and toxic chemicals released into the air. You may have to decide on short notice whether to *leave* or *stay.* In some cases you may have no choice but to leave; in others you may have no choice but to stay. If you leave, you can take some belongings and will likely escape the danger. If you stay, usually at home, you'll be familiar with your surrounds, you may be able to save some of your property, and you'll conserve energy by staying in one place.

Leave if ordered by authorities, because they know the big picture better than you. Also leave if you live in a mobile home, if you are unprepared for what may arrive, or if your understanding of the situation scares you —as happened to the mother in Moore, Oklahoma, who believed she and her son should leave their house before the tornado arrived as described on page 25. The things you should do before, during, and after you leave are detailed beginning at **K** on page 112.

Stay if the authorities allow it, you believe you'll be safe where you are, and you will have enough water, food, tools, and other supplies to last until things return to normal. If you have time …

☞ Move vehicles indoors, seek shelter in your safe room or similar sanctuary, and listen to the radio.
☞ Make sure you have a flashlight, a bucket for bathrooming, and a large plastic bag for trash.
☞ Assign tasks for each member of your party, and alert friends and relatives of your decision.

If a tsunami approaches

If you are at the beach, perhaps enjoying a well-deserved vacation at a coastal resort, and you see the surf recede with an ominous low sucking sound, don't wait until it has exposed the ocean floor for hundreds of feet from shore —flee quickly inland to high ground, because during the next several minutes the sea will return and build to a mountainous crest as much as 100 feet high that moves forward at 50 miles an hour. You may hear civil defense sirens wailing. If you are far enough inland so the wave's crest has broken and fallen forward, you may encounter acres of sloshy surf 10 to 20 feet deep that no longer packs a lot of power but may be floating with chunks of bobbing debris. Listen to the water rushing by … it might move inland for several minutes. Then all may be calm —but don't be fooled, for the flow may be about to reverse before returning to the sea. Then listen to the water flowing the other way, as it rakes flooded areas with a ferocious undertow that erodes building foundations and carries away buildings weakened by the original wall of water. Then all may be calm again. Still don't be fooled —because several waves may arrive often 20 to 30 minutes apart, and the second or third one may be stronger than the first.

☞ If you live in a lowland area near a body of water, know the quickest route to the nearest high ground you could flee to if a huge wave should approach.
☞ If you see a concrete building at least three floors high (at coastal resorts the beaches are often lined

with high-rise concrete buildings) enter it and climb quickly to the third floor if you can, then hide in a small room near the center of the floor. A stairwell or rest room is better than a room with windows. If you are in a stairwell, hold onto a railing. If in a bathroom, enter a toilet stall and kneel and hug the toilet. You want to keep from being tossed around if the building is shaken by the impact of the water.

☞ Afterward, after you have crawled out of hiding, stay away from buildings and bridges that could be damaged. Continue walking inland, until you have passed the line where the water advanced the farthest. There you may be surprised at how normal everything looks! Not a power line will have fallen, not a storewindow will be cracked, not a strip of decor will be out of place. Find a radio if you can, and listen for any news or updates. Heed the advisories, buy some water and food, help the injured, and wait until help arrives.

To read how to prepare for a tsunami well before it occurs, turn to page 84.

If nuclear fallout is a danger

If you are caught above ground, seek shelter in a windowless central area on a middle floor in a multistory building. Otherwise, quickly gather what you will need for three days and enter a fallout shelter, basement, subway, tunnel, or other underground area. Bring a flashlight and a battery-powered radio.

☞ Listen to radio or TV broadcasts for evacuation routes and other advisories. Try to learn what caused the emergency, how much radiation might be released, and when it will reduce to safe levels. If you have a radiation detector you can determine some of this yourself.

☞ If you stay where you are, stay indoors and …

- Close all the doors and windows.
- Turn off any air conditioners, furnaces, and fans that draw air from outdoors.
- Seal the seams around every door, window, and other openings with duct tape.
- Do not use the telephone unless absolutely necessary. Leave lines open for emergency calls.
- Put the food you will eat during the next three days in covered containers or in the refrigerator. Wash any food previously not in covered containers. Water in plumbing is usually safe to use.
- Shelter pets and give them stored or canned food.

☞ In case you may need to go outdoors, have the gloves, thick clothing, aluminum foil, and ski goggles needed to make the "fallout suit" described on page 138.

☞ If advised to evacuate and you drive, keep your car windows and vents closed and drive at least 20 miles away. If you ride a bike or run or walk, do not exhaust yourself, wear goggles and gloves, and cover your head. If you have a turtleneck sweater, slip it over your head until its neck rests on your nose and the rest of the shirt falls about your neck. Two turtlenecks worn like this are better than one.

To read how to prepare for a nuclear emergency well before it occurs and if one suddenly occurs, turn to page 105 and **O** on page 138.

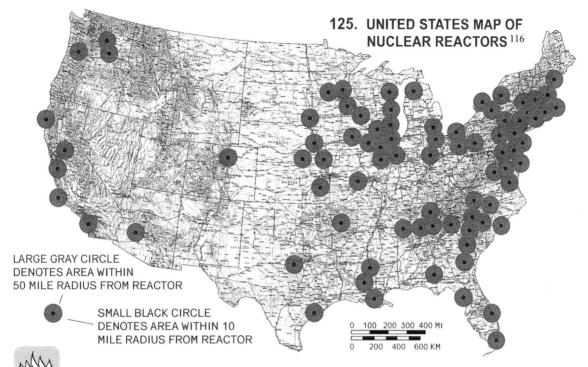

125. UNITED STATES MAP OF NUCLEAR REACTORS [116]

LARGE GRAY CIRCLE
DENOTES AREA WITHIN
50 MILE RADIUS FROM REACTOR

SMALL BLACK CIRCLE
DENOTES AREA WITHIN 10
MILE RADIUS FROM REACTOR

0   100   200   300   400 MI
0   200   400   600 KM

If a wildfire approaches

As mentioned on pages 102 and 103, wildfires can spread via *surface fires, crown fires, firebrands*, and *flame fronts*. Wind-driven flames can race across the ground faster than a horse can gallop, and the air around a large fire can be so hot that a building will combust before flames reach it, plastic gutters and siding will melt, and metal roofing or siding will ignite the plywood sheathing underneath. Large fires can also suck oxygen from the air for hundreds of feet around, so even if you find a damp or cool place to stay you could suffocate.

Since it normally takes two to three minutes for fire to ignite wood and a flame front usually passes through a given area in one to five minutes, an effective firefighting strategy is to hose down a house's wooden surfaces that face an approaching fire, then put the hose on the roof with the water running and leave before the flames become hot enough to burn or asphyxiate anyone. The dampened exteriors will be less likely to ignite when the flames pass. When a wildfire torched 60,000 acres (that's 940 square miles) in Big Sur when I lived there in 1970, I saved a house by starting a backfire on the house's lawn and controlling the blaze completely around the house with a garden hose until the whole lawn was charred. Then I went into the kitchen, got an icepick, stabbed dozens of holes along the hose, climbed a ladder onto the roof and looped the hose back and forth along its peak, then turned on the hose before evacuating. The wildfire swept through the area and burned every house to the ground within a half mile but this one.

The moment you learn that a fire is approaching your house, do the following...

☞ Turn on your radio or TV to obtain the latest updates and advisories.

☞ Move the furniture toward the center of the house so it will be less likely to catch fire if flames enter a window.

☞ Pack important papers and possessions.

☞ Close every door and window to prevent drafts, and remove curtains and drapes.

☞ Turn off fuel lines, gas valves, pilot lights.

☞ Leave the building's entrances unlocked and accessible to firefighters.

☞ Do not plan to use electrical tools to prepare for an approaching fire, because power lines miles away may be severed by the fire.

☞ Don't assume a nearby creek will be a water source, because a sizable fire upstream can suck it dry. Also a stream less than 30 feet wide is often a poor fire barrier since foliage growing high along its banks can fuel advancing flames that leap across the water.

☞ If you have a hose and water, hose down any part of the house and grounds that could burn, then leave a sprinkler or soaker hose with the water running on the roof.

☞ If you have a swimming pool, toss in any heavier-than-water valuables that won't be damaged by the water.

☞ Before leaving, load in your car an axe, chainsaw, brush saw, shovel, and hoe if you have them, so if you come to a burning tree fallen on the road you may be able to remove it. Also bring a hardhat, first-aid kit, towels, and a couple of friends. Know what evacuation route you will take and listen to the radio as you leave.[74]

To read how to prepare for a wildfire well before it occurs, see page 102.

If a tornado threatens

If the sky is filled with low dark clouds, a tornado could be near even if you can't see it. Some twirl down from the clouds without warning, and some don't even have a funnel, the only clue to their presence being whirling dust or debris on the ground below. You also won't see one at night, if it is hidden by trees, or it is raining. But if you hear a roar like an approaching freight train, do the following…

☞ Close the shades and curtains, unplug electrical equipment, and head for your safe room.

☞ If you have no safe room, hide in a bathtub or closet, or under a heavy table, or flip a sofa upside-down and crawl under it. If you have a protective helmet, put it on and cover yourself with whatever cushions, pillows, coats, sleeping bags and other soft things you can find.

☞ Stay away from windows, mirrors, refrigerators, pianos, and other heavy and glassy objects.

☞ Once in your shelter, listen to the latest updates and advisories on your radio.

☞ If caught in a public building, go to a designated shelter or small central room such as a bathroom on the lowest floor, crouch against the base of a wall, and cover your head with an overcoat or other padding. Avoid large rooms. Don't enter an elevator; if the power fails the cab could get stuck and you'd be trapped.

☞ If you can clearly see which way the funnel is moving and can drive away from it, do so. If possible, drive into the center of a concrete parking garage or similar structure, huddle low below the windows, leave two opposite windows slightly open to equalize pressure inside and outside the car, and cover your head with your hands, clothes, maps, floormats —anything you can find. Parking under a bridge is chancy. If the storm is weak, a bridge is adequate shelter; but if the storm is strong, the bridge could become dislodged, a large tree could fall and topple it, and flying debris could blow under it.

☞ If you can't see the funnel and are on the road, drive into a strong building if you can quickly do so. Otherwise leave the vehicle and lie in a ditch or other depression and cover your head with your arms.

To read how to prepare for a tornado well before it occurs, turn to page 83.

If a thunderstorm is near

This weather produces lightning, strong winds, hail, floods, and sometimes tornadoes. In hot dry areas a storm's raindrops may evaporate before they reach the ground, but bolts of lightning can still kill you and start wildfires. It is a myth that lightning doesn't strike the same place twice: the Empire State Building has been struck more than 200 times.

If you are at home and the sky fills with dark clouds flashing with lightning and rumbling with thunder and the wind picks up…

☞ Quickly move any cars into the garage and take any lawn furniture or other loose objects indoors.

☞ Remain indoors, stay off porches, and keep away from exterior doors, windows, and skylights.

☞ Don't lie on concrete floors or lean against concrete walls. If lightning strikes the building its electricity can pass through concrete, especially if it contains steel reinforcing.

☞ Unplug appliances and electrical equipment, don't touch any cords or equipment, and don't use the phone. A lightning surge could enter the wiring and shock you.

☞ Don't touch any plumbing. Don't wash your hands, take a shower, wash the dishes, run the dishwasher, or use the clothes washer or dryer. If lightning strikes the building it can send a few million volts through every metal pipe and drop of water pouring from them —and through you.

☞ Listen to a radio for weather updates.

☞ If you are caught outdoors, stay away from trees, lamp posts, power lines, golf clubs, fishing rods, and anything that is tall and has metal or water in it. Cars are a safe place if you are completely inside, the doors are closed, and you don't touch any metal.

☞ If you feel your hair stand on end —lightning is near. Crouch low with your hands on your knees (if you are struck, the current will more likely pass through your limbs than your torso). Do not lie flat on the ground (this will make you a larger target and the electricity may pass through your torso), and stay out of depressions with water in them.

☞ If you can find a dry ditch or culvert, lie in it and cover the back of your head with your arms. If a vehicle is near, climb in, close the door, huddle as low as you can and don't touch any metal. If you feel like you may be sucked out of the car — possible in a tornado— grab the brake pedal on the floor and hold on for dear life. Stay inside until the storm passes.

☞ If lightning strikes the building you are in, it could set it afire. If this occurs, leave and call 911. If the fire is small and is indoors, open the nearest windows and try to put it out with water and fire extinguishers. Otherwise run to the garage, climb into your car, and drive a safe distance away. For more information on how to fight a fire that has erupted indoors, see pages 130 to 133.

☞ If you are driving, pull well off the road so other cars won't crash into you. Park on a wide shoulder or under a bridge, pull into someone's driveway or a service station canopy, or drive into a concrete parking garage or other strong structure. Don't park near a stream or storm sewer that could fill with floodwater. Stay away from trees, power lines, and other overhead objects that could fall on you due to wind or lightning. If you can't pull off the road, slow way down, turn on your headlights and emergency flashers, stay away from other cars, and approach intersections slowly.

☞ If someone near you has been struck by lightning, first know that a person struck by lightning carries no electric charge that can shock others. Look for burn marks where the lightning entered and exited the body. If the person is burned, treat them as well as you can and call 911. If the person's heart or breathing stops, administer CPR and call 911.

Another thunderstorm danger is *hail*. These pellets of ice usually range from pea to softball in size. The largest hailstone recovered in the United States fell in Vivian, South Dakota, on June 23, 2010; it was 8 inches thick and weighed 1 pound, 15 ounces. Most hailstorms occur between one and nine p.m. and rarely last 15 minutes. The hailstones can pile so deep that they are best removed with a snow plow; but since these storms typically occur in the summer the hail usually quickly melts. In the United States these storms are most common in the area where Colorado, Nebraska, and Wyoming meet. This region, about 6,000 feet above sea level, is nearer the atmosphere where rain freezes to form hail which has less time to melt before reaching the ground. This region experiences hailstorms an average of seven to nine times a year.

Here is a sample of the destruction a hailstorm can wring. On July 11, 1990, a Ferris wheel was operating at an amusement park in Denver, Colorado, when an approaching thunderstorm caused the power to fail and the passengers trapped in their seats were battered by softball-sized hail. 47 people were seriously injured. Sometimes it doesn't pay to get out of bed. [75]

☞ If you are at home when a hailstorm begins, close the drapes or shades so they will contain any shattered glass. Stay away from windows and skylights.

☞ If you are caught outdoors, seek shelter quickly. If none is nearby, cover your head somehow, even if with clumps of grass or a flat rock. If you have any pets, take them quickly into a shelter.

☞ If you are caught while driving, drive slowly, because the faster you drive the greater will be the hail's impact against your windshield. As quickly as you can, park well off the road under a bridge or service station canopy, in a building, or under a tree if this is all you can find (you're less likely to be struck by lightning than hail). If you find no shelter, try to park your vehicle so the hail hits its front, because windshields are made to withstand pelting objects better than side or back windows. Inside, keep as far as possible from the windows and cover your eyes. If you can, lie face down on the back seat, keep any children under you and cover their eyes, and protect yourself with a blanket or overcoat. Even if hailstones pound the vehicle's body and smash its windows, its metal shell and shatterproof glass will likely protect you from serious injury. Do not open a door or window until the pattering or pounding has stopped.

Suddenly

In some disasters you have no warning at all. Perhaps you're enjoying life in the comfort of your home, or your workplace, or your car while driving, thinking of how marvelous modern society is with all its amazing devices —when suddenly your feet are yanked from under you or the ceiling falls in or your face sears with pain or you suddenly can't breathe.

Think of what it was like for 42 people who were driving on the Nimitz Freeway along San Francisco Bay the afternoon of October 17, 1989, glancing out the windows at the lovely bay alongside and the cityscapes laid like sequined carpets beyond —when suddenly the pavement shook beneath their tires and the freeway overhead thundered upon them and an instant of crushing pain may have been the last thing they remembered while millions of people nationwide watched the tremors on television as the Oakland Athletics and the San Francisco Giants were playing the World Series until the screen went blank. [76]

When a sudden disaster catches you completely off guard, in the most elemental terms your immediate response depends on two things:

Where are you?

What happened?

As for where are you, are you at home? In a suburban residence. A sixth-floor urban apartment? Are you at work? In an office? Factory? Retail store? First floor? Tenth floor? Are you shopping? In a store downtown? Suburban shopping mall? Flea market? Near your car? Far from your car? Are you driving? On a city street? Expressway? Country road? Might you be biking? In a plane or train? On a ship?

As for what happened, is the disaster still happening or has it stopped? Can you breathe? Is the ceiling above or the floor below teetering? Are you freezing cold and don't have a jacket? Are you in ten feet of water? Can you see? Do you have time to get dressed? To turn off the electricity and water? To close the doors and windows and curtains and drapes? To take a few belongings to a safe place?

Here all the crisscrossing possibilities between where you are and what has happened are so innumerable that no thin book could encapsulate them all. Rather than provide you with all manner of lists of things to have and pages of explanations for every exigency that could arise, better would be to improve your ability to think creatively, use your imagination, increase your confidence, maximize your knowledge, and act resourcefully —so in seconds you can convert your desperation into effective action in any misfortune you may face.

If you are at home

If a disaster strikes you suddenly while you are at home or you wake up in the morning and discover something terrible has happened during the night, if you can, quickly dress in comfortable work clothes and sturdy shoes, grab a flashlight and see if everyone else inside is safe, then turn off the electricity, water, and gas. If any floors are wet or covered with water, be wary of electric shock. Turn on your battery-powered radio. If you don't already know what happened, try to learn what did.

128

S
U
D
D
E
N
L
Y

☞ If any floors, walls, or ceilings are seriously damaged, try to assess how safe they are. If you have any doubts, leave the premises if you can and have a professional assess the damage for you.

☞ If you are trapped indoors, in some scenarios it is safer to move to a second floor, attic or rooftop and wait for help; in others you should descend into a basement.

☞ If there is smoke or the fire is bigger than a chair, get everyone outside fast. Don't risk being asphyxiated by the toxic products of combustion.

☞ If carbon monoxide is a threat or you smell propane or other fuel gas, quickly open every door and window to ventilate the building and get everyone outside into fresh air. Do not re-enter until you are certain there is no longer any danger —preferably until an emergency rescuer or professional tells you so. For carbon monoxide poisoning, quickly seek medical attention because immediate treatment is important.

☞ If the room you are in is flooded, your immediate response will depend on deep the water is, how much more it may rise, how safely you can reach the second floor and possibly the roof, how shallow is the water outside, how swiftly is it flowing, and how easily you can find something that floats.

☞ If the weather is freezing cold, open every faucet whose pipes could freeze until the water trickles at about one drop per second, and open any cabinet doors below to expose the plumbing to the room's heat. If a pipe bursts, quickly shut off the water at its source to minimize flooding indoors and call a plumber. Never thaw a pipe with an open flame or torch. If you leave the building for several days, either have someone check your house daily or consider draining the plumbing.

If trapped in a city

In an urban disaster, many people living in a small area typically vie for goods, services, and supplies that may quickly run out. Here are your chief concerns and remedies…

☞ Drinkable water can be hard to find. In a landscape of pavements the biggest body of water may be in a building's plumbing. One several stories tall may hold hundreds of gallons. See page 160 for how to obtain it. If any lakes, rivers, or even storm sewers are within a few blocks, have buckets that you can carry water in. Even if the water is impure you can use it to flush toilets, or boil it if you can find the fuel. Other water sources are cans and bottles of water, soda, and fruit juice.

☞ A city typically has only a three-day supply of food. If you find a store that has food, buy all you can carry. If you have a slingshot and a few marbles or pea gravel, you can kill pigeons, seagulls, and rats. If a park is nearby and you have a book on wilderness foods, you can forage for edible plants. If the park has a creek or pond, look for crawfish, frogs, minnows, and larger fish.

☞ Traffic may be so congested that "getting out of Dodge" isn't an option. If you stay at home you'll be familiar with your surrounds, will save energy by not traveling, and can better protect yourself from outsiders. If your home is unlivable, make a temporary camp in a strong commercial building, preferably in a bedroom-size area on the second floor that has a window and a kitchen or bathroom (the basins and cabinets will be useful even if you have no water).

☞ Garbage can pile up and become a source of rapidly spreading disease. Stay away from piles of garbage, and bag your own carefully.

☞ City streets may be cruised by law-breakers who will take whatever they can from others. Stay off streets as much as possible, avoid strangers, and stay above the first floor which is where most undesirable activity usually occurs.

☞ Hospitals and staffs can become overwhelmed with victims, so don't go unless you have a real emergency. Having a well-stocked first-aid kit and plenty of isopropyl alcohol can be a lifesaver.

☞ Apartments and businesses above the third floor can be traps if the power fails. Elevators and plumbing won't work, heating and air conditioning won't work, and if the windows won't open (common in tall buildings) the air can become unbearable in a few hours. If this happens, descend to the entrance with as many important things you can carry and try to find a safe place to stay.

Here is how one 94-year-old widow living on the 26th floor of an apartment in lower Manhattan coped with hurricane Sandy. When it was forecast she stocked up on bottled water and foods that needed no cooking. After the power failed, she managed with what she had. A few days later when supplies ran low and things were getting rank, she packed a few bags of belongings, left them in her apartment and carefully descended the 25 flights, checked into a generator-operated B&B around the corner, then walked slowly back up and packed her bags.

☞ On the plus side, urban dwellers are often quick to help each other. Know who your dependable friends are, and discuss how you can team together to meet your common needs.

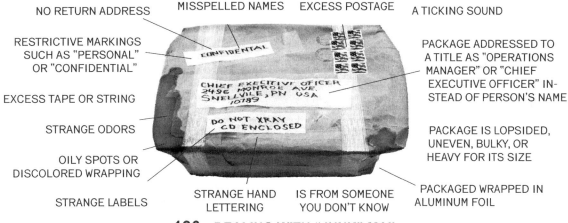

126. DEALING WITH "JUNK" MAIL

If you receive a threatening phone call or mail

If you receive a *threatening phone call*, get as much information as you can, try to record the conversation, and call the police. If you receive a *package that could be dangerous* as appears in figure 126 above, don't open it —throw a blanket over it, take it quickly outside and place it on the ground away from the house, and call the police. If a puff of *dust rises from a letter you open*, delicately set the letter and envelope in a sealed plastic bag, thoroughly wash your face and hands with warm soapy water, put on clean clothes, put your previous clothes in a sealed container, and call the police.

If you are in a burning building

We've all seen news videos of flames billowing from a furiously burning building. But even more deadly are gases generated by the fire which swiftly spread far beyond their source. Consider the Happy Land nightclub fire near New York City in 1990 in which 87 people breathed their last. Some who died on the lower floor were found slumped in their seats at the bar with cigarets and drinks in their hands — because they inhaled a colorless, odorless, toxic gas and one lungful was all it took. [81]

And consider the Stouffer's Inn fire near White Plains, New York, in December 1980 that killed 26 people attending a management seminar on the third floor. When a woman saw smoke seeping around a closed hallway door she shouted, "Get out of here!" When someone pushed the door open, flames billowed inside. Some victims were felled instantly; others succumbed to the fire and fumes in minutes. Firemen said, "The blaze erupted with the force of an explosion and spread with the speed and intensity of a flamethrower." One who escaped said, "We thought we had more time." Some who escaped didn't rush out the main door but "moved toward the rear," and fled through "a second set of double doors into a hallway quickly filling with dense smoke." Others "smashed plate-glass windows with furniture and leaped 35 feet to the ground. They suffered burns, cuts, and broken bones." Seven victims "were found in a walk-in closet whose door they mistook for an exit door." [82]

Even the mighty strength of steel and concrete will desert those who seek its refuge in a fire. Intense heat weakens steel until it is as limp as soft chocolate, and it weakens concrete until its massive spans droop like wet spaghetti. When fire broke out in the World Trade Center towers in September 2001, the intense heat so reduced the strength of the steel and concrete supporting the uppermost floors that they failed — then their downward momentum pancaked dozens of floors below that hadn't seen a spark of flame.

A fire can fill a room with smoke in minutes, leaving little time to grab valuables or call 911. Smoke, being lighter than air, initially collects on the ceiling. As its underside lowers, first it hides any EXIT signs mounted high on the walls and you can't see them. As the smoke lowers to eye level it will sting your eyes —then they close, because this is how your body protects them, and *you can't open your eyes and see where you are*. And smoke is hot. By the time it reaches the floor, the temperature at eye level may be 600 degrees —it makes little difference whether the degrees are Fahrenheit or Centigrade. Such rooms are little more than big coffins. Here's how to escape them and live another day...

If you are at home or in a small building ... You may have only a moment to decide whether to *fight* or *flee*. If a frying pan of grease on the stove erupts in flames and an extinguisher is close by you fight. If a fire is bigger than a chair, forget the extinguisher and get everyone outside fast. But if smoke fills the second floor and your children are sleeping upstairs, no book is going to persuade you to flee. Between these extremes decide what is rational. Be guided by what you hear and smell as much as what you see.

If you are in a room whose door is closed and smoke is seeping around the door, keep it closed. No smoke around the door? Feel the knob and the top and bottom of the door with the back of your hand — not your palm or your fingers, because if they get burned you may not be able to crawl on the floor or grab any doorknobs and ladder rungs.

The knob is cold? Take a deep breath and set your foot firmly behind the door, open it an inch, and peek outside. If smoke swirls against the ceiling outside and you see no fire, crawl on the floor until you are outdoors. Is smoke near the floor? Close the door and soak a washcloth, paper towel, or newspaper with water and hold it in your teeth and breathe through this filter, not your nose, and crawl on the floor outside as low as you can.

The knob is warm? The fire could be just outside. Open a window and jump out if you safely can. If the window is high above the ground, grab everything soft inside —curtains, rugs, clothes, bedding, the mattress— and throw them outside to create a softer landing if you jump. If you can, roost on the sill, breathe the fresh air, and wait till the fire trucks arrive. If smoke is seeping under the door and the window is unsafe, stuff wet fabrics under the door to keep out the smoke and hang a sheet or light-colored fabric out the window and yell to anyone outside to alert firefighters.

1 LOOK AROUND THE EDGE OF THE DOOR. IS SMOKE SEEPING IN BETWEEN THE DOOR AND ITS FRAME?

2 FEEL THE BACK OF THE DOOR AT THE TOP, ALONG THE SIDES, & THE BOTTOM. IF THE DOOR IS WARM, DO NOT OPEN IT

3 FEEL THE KNOB WITH THE *BACK* OF YOUR HAND

4 IS THE KNOB COLD? SET YOUR FOOT FIRMLY BEHIND THE DOOR, OPEN IT AN INCH, & PEEK OUTSIDE.

127. HOW TO OPEN A DOOR IN A FIRE

☞ Call 911. Some authorities say wait until you're safely out of the house and use a neighbor's phone, but this delays the arrival of the fire department and is a bad idea if the nearest neighbor is far away. If you have a cellphone, call 911 from outside.

☞ If you have time, close all the windows and doors to prevent drafts from spreading the fire, leave exterior doors unlocked so rescuers can enter, and disconnect automatic garage doors so rescuers can manually open them.

☞ If you are sleeping and an alarm awakes you, don't stand up —crawl out of bed onto the floor, because toxic gases may have filled the upper part of the room.

☞ If you have a fire extinguisher, use it as described on page 43.

☞ If a brush fire nears your home and you have time, hose the ground around the house, set lawn sprinklers between the fire and the house and any above-ground fuel tanks, or set them on the roof.

☞ Once you've left the building, park your car a safe distance away, close the doors and windows, and leave it unlocked so emergency responders can remove it if you aren't around.

If you are in a motel or hotel ... Before entering your room, locate the nearest emergency exits. If you are with another person, talk the situation over as you look around. Usually the biggest danger is not fire but smoke —which could come from anything from an explosion to a smoldering mattress down the hall. Pretend you are blindfolded. Count the steps from your door to the exit door in case it will be dark or smoky. How many doors will you pass? Any corners? Stairs? Anything that could get in your way —like an ice machine? Imagine crawling on the floor next to the wall on the side of the exit, feeling and counting the doors and noting the corners as you go. Don't think of using an *elevator*. (1) They won't work if the power fails. (2) Life-snuffing smoke and hot gases often rise through the shaft. (3) The cab could stop working between floors and you'd be trapped. (4) If many people board the cab it can overload which makes it stop. (5) Smoke can obscure the photocell light that keeps the door open. (6) The smoke can cause the cab's electronics to malfunction. There have even been cases where a passenger pressed the DOWN button and the cab *rose* to the floor where the fire was!

After returning to your room look around. Find the bathroom. Turn on the faucets. Turn on the vent fan. Note where the ice bucket and the waste basket are. Find the air conditioner and work the dials. Open and close the windows. How high above the ground are you? Any ledges outside? When you go to bed, keep your room key and a small flashlight on the nightstand.

☞ If you smell smoke or hear a voice yell "Fire!" or someone bangs on your door —grab your room key and flashlight (in case the power is out), crawl to the door and feel the knob with the back of your hand. Is it hot? Don't open it. Is it cold? Open it slowly as earlier described and peek outside. Smoke on the ceiling? Escape if you can. If you can't, close the door. Don't lock it, so rescuers can enter.

☞ Telephone the front desk and tell where you are, then call 911 yourself. Many hotels won't call 911 until they are sure there is a fire and by then it may have spread. There

BATHTUB
FILL IT FAST BEFORE THE PLUMBING FAILS!

CHAIR USE IT TO SMASH A WINDOW IF YOU HAVE TO

WASTE BASKET OR ICE BUCKET SCOOP WATER FROM THE TUB & THROW IT ON HOT SURFACES

WASH CLOTH WET & STUFF IN MOUTH & BREATHE THRU IT

CURTAINS, TOWELS WET & STUFF AROUND DOORS WHERE SMOKE ENTERS

MATTRESS PAD LAY IT ON JAGGED GLASS IN A WINDOW

MATTRESS PRESS AGAINST DOOR & HOLD WITH BUREAU

BEDSPREAD IF AIR IS HOT, DUNK IN TUB & WRAP AROUND YOU

YOUR LUGGAGE WHAT DOES IT CONTAIN THAT CAN HELP YOU?

128. HOTEL ROOM FIREFIGHTING TOOLS

have been incidents when a guest called the front desk to warn of a fire and the manager sent a staff member to investigate —but ten minutes later he hadn't returned because he was asphyxiated.

☞ If the water is running, quickly turn on the bathtub water to fill the tub.

☞ Turn the air conditioner to MAX COOL and open any windows if no smoke is outside.

☞ Wet a washcloth and hold it in your teeth and breathe through it.

☞ If the air is hot, dunk your bedspread in the tub and wrap it around you.

☞ With a waste basket, ice bucket, or coffee pitcher bail water from the tub onto any hot surfaces to keep them cool.

☞ To reduce any smoke, swing a wet towel above your head around the room.

☞ Wet sheets, curtains and towels and stuff them in cracks where smoke enters.

☞ Place your mattress against the door and hold it in place with a table or dresser.

☞ Keep thinking and fighting until the fire trucks arrive. [83]

If you are in a commercial building…

When you arrive, find the emergency exits and walk the routes as in a hotel. If a fire breaks out …

☞ If you have a cell phone call 911.

☞ Look for wall alarms to turn on and emergency exit signs that will lead you outdoors.

☞ Look for a fire extinguisher. If the fire is small, put it out. If not and you can flee the area, take the extinguisher with you; you may need it along the way. Call for others to follow if you know where you are going.

☞ Don't run through the first exit you see. Look quickly around. Any other exits? Before you open a door, feel it and the knob with the back of your hand. If it's hot don't open it —the heat could burst it open as occurred in the Stouffer Inn and fell you in seconds. If the door isn't hot take a deep breath, set your foot firmly behind it, open it an inch and peek outside. Smoke on the ceiling? If you can see under it, crawl on the floor to an exit.

☞ If you stay inside, find a faucet or other water (in the Stouffer Inn conference there were "water pitchers on the tables"). Soak a cloth napkin, paper towel, or newspaper in water, then hold it in your teeth and breathe through it and not your nose. Keep your hands free for other things.

☞ If you must smash a window to escape, see how far below the ground is. Is there a balcony or ledge outside where you can wait till the fire trucks arrive? A smashed window's edges may be lined with jagged pieces of glass. Pull any drapes off the windows and cover any glass in the open window with fabrics, and throw the rest outside to create a softer place to land.

If you are driving

L FROM 113

With increasing traffic our vehicles and freeways often become traps from which we cannot escape. In late January 2014 icy weather in Atlanta, Georgia, so paralyzed traffic that some drivers were trapped in their traffic lanes like prisoners in cells for 22 hours, "too scared to step out of the car and too nervous to sleep for fear that traffic would start moving at any moment." Passengers had no food, no water, no bathrooms. Some cars overheated in the icy weather and some ran out of gas. Two babies entered the world in trapped cars. [84] Clearly today's drivers need new strategies for coping with these scenarios. So here are the new "Robert's rules of order" for today's mobile society…

If it is raining heavily ... turn on your emergency flashers and your headlights at low beam; this reveals more of the road ahead. If you pull off the road, park well away so other cars won't crash into you. Park on a wide shoulder, in a driveway, under a bridge or gas station canopy, or in a parking garage (not on the lowest level if it could flood). Don't park near water, and stay away from trees, power lines, and other tall objects that could fall on you due to wind or lightning.

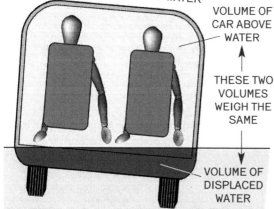

ALL THE EMPTY SPACE IN A CAR MAKES IT WEIGH A QUARTER AS MUCH AS AN EQUAL VOLUME OF WATER

VOLUME OF CAR ABOVE WATER

THESE TWO VOLUMES WEIGH THE SAME

VOLUME OF DISPLACED WATER

BUT LONG BEFORE THE CAR BEGINS TO FLOAT, ITS TIRES LOSE TRACTION WITH THE ROAD —THEN YOU LOSE CONTROL

129. THE PHYSICS OF FLOATING CARS

If part of the road ahead is flooded with water whose bottom you can't see, do not enter even if you are familiar with it, because what you cannot see may have washed away. A car or truck from the doorsills up contains much less solid than void, so it will float like an inner tube if its body is only a few inches deep in water. If you enter deeper water, your tires may suddenly lift from the road. If you try to steer upstream, you drift the other way —you're a raft now. The current

washes you off the shoulder and before you know it you're bobbing like a cork in a flooded creek. Even if you leave your car while it's on the road, you could suffer the fate of one victim in our grim list who "died when his car stalled in flooding water and he got out to flee and slipped in the water." Shallow water can also flood your engine's air intake and ruin the engine (diesels are especially vulnerable to this), if water enters the exhaust it can ruin the catalytic convertor, and if another car approaches it may create a bow wave that floods your engine.

One way to tell how deeply a road is flooded is to look carefully at any other vehicle entering or in the water (if nobody else is foolish enough to do this, don't you be the first). How high is the water against its tires? Up to the hubcaps? Below this level you're safe. Above this, your car becomes more buoyant and you lose control. Do the wheels plowing through the water create bow waves that splash over the curbs? Don't be intimidated by horns honking behind you. Wait till the wheels pass and "the coast is clear," literally, then enter the water near the center of the road, because the crown is higher than the curbs. Shift into low (this revs the engine faster and keeps the exhaust clear), do not change gears (this can cause water to suck into the exhaust), and move slowly so you don't create a bow wave. After leaving the water, test your brakes if no cars are nearby.

If your car stalls and won't restart, don't get out and open the hood; the rain could soak the engine. Leave the vehicle, seek high ground, and wait for help. Find a long stick, and before you step in any water probe it with the stick. Look at anything floating in the water; this may tell you how deep it is and how fast it flows.

ABOVE THIS LEVEL, YOU'LL BE SORRY

BELOW THIS LEVEL, YOU'RE SAFE

130. THE HUBCAP TEST

Stay away from any water with a ripple in it. That ripple says the water is *moving*—and even if only six inches deep it can sweep you away as it did to one victim in our grim list who "died when a surge of water swept him off a sidewalk." Stay 30 feet from the end of culverts; water swirling into them can suck in pets, children, even adults. Two-thirds of the people who die in floods drown in floodwater —many within 10 feet of safety. Other tips …

☞ Wherever you drive, carry water, food, toilet paper —and diapers. In Japan and China, some drivers wear diapers in case they get stuck in traffic for several hours.

☞ If trapped in traffic turn off your engine. If you don't move for 20 seconds you'll save more energy than you'll use by restarting.

☞ Be wary of rear-end accidents. If you are bumped from behind and do not feel comfortable stopping where you are, motion to the other driver and drive to the nearest service station, police station, hospital, or other public building that is open.

FENDER

1. EXHAUST IS BLOCKED BY SNOW   **2.** EXHAUST IS CLEAR OF SNOW

131. CLEARING THE EXHAUST

If heavy snow traps you in your car … When the snowflakes are thick and drifts pile on the road, pull off the road —far enough so other cars won't hit you, but near enough so they can see you if you need help. Turn on your hazard lights. Hang a help flag or brightly colored (not white) distress flag from the antenna or window. Then assess your situation …

☞ Can passing drivers see you? Any buildings you can walk to? Is it day or night? What will the weather be like the next few hours? If you have a cellphone call 911. Call anyone on your contact list who could help. If your cellphone is too weak to make a call, leave it on; rescuers may detect its signal and proceed to its source.

☞ On your roadmap locate where you are and the nearest town. Don't leave the car unless you see a building where you can take shelter. Blowing snow distorts distances, and it may be too deep to walk far.

☞ Listen to the radio. When you hear the information you need, turn the radio off to conserve electricity.

☞ If stranded in a remote area, try to find a clearing nearby and stomp a large **SOS** in the snow. If you have potassium permanganate or other dye, sprinkle a big SOS on the depression so the letters will be visible to a search helicopter or plane. If possible, build a fire to warm yourself and attract attention.

☞ Get out and look at the exhaust pipe. Is it blocked? Unblock it with your hand, foot, a shovel —whatever it takes to keep your car from filling with carbon monoxide.

☞ If stranded at night, when another car approaches turn on your dome light, honk the horn, and turn your headlights on and off in hopes they will help you. If the weather clears and you must stay where you are, get out and raise the hood; this signals that you need help.

☞ If the weather is cold, run the engine five or ten minutes each hour to keep warm. While the engine runs, open a window on the downwind side (the side away from where the snow is blowing) a half inch to provide ventilation and protect you from carbon monoxide poisoning. Don't lower the window all the way; if the battery dies you may be unable to raise it.

OPEN
WINDOW
1/2 INCH

132.

☞ If others are with you, take turns sleeping so one person can look for rescuers.

☞ Exercise slightly: clap your hands, move your limbs vigorously, imagine you're dancing with Elvis Presley. Huddle with other passengers and cover yourself with maps, seat covers, floor mats, and coats to conserve body heat.

☞ Drink fluids to avoid dehydration. If you have food, eat small amounts every few hours. Do not eat snow as it will lower your body temperature. Melt it first.

☞ If you need to go to the bathroom, leave the car on the downwind side, quickly close the door, and stomp a depression by the car. Cover with snow and mark the area with an object for the next user and quickly return inside.

☞ Leave the car on foot only after the storm ends and you know where you are going.

LosT
Robert
Butler
Was here
1:20 PM
3/16

133. THE BLAZED TREE NOTE

Here's a recipe a disaster-stricken father cooked up in December 2013 when his car broke down in the snowy Rockies of Nevada in minus 15 degree weather that saved the lives of his wife and four children: Lay your spare tire in the snow, fill its hub with nearby grass and wood and build a fire, toss some nearby rocks in the fire, and put the heated rocks in the car. His cellphone was too weak to make calls but its beam was strong enough for rescuers to detect and locate him in two days. Most important, the family didn't leave the car. [85]

If you leave your vehicle to escape or find help

… Look around in every direction. If you can see in the distance and have a map and binoculars, get an idea of the safest direction to leave. If your car is equipped as described on page 70 to 73, sheath your hatchet and hunting knife on your belt, slip your notepad and a pencil or pen in a pocket, wear your car kit on your back, carry your personal relief kit on your side so your arms are free, then with your hatchet and hunting knife fashion a nearby sapling into a stout walking stick.

☞ So you can find your way back to your car if necessary and others can find you, leave a virtual *breadcrumb trail*. If trees are around, every fifty yards or so break a branch on a bush, or blaze a tree with your hatchet and on the bare wood write the date, time of day, and a *note*. This idea isn't farfetched when you think that notepaper is made of wood. Or wrap a strip of duct tape around each tree and write on the tape. No trees or bushes? Make a series of landmarks by piling a few rocks around a written message every fifty yards or so, or set a strip of tape on the ground, weigh its ends with rocks, and write a message on the tape. Number the marks as you go and record them in your note pad.

134. THE PILED ROCKS NOTE

☞ As you walk, note any ponds, creeks, unusual trees, old or damaged buildings, and other significant landmarks; don't depend on your memory. Sketch a map of the area.

135. THE DUCT TAPE NOTE

If you hitch a ride to get help … on your vehicle's dash leave a police note that describes your dilemma, where you are going, any emergency contacts, the make and license number of the vehicle you'll ride in, and the name and a description of the driver and any passengers.

If an explosion occurs

Explosions typically result from industrial events or terrorist acts. The former may occur at factories and along railroads, highways, and seaways where explosives are conveyed; the latter may occur at government institutions, corporate centers, and public gatherings. Though either may possess the power of a bomb, it makes little difference to victims that one is an accident while the other is a premeditated act of war. If an explosion occurs near you…

☞ Crouch quickly behind a wall or similar barrier and cover your head with anything you can find —waiter's tray, coat, desk blotter, etc. Indoors, hide under a table or desk or in a closet, or run into a bathroom since they are small strong rooms with toilets and water you can drink and use to clean injuries. If the air is dusty, unbutton a shirtsleeve and breathe through it or dampen a paper towel and cover your face.

☞ If you smell gas or hear a hissing noise, open the windows, get everyone outdoors, turn off the gas main valve if you can, and flee to a safe area.

☞ If you are trapped in debris, signal your location to rescuers by waving a flashlight, tapping a wall or pipe, or blowing a whistle. Do not light a match. If the air is dusty, cover your nose and mouth with fabric, and avoid any movement that could stir up dust. Shout as a last resort, as you could inhale dangerous dust.

☞ If and when you can leave, do so quickly. With every step watch for falling debris, teetering walls, weakened floors, and damaged stairs. Don't use elevators, don't stand near walls or windows or glass doors, and don't linger on sidewalks or roads that may be used by emergency rescuers or others fleeing the area.

S
U
D
D
E
N
L
Y

I
FROM
107

O
FROM
123

☞ If you're driving and the road is not littered, drive swiftly away. If the blast suddenly throws debris in front of you, brake and duck below the windows. Escape quickly away from the blast.

The worst explosion of all is a *nuclear blast*. This creates a huge fireball that is so bright it can blind you for life if you look at it. The blast also emits clouds of radioactivity that can contaminate the air, water, and ground for miles around; and it creates a wave of intense heat that travels at nearly the speed of sound which can ignite buildings, flatten everything in its path, and sear the skin and tear the clothes off people miles away. The blast wave is immediately followed by a reverse wind of nearly equal strength that sucks everything back toward the explosive core. If you ever experience a blast wave, even from a small explosion, don't just turn away; protect your front *and* your back.

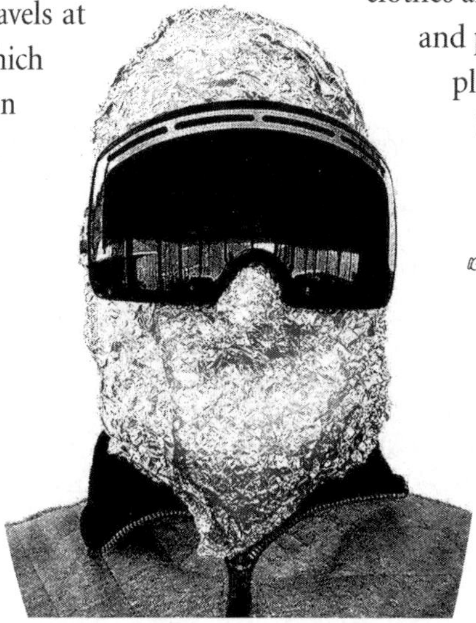

136. NUCLEAR FALLOUT MASK: PORTRAIT OF THE AUTHOR AS AN OLD MAN

A nuclear blast can be triggered by a bomb dropped from a plane, a warhead mounted on a missile, even a suitcase-size device planted in a building. You can reduce this damage in three ways: *distance* (the more between you and ground zero the better), *shielding* (the denser the materials between you and the radiation the better), and *time* (the longer you remain in a fallout shelter the better).

☞ If a huge fireball explodes in view, quickly shut your eyes and duck as low as possible. Unless you're looking straight at it you may only see reflective surfaces around you. If you can walk, flee to a subway, basement, or underground area to shield yourself from radiation. Remain inside until advised to do otherwise.

☞ If caught outside, take cover behind anything solid that might offer protection. No cover? Lie flat on the ground and cover your head.

☞ If exposed to nuclear radiation, change your clothes and shoes, take a thorough shower, and put the exposed clothes in a sealed plastic bag (in a month they'll likely be safe to wear again). Seek medical treatment for burned skin or nausea.

☞ If you must go outdoors, wear thick apparel (a light jacket and work trousers are adequate) that covers all of your body but your hands and eyes, then cover these with thick gloves and ski goggles. You can also make a protective suit of tin foil and duct tape and cover your head and eyes as appears at left. Go outdoors as little as possible. After returning indoors remove your apparel and rinse it off, and wash any exposed skin and hair.

☞ Don't eat food exposed to radioactive air. Wash, seal, and/or store food in the refrigerator. Safe-to-eat foods include bagged or packaged foods such as potato chips, cereals, and peanut butter. As for water, the safest is in your plumbing. Wash your hands before eating and drinking.

To read how to prepare for nuclear fallout well before or just before it happens, turn to page 105 or 122.

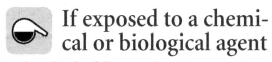

If exposed to a chemical or biological agent

In these kinds of disasters the air is contaminated with a toxic or sickening gas or mist that can contaminate food and water, cause death or serious injury, and create long-lasting health disabilities. These disasters can cover large areas and are often bewildering because it takes time for authorities to determine what happened —which may not occur until they detect a pattern of unusual illness or many sick people seeking medical aid. Often the first sign of danger is that you feel strangely sick, dizzy, nauseous, feverish, or faint and others nearby are similarly overcome. The room may look a little hazy, a slightly oily film may appear on tables and other surfaces, or gasping animals may lie about. Some agents break down quickly when exposed to the air, while others such as anthrax spores are long-lived. To prepare for such rare but terrible events …

☞ If you suddenly feel strangely ill, cover your mouth and nose with a respirator, napkin, handkerchief, sleeve or wet paper towel. If you can, call 911 and listen to the radio or TV.

☞ Try to learn what has happened, what the agent is, where it originated, its concentration, the areas affected, its symptoms, what medications may be required, and where you can find them.

☞ Learn if the agent is lighter or heavier than air. If lighter than air, descend underground; if heavier than air, go well above ground. In both cases move away from the agent's source.

☞ Learn if your skin could absorb the agent. If so, cover with apparel, towels, or blankets and flee to a safe place.

☞ Learn if the agent reacts adversely with water. If so, don't drink it or wash with it. If the agent doesn't react adversely with water, once you've reached a safe place scrub exposed areas with warm soapy water or a solution of $1^1/_2$ cups bleach per gallon of water. No water? Sprinkle flour or talcum powder liberally over the area, wait 30 seconds, and vacuum or brush off with a rag. Wear rubber gloves, and practice good hygiene to avoid spreading chemicals or germs.

☞ If you have been contaminated by the agent, stay away from other people, cover yourself with protective clothing, touch as few objects as possible, and go to a hospital. If medical help is unavailable, find a safe place and remove your clothing, shower thoroughly if the water is safe, change into fresh loose clothing, and seek medical help as soon as possible.

☞ If you are exposed to a chemical spillage, put on protective clothes, thick gloves and ski goggles, then clean the spillage quickly or leave the area. If you clean the spillage, take the cleaning materials outside and allow any fumes to dissipate, then wrap the materials in newspaper, place in a sealed plastic bag, and dispose according to any official instructions.

☞ If you stay where you are, close all doors, windows, dampers, and vents. Tape seams around windows, ducts, and pipe entrances. Turn off air conditioners, and set ventilators to 100 percent recirculation so no outdoor air is drawn indoors.

☞ If caught outside, stay upwind (hold a wet finger above your head to determine its direction) and flee at least one-half mile or eight to ten city blocks from the danger. Do not walk into any airborne mists or touch any spilled liquids or chemical deposits. Head for a hospital if one is nearby.

☞ If you evacuate, bring a battery-powered radio, water, and food, and wear comfortable clothes that cover your body. If you're in a car, quickly roll up the windows, shut off the air conditioner or heater, and close all vents. If you know the agent's source, drive quickly the other way and/or to a hospital. Listen to the radio, and return only when authorities say the afflicted area is safe.

☞ When you return, air out interiors by opening all the doors, windows, and vents and turning on ventilation fans. If you detect lingering vapors or other hazards, call 911. Find out from local authorities how to clean your house and property. Place any exposed clothing and shoes in sealed containers so they don't touch other materials, and ask local authorities how to dispose of them.

To read how to prepare for a chemical or biological agent well before it happens, turn to page 104.

If an earthquake strikes

If you are indoors…

☞ Hide under a heavy table or bench, against an interior wall or corner, or in a doorway. Cover your head and hold onto something. If in bed, hold onto the sheets and blankets and cover your head with a pillow. If you can slide under the mattress, do so.

☞ Keep several feet from windows, exterior doors, walls, and tall or heavy objects like bookcases, refrigerators, mirrors, and pictures with glass over them.

☞ Stay inside until the shaking stops. Many victims are killed or injured when struck by falling objects as they leave a building.

☞ Don't use an elevator, as the cab could get stuck between floors.

☞ If trapped under debris, do not light a match to see around you (there could be a gas leak) and do not move about

or stir up dust. Cover your mouth with a handkerchief or clothing. Tap on a pipe or wall so rescuers can find you. Use a whistle if you have one. Shout only as a last resort because this can cause you to inhale dangerous dust.

If you are outdoors …

☞ Move away from bridges, buildings, streetlights, power lines, trees, and anything that could fall on you. Move toward open areas and drop to the ground. Don't enter a building because it may be damaged and could collapse. If you smell gas, move to fresh air.

☞ If you are near a sea or lake, flee to high ground or until you are two miles inland due to the possibility of a tsunami.

☞ If you are driving, you may feel like you're driving on four flat tires. Overhead lights, trees, and power lines may sway or snap, and you may be shaken out of your lane into adjacent vehicles. Slow way down, steer away from other vehicles, pull well off the road, and park well away from bridges, buildings, power lines, trees, and anything else that could fall on you. Keep your seatbelt on, duck as low as you can, and stay inside until the shaking stops. Turn on your radio and listen to emergency information. When the shaking ends, proceed cautiously and watch out for fissures, cave-ins, and tilts in the pavement.

☞ Watch for aftershocks. They are usually less violent than the initial tremor, but they can collapse weakened structures. If you drive, avoid rockslides and bridges or ramps that may have been damaged.

To read how to prepare for an earthquake well before it happens, turn to page 91.

If a volcano erupts

If one of these mammoth cones near you starts rumbling or puffing smoke, do the following…

☞ Since ash usually spreads in a long narrow plume in the direction of prevailing winds, determine the wind's direction by holding a wet finger above your head; it will feel cool on the side facing the wind. Do not move toward or away from this direction but sideways.

☞ If you evacuate, don't drive through clouds of ash, because this will draw ash into the carburetor which can stall the vehicle and stir up ash on the road, clogging vehicles behind you. If you must drive in ash, don't exceed 35 miles an hour. Stay away from slopes, streams and low-lying areas. Look up-stream before crossing a bridge. If you see any moving earth or flowing lava, race across or back up. Flee to where you will be safe indoors, even if hundreds of miles, and stay until any ash has settled.

☞ If you will stay in the building you are in and have time, close all the doors, windows, dampers, and vents and cover their seams with duct tape, because volcanic ash as fine as dust can enter the tiniest seam in a building's shell.

☞ Wear a dust mask or respirator to filter your breathing, and wear goggles, gloves, a long-sleeve shirt, trousers, and hiking boots. Don't wear contact lenses, as the ash can grate in your eyes. If significant amounts of ash could pile on your roof, have a method of raking, scraping, or shoveling it off.

☞ One way to ro remove accumulating volcanic ash from a sloping roof is to fell a thin sapling, trim the minor branches until you have only a shaft and a few stubs for handles, and firmly fasten the thin end to the handle of a rake with electric wire and duct tape as sketched below. A few adults standing on the ground can use this long rake to pull volcanic ash from a pitched roof, and also to remove an object in a fire, help someone who has fallen through thin ice on a lake, or lift an object submerged in several feet of water. And it floats.

To read how to prepare for a volcanic eruption well before or days before it may occur, turn to page 90 or 120.

1 TRIM THE TRUNK OF A LONG THIN SAPLING

2 TRIM A FEW BRANCHES TO STUBS FOR USE AS HANDLES

3 FASTEN RAKE FIRMLY TO END OF SAPLING WITH WIRE & DUCT TAPE

… AND IT FLOATS

137. THE RUBBLE RAKE, FOR REACHING DISTANT OBJECTS

If a landslide or mudflow occurs

In these disasters masses of earth, boulders, and trees flowing downhill crush buildings as if they were made of cardboard and vehicles as if they were made of tinfoil. If you ever see a mass of earth descending toward you, quickly move laterally from its path because you won't outrun it. If you are lucky enough to escape entombment, look for injured and trapped victims, and watch for broken electrical, water, gas, and sewer lines. Since these masses of earth are usually saturated with water, they often flow like wet cement and when freshly settled they often have the consistency of quicksand. If you can find any planks, sheets of plywood, small trees, or similar long flat objects to walk on, create a path with these to any trapped victims. Do not step on what looks like earth —or you may suddenly be chest-deep in mud. Even when you think the slide has ended, adjacent slopes may suddenly give way, and many slides creep for days afterward.

To read how to prepare for a landslide well before or days before it happens, turn to pages 86 or 120.

If a meteor arrives from space

In February 2013 a 60-foot-diameter meteor traveling 42,000 miles an hour streaked over central Russia, its contrail looking like cotton candy on a skewer, until it heated up and exploded 15 miles above the earth. This created a blinding fireball seen for miles around that scattered meteor debris over an area 600 miles long and initiated a shock wave that when it reached the earth's surface peeled roofs from buildings and shattered windows, exposing interiors to icy cold, freezing plumbing systems, and injuring 1,500 people —most of whom were gazing at this rare event through windows which the shock wave shattered in their faces.[77]

Our planet is occasionally visited by stellar objects. In November 1954 a grapefruit-size meteorite crashed into a house in Oak Grove, Alabama, and struck Ann Elizabeth Hodges as she was napping on her living room couch.[78] In June 1908 a meteor crashed in central Siberia and flattened trees over an area of 800 square miles. 50,000 years ago a meteor slammed into Arizona and left a crater 4,000 feet wide. And 65 million years ago a huge meteor landed off the coast of Yucatán and destroyed everything for hundreds of miles around, changed climates worldwide, and killed the dinosaurs.

Three kinds of stellar objects enter the earth's atmosphere: *asteroids*, *meteors*, and *comets*. An asteroid is a chunk of rock or metal that orbits the sun, usually between Mars and Jupiter. If one enters the earth's atmosphere it becomes a meteor. A comet is a mass of rock, ice, and frozen gases that usually orbits elliptically around the Sun, is bigger than an asteroid, and has a luminous tail.

If you ever see a fireball or a contrail streak across the sky, resist looking at it and quickly turn away. Also …

☞ Back away from windows, run into a bathroom or similar small room, and crouch close to the floor.
☞ If you are outdoors, quickly seek the nearest shelter, even if it's standing behind a thick tree. Or lie face down in a depression and cover your head with your hands.

During

It is this you have carefully prepared for in hopes that it would never happen! Perhaps the danger lasts only a few terrifying seconds as the floor joggles and pieces of furniture shake like dice in a cup. Or maybe it takes several anxious hours to build to a howling hurricane and several more to diminish to an occasional gust. There is little to say here, between all the preparations you have made beforehand and all the work you may have to do afterward, other than …

Stick to the game plan … If your fear increases as the disaster strengthens, don't second-guess yourself. Don't suddenly decide you had better move your car —as did one victim in our grim list who died "when struck by a falling tree while trying to move his car;" or change your mind about staying as did another who died "when struck by a falling tree while helping his family into their car to evacuate." Be guided by your judgement, not your fears.

Stay in small rooms … In wood stud framing, a room's corners have three studs nailed together, which makes them eight times stronger than the studs in the walls between the corners. And the rafters above a bathroom and other small rooms are typically the same size as the rafters above a living room and other large rooms, but the rafters spanning the smaller rooms are shorter —and a shorter span of equal size is stronger. So in smaller rooms the corners and ceilings are stronger, which makes them safer sanctuaries in a disaster. Bathrooms are stronger still, since their walls contain metal pipes that give them a cage strength which other rooms don't have.

Don't get upset … No matter how prepared you are, if a disaster happens you will likely be overwhelmed with fear, anger, and sadness. These terrifying events will strain your nerves, they will test your patience, they will wear you down. This is only natural. Take solace in the fact that, thanks to the news media, your fellow citizens are saddened by what you are going through and a well-trained portion of their numbers are on the way to help you.

Do everything slowly … When disaster strikes, tasks you may have done hundreds of times and look exactly the same will seem different and may take longer —and any mistakes you make will be greatly magnified. Remember that one victim in our grim list "died when she cut her arm and bled to death after shutting off the gas to her house" —a simple act that shouldn't have caused her to die. So think about everything you'll do a few extra seconds before doing it. Envision the related possibilities. Do everything deliberately —and well. Don't just look: observe. Don't just hear: listen. Don't just touch: feel.

Don't drive … Steer your thoughts with these deathly scenarios drawn from our grim list: "A section of a building detached by a strong wind crashed into the windshield of her car" … "His car struck a tree that had fallen across a road" … "A falling tree crushed their car." Another reason to avoid driving when a disaster rages is to leave the roads clear for highway departments to clear them of debris, rescuers to reach other victims, and public utilities to repair power lines.

Don't go outdoors to see what is happening … In disasters this is a big killer. Consider the sheet of plywood that cleaved the tree trunk that appears on page 82. You wouldn't want to get in the way of something like this if you stepped outdoors. Even after the disaster has passed keep your curiosity in check —or you may suffer the fate of another victim in our grim list who "was killed when she stepped on a downed power line in front of her home while taking pictures of the damage." Here's another scary tale about downed power lines. In the summer of 2013 a violent thunderstorm struck a small town in the South after which a woman stepped out to the street in front of her house to survey the damage. The heavy rain draining from the road had formed a rivulet of water a few inches wide and a quarter inch deep along the side of the road, and fifty feet up the road a downed power line had fallen in the water. When she stepped in the water in front of her house —fifty feet from the fallen power line, mind you— she was electrocuted. [86] If she had worn rubber boots, looked where she was stepping, or stayed inside, she would be alive today.

The role of government in a disaster [87]

When disaster strikes a region of the United States, if the afflicted states, counties, and communities of the region haven't the resources to respond to the disaster themselves, one or more local government leaders make a formal request for aid to the President. Then the President declares either an *emergency* or a *major disaster* as follows:

☞ A declaration of an *emergency* authorizes the President to send supplementary funds and other resources to state and local efforts to save lives and protect property. This involves …

- Mobilizing search and rescue operations.
- Detecting and fighting fires.
- Establishing emergency communication systems.
- Involving the news media so they can inform the public.
- Eliminating any duplication or misdirection of emergency services.
- Restoring essential power systems, fuel supplies, and public services to communities.
- Distributing water, food, clothes, first-aid, and other relief supplies to victims. Much of this work is done by the American Red Cross. They also create a database to help people find other members of their families, and they and other volunteer organizations set up shelters for people who can't return to their homes. If you need their help, listen to the radio, watch TV, and read newspapers for locations. You will have to find a way to get to their facilities.

☞ A declaration of a *major disaster*, in addition to the above, authorizes the President to send funds to state and local agencies through the auspices of the Federal Emergency Management Agency, known as FEMA, to provide aid and relief to disaster victims.

The above activity is the *Disaster Response Phase*. After the disaster has passed, victims and communities must rebuild. This is the *Disaster Recovery Phase*. This can take months, even years, to complete. For this the federal government may extend loans and grants to certain organizations to do the following …

☞ State and local governments to clear fallen trees, remove debris, repair roads and bridges and other infrastructure, restore water and sewage and other essential services, provide equipment and technical assistance, provide housing where homes have become unliveable, and otherwise preserve life and property. Federal funds are also available for repairing, restoring, or replacing damaged dikes, levees, drainage systems, parks and recreational areas, public buildings and related equipment, as well as nonprofit educational, medical, and custodial care facilities.

☞ Communities and nonprofit institutions to reinstate public transportation systems, restore schools and other public facilities, and provide educational, utility, medical and other community services.

☞ Individuals, families, farms, and businesses to help return their lives and livelihoods to nearly normal. In addition to low-interest loans and cash grants of up to $12,900 to help repair, replace, or rehabilitate homes, farms, and businesses, this assistance may include temporary housing for up to 18 months, payments of mortgages and rents, tax refunds, unemployment relief, veteran's benefits, legal services, and crisis counseling. The SBAH (Small Business Administration for Homes) extends loans to homeowners, and the SBAB (Small Business Administration for Businesses) extends loans to small businesses.

To apply for disaster assistance, a victim typically visits a disaster application center, often known as a DAC, that has been established in the area by FEMA in partnership with state and local emergency management offices after the President has declared a major disaster. Here representatives from federal, state, local and volunteer agencies will explain what assistance is available and help you apply for the assistance you may be eligible to receive. You can also call 800-462-9029 or 800-462-7585 for further information. Below is an idealistic script of what will happen. In reality some facilities may be disorganized due to the hurried nature of setting them up quickly, some staff members may be unknowledgeable because they haven't had time to learn what to do, you may have to wait in a long line before getting to talk to someone, and the authorities may have to rush you through the process if many victims are waiting behind you.

☞ Your first stop will be at a registrar who will discuss your needs. Together you will fill out a one-page application for assistance. Be prepared to provide the following information. If you do not have it when you apply, usually you may supply it later …

119

- Your name and social security number.
- Telephone numbers where you can be reached.
- Names and ages of those living in your home during the disaster.
- A summary of your damage and a rough idea of costs for repairs and replacement.
- The total amount of your living expenses.
- Insurance papers including proof-of-loss forms.
- Information regarding your income and debts (mortgages, car loans, etc.).

☞ After discussing your needs, the registrar will indicate which agencies may be able to assist you. Representatives from each will be there to answer questions and make arrangements for assistance.

☞ When leaving the DAC, an exit interviewer will make sure you have spoken to everyone who can help you, and a representative from FEMA will verify the information you provided at the DAC. If you applied for financial assistance and you qualify, FEMA will later mail you a check to the address on your application. "Later" may be a few days or several years. As a sample, as of late 2013, FEMA was still processing claims from victims of Hurricane Katrina that occurred in 2005.

In summary, when you need help from the Big Hand in Washington, it is rarely the fairy godmother you fondly hope it will be in your moment of distress. To metaphorize the situation: it may help you get back on your feet, but you may have to walk with a cane.

How the public can help disaster victims [88]

After a major disaster citizens, businesses, churches, radio stations, and other groups throughout America often offer their assistance, usually by raising funds or collecting needed supplies in their community and sending them to the disaster area. If this interests you, contact your local Red Cross, Salvation Army, United Way, Catholic Charities, Adventist Community Services, and similar organizations and ask how you can help. Also contact your municipal or county government and ask the same.

Usually what disaster victims need most are *money* and *blood*. Regarding money, you can write a check or make a credit card transaction through a recognized volunteer agency and earmark your funds to be distributed by a particular agency in the disaster region. Regarding blood, you can give this at the your local chapter of the American Red Cross or often a local hospital.

Donations of food are usually discouraged, due to the quality and perishability of the food and the difficulty of setting up facilities to receive, store, and distribute it. If food is requested, the first is usually baby food, then cans and boxes of ready-to-eat or nonperishable foods that are protein-rich and help build energy. All donated foods should be clearly labeled to facilitate distribution.

Donations of clothing and shoes are also discouraged because it is difficult for disaster relief operations to fit victims with the right size. If clothing is requested, it should be new or freshly washed, and be wrapped in a simple lightweight manner that keeps each article of clothing from contacting other apparel.

Donations of medical supplies are also discouraged because they are specialized commodities that must be distributed by qualified personnel. If medical supplies are requested, each must have a shelf life of at least six months after arriving at the disaster site and must be clearly labeled. Never send prescription medications. If the donations are other than blood or money, donors should be prepared to transport the goods and arrange for their unloading at a specified location.

It is not usually a good idea to visit the disaster scene in order to help. Unless you have a specific occupation or ability that disaster relief operations have requested, usually your presence would only add to the confusion of logistics and transportation. If you want to go, first call either the American Red Cross or the Salvation Army and follow their instructions. The American Red Cross also conducts a basic training program for volunteers and usually sends only people who have completed this training. If this appeals to you, get in touch with them. If the disaster is local, contact emergency service organizations about volunteering for disaster relief efforts.

Just After

When you think the worst is over, beware —because *many disaster fatalities occur just after the disaster "ends".* Sure, you're anxious to see the damage. But if you venture outside, look below your feet —lest you suffer the fate of a victim on our grim list who "was killed when she stepped on a downed power line in front of her home while taking pictures of the damage." And look overhead —lest you end up as did another victim who died "after being struck in the head by a broken tree limb." You want visual proof? Look at the tree below. Three widowmakers lurk high in its branches that could kill or maim an unobservant person venturing below at the wrong moment.

Indoors is no safer. Things that may *look* the same may not *be* the same. A vibration soft as a footfall —yours— can send a piece of debris teetering overhead to topple, as occurred to two more victims in our grim list who "were crushed by falling debris in their basement." You step down a flight of stairs you've used hundreds of times —and you slip as did four more in our grim list who "died in falls down stairs in homes that had no electricity." Or you descend to a basement whose floor is under a few inches of water to inspect the damage —and you expire as did another victim in our list who "was electrocuted while wading in his basement."

If you inspect a building afterward, inside or out, wear a protective helmet, carry a walking stick, have a notepad and pencil in one pocket, work gloves on your hands, and rubber boots on your feet if water is present. Go outside and look at the chimney, the roof, the facades, the foundation all around. This inspection is explained in greater detail beginning on page 179. With every step watch for broken glass, nails, sharp objects, puddles with wires in them. Flip debris over with the walking stick to see what's underneath. After dark don't use matches or lighters, lest there is any leaking gas nearby. Right now you're not thinking of repairing anything; you're only determining if your premises are livable or unlivable, as this is another of those critical moments where you must decide whether to **leave** or **stay**, as follows …

139. THREE WIDOWMAKERS LURKING IN ONE TREE

Are your premises *livable*?

Here are the possibilities: (1) you never left while the disaster was happening, (2) you're returning afterward, (3) the premises are undamaged, and (4) if partly damaged the undamaged part is livable. Whatever combination you are confronted with, compared to dwelling elsewhere you will have a familiar center of operations, you will own what you have, and you can stay indefinitely. Your biggest concern will be if any supplies run out. If you have plenty of the calamity commodities described earlier in this book, you're in good shape. Otherwise you may be at the mercy of bad roads, empty gas stations, and bare store shelves.

    If your premises are livable, here are a few advisories …   120

☞ Be wary of further disasters spawned by the first one —earthquake aftershocks, subsequent landslides, weakened buildings that fall, levees that failed after a hurricane occurred, nuclear reactors that exploded after a tsunami roared ashore, and other secondary disasters. As you know by now, these things can happen.

☞ Cooperate fully with local authorities and rescuers, and obey health regulations for personal and community protection against disease epidemics. Report any violations.

☞ Help locate victims and lead them to shelter, food, clothing, transportation, and medical supplies.

☞ Never leave children alone or let them play in damaged buildings or areas that might be unsafe.

☞ Even if your premises seem undamaged, open exterior doors, turn off any gas lines, and let the house air out. Don't use matches or an open flame to help see better. Use a flashlight, and turn it on outside the building, because turning it on creates a tiny spark between the switch and battery that could cause any leaking gas to explode. Examine foundations, floors, walls, ceilings, and roofs for structural damage as detailed beginning on page 179. Look for nails, broken glass, sharp pieces of metal, damaged woodwork, holes in walls or floors, wet or falling construction materials, leaky plumbing, spilled chemicals and poisons, and damaged furniture. Walk cautiously, because snakes, rodents, and other wild animals may have taken up residence in your absence.

☞ Do not use the electrical system in a damaged building until it has been inspected by a licensed electrician. If a building is only partly damaged, it may be safe to use the undamaged circuits.

☞ Control intruding rodents and insects by trapping, screening, and the like.

☞ Sanitize dishes, cooking utensils and food prep areas as detailed beginning on page 168.

☞ If the premises have been flooded, you have a lot of work to do, as detailed beginning on page 181.

☞ Know what stores are open, how to reach them (drive, bike, walk, ride a bus?). If you drive, will gas stations have gasoline? Whatever transportation you use, beware of debris on streets, fallen power lines, trees across roads, washouts, and weakened bridges. Especially beware of traffic lights that don't work. When they don't, they can change from lifesavers to lifetakers for drivers and pedestrians alike —as happened to one driver in our grim list who died "after his motorcycle crashed at an intersection whose traffic light didn't work" and one pedestrian who perished "when he was struck by a car while crossing a street where a traffic light was out." Also resist the urge to sightsee, as this may impede the efforts of police and rescue operations to help victims.

Are your premises *unlivable*?

Again, here are the possibilities: Can you leave? Are you forced to stay? How near is safe ground? As a sample of the last concern, the tornado that struck Joplin, Missouri, in May 2011 destroyed everything in its path; but though the damage track was 22 miles long it was less than a mile wide, so every victim was within a half mile of safe ground.[91] At the other extreme, the eruption of Mount St. Helens in May 1980 covered 100,000 square miles with volcanic ash including four inches that fell on the city of Yakima, Washington, 110 miles away.[92] Many homes in this vast area were unlivable and residents had nowhere to go.

If you can leave

This possibility fathers further questions: *Where will you go?* To a public shelter? To the house of a neighbor or distant friend? And *How will you go?* Will you drive? Bike? Walk? Take a bus? The parts of this book that describe these possibilities are listed below. Are the roads clear? Littered with debris? Congested with traffic? Listen to radio traffic reports that describe local road conditions, both nearby and far away. Three traffic information websites on the internet are www.traffic.com, www.beatthetraffic.com, and www.fhwa.dot.gov/trafficinfo. Available for mobile devices is http://www.inrixtraffic.com. These resources typically describe road conditions, closures, alerts, construction zones, and expected weather. However you leave, post a police message on or near the front door that lists the names of the people in your party, your planned route, planned destination, vehicle license number if you're driving, and phone contact numbers.

Where will you go?

To a public shelter … See page 150. *To a house of a neighbor or distant friend* … See page 173.

How will you go?

Drive … See page 112.

Bike … Equip it with a basket over the front wheel, a handlebar bag, a rack over the back wheel and saddlebags on each side, and a trailer behind like the one appearing on page 113. For a "complete bicycle touring gear checklist", visit http://bicycletouringpro.com/blog/jim-dirlams-complete-bicycle-touring-gear-checklist/. Before you step on the pedals, spin the wheels to make sure they're true, make sure the brakes pull correctly and the pads align on the rims, and you have a patch kit and hand pump for flat tires.

Walk … If the terrain will be rough, don't bring a suitcase with telescoping handles and small wheels; wear a knapsack and carry two large handbags that won't come apart if they get wet. Have everyone in your party, children too, carry what they can. Every pound each person takes will make everyone else's load a pound lighter. Wear lightweight hiking boots or jogging shoes, gloves, sunglasses, bandana, and a hat or protective helmet.

Bus or public transportation … Whatever your destination, ask where you are going and what you should take, and carry all you can. Have funds to pay your fare.

If anyone is injured, you must transport them as well. You may first go to a medical facility, then the injured may be moved to a hospital or an official shelter, or be taken in by friends, church groups, etc.

J
U
S
T

A
F
T
E
R

If you go to a public shelter

If authorities order you to evacuate, they may take you to a public shelter, also known as a mass care facility, or you may go on your own. This could be a public auditorium or other large building, or a tent city with rows of canvas tents mounted on wood platforms. Before you go, try and find what the place is like. They usually have water, food, first aid, bathing, and often an assembly area, laundry, and electricity to charge laptops and cellphones. Is there public parking? If so, fill your car with all you can. If not, bring your go bag and pack a suitcase as if you're taking a week's vacation. What food will the facility have, and how will it be served? You may want to bring dried fruits, nuts, crackers, peanut butter and jelly. Will there be towels, linens and blankets? If not, bring your own. What will the lighting be after dark? Bring flashlights, batteries, and a radio. Know that your questions may be answered inaccurately because disaster shelters are often set up quickly and staff members may know hardly more than you do; so probe a little. When you arrive, find the rest rooms, eating, and sleeping areas. When you find where you will stay, have the members of your party take turns watching your belongings. Since many people may live in a small area, to minimize conflicts the staff may impose disciplinary measures as…

☞ No alcohol, drugs, weapons, or pets.
☞ No violence, stealing, or loud noises.
☞ No smoking except in restricted areas.
☞ Strictly rationed supplies.
☞ Assistance in facility maintenance: distributing food, sweeping floors, collecting trash, and the like.

The time you stay may be short (as during a tornado) or long (as during a hurricane). Stay until authorities say it is safe to leave, and listen often to your radio.

If you are forced to stay

If everything for miles around is devastated and your only choice is to stay where you are, your chief concerns are *staying alive* and *making yourself visible to rescuers*. Your first task is to set up a camp. This is detailed beginning on page 152. Try to team with at least two others so if one is hurt, a second person can tend the injured while the third seeks help. Assess each person's abilities and assign tasks so everyone will work efficiently. Make alternative plans in case something goes wrong.

Next, make your location visible to rescuers.

140.⁹³

Find an open area if you can, so rescue helicopters can see you from the air. If you are in a forest or jungle, find a way to make yourself visible. A few possibilities …

☞ In a clearing, create a large **S O S** with rocks or other items.
☞ Beside a road or river, erect a pole with brightly colored cloth on it.
☞ If someone approaches by land, sea, or air, flash a mirror at them, or fire a flare (smoke in day, incendiary at night). Never fire a flare directly at an approaching vehicle or helicopter. At night don't shine a spotlight at one that is nearby, as this can blind the driver or pilot.
☞ Hang an American flag upside-down. U.S. Code of Laws §106 says: "The flag should never be displayed with the union down, except as a signal of

dire distress in instances of extreme danger to life or property."

If your rescue will be by helicopter and you can walk or hobble, as the helo approaches, move to a clearing with no overhanging branches or other obstructions that could snag the winch cable as it is lowered to you. When you see the helo, stand with both hands raised above your head: the universal signal for "Pick me up." Do not raise one hand only —this is the signal for "Do not pick me up." If one arm is injured and you cannot raise it, attach a bright fabric to a long stick and wave it over your head. Remove or batten all small objects around you, such as hats that could fly off in the rotor wash and any chairs and other furnishing the rotor wash could flip over. Gather the belongings you will bring. When the helo is hovering about 50 feet above you, a rescuer will descend on a winch cable with a basket stretcher. When the rescuer reaches the ground, he will grab something immovable to anchor himself, then scramble to your side. Never grab the winch cable and attach it to anything around you. The rotor will create lots of noise and a hurricane-like downwind that will throw grit

141.[94]

in your face and blow everything about.

The rescuer will help calm your nerves and provide mission info, and he will communicate via headset with the winch operator in the helo as he organizes the hoist. He will help you into the basket stretcher where you will lie on your back, then he will strap you in and signal to the helo when it is safe to hoist. They have to hurry lest they run out of fuel. As you lift off, you may suffer a queasy feeling as you dangle in the air. As you near the side of the helo, do not lunge for the door; let the crew pull the basket into the cab. Then they will close the doors, unstrap you, and help you to your feet. [96]

If you will be hoisted in a *helicopter rescue sling* (see figure 142) the rescuer will help you in, buckle you, and signal the helo to hoist.

142.[95]

You might pause for a moment and think how amazingly skilled these rescuers are, and how they perform their high-wire acts so casually!

If your evacuation is on land, a party of trained rescuers will arrive with whatever tools and medical supplies they need to help you. First they will stabilize any injuries you have. If you are trapped under debris, they may employ a *lift-and-crib operation* to extricate you. This involves levering the entrapping debris upward or sideward and sliding pieces of wood or other wedges into the space created by the levering, the mantra being "lift an inch, crib an inch" to minimize the risk of any debris falling on you, until you are free. The rescuers may hand pieces of debris from one person to the next away from the site until it is safe. Afterwards, if you can move unassisted, you will gather any belongings you can easily carry and walk out with the rescuers. If you require assistance, the rescuers will remove you in a stretcher or other method usually to a nearby boat or land vehicle. [97]

143.[98]

Roughing it in the rubble

If you must "go on your own hook" until you are located and rescued, you must first determine how to fashion a functional shelter out of seemingly nothing.

As a sample, ponder the rubble above. This jumble of destruction is like the pieces of a jigsaw puzzle waiting to be assembled. You could create a small shelter with the studs. Even splintered ones would serve as seasoned firewood. You could pull a damaged sofa out of the debris, collect a bunch of bricks and concrete blocks and build a waist-high wall in front of the sofa, then lay some plywood over both to create a shelter a family could huddle in. Or you could rip open a sofa and spread its stuffing on the ground to make a mattress that will insulate you from the clammy earth, and you could fill a tee-shirt with more stuffing to make a pillow. Chairs and tables may be sturdy enough to sit and work on. Cabinets may be strong enough to store things in. Even such seeming trash as an empty cardboard toilet paper holder and clothes dryer lint can become useful by stuffing the lint into the cylindrical holder and using it as a fire starter. With these resources the possibilities are endless. When performing this labor wear gloves, beware of sharp pieces of metal and broken glass, and try to clear away the kitchen area first because food prep is a top priority.

A wrecked car is another trove. First check the gas tank. If it is leaking or the vehicle is tilted and could roll over, steer clear of this resource. Otherwise look under the seats, in the console, the glove box, the trunk. Grab a crowbar and hammer and mine this motherlode of metal, plastic, fabric, and glazing for all it's worth. If you know how to siphon the gasoline (if not, see page 57), use this fuel to clean and burn things.

Check the radiator for water, the crankcase for oil, the battery for electricity. Siphon the wiper fluid to clean dirty surfaces. Intact, the interior could make a safe and cozy bedroom for children.

But your biggest bonanza may be the tons of materials around you that have existed ages before the disaster. Trees. Rocks. Earth. Before the pyramids of Egypt these building blocks, leavened with imagination and crafted with committed hands, have been used by people no different than you to fashion habitable shelter for centuries everywhere around the globe.

Whatever materials you build with, first choose your site. Begin well before sunset if you can. Water nearby is the prime essential. Close to this find an open area about twenty feet square that has no trees and no branches within about twelve feet above the ground, and whose surface is generally free of roots and rocks. Ideally the area should be nearly level) perfectly level areas don't drain well and steep ones will slide you out of bed at night), slightly above its surrounds on at least two sides (such a site is less likely to be soggy in wet weather), and have no holes in the ground (mice, snakes, and ants may live in them). Avoid sandy areas (these won't hold tent pegs and stakes), ravines (these trap dampness and fog), dead or leaning trees (these can fall on you), thickets (these are lairs of bugs), and marshes or swamps (these swarm with sanguinary mosquitoes and biting bugs). Allot space for cooking, dining, sleeping, sanitation, and storage. Locate the cooking in the center, the dining close by, storage on one side, sleeping on the most level area, and sanitation farthest away downhill. Leave at least six feet between the campfire and the beds. Also …

☞ If the ground is covered with leaf litter, clear it down to bare earth since it may be infested with insects, spiders, and ticks. Be wary of briars, nettles, poison ivy, poison oak, and poison sumac.

☞ Know the general direction of prevailing winds. Locate the sleeping area downwind of the campfire area, and the bathroom area downwind of the campsite.

☞ Know the general time and direction the sun will rise and set. Ideally you want morning sun, sunshine sometime during the day to dry things out, and evening sun.

☞ If you can find a rug, part of a carpet, or even areas of underlayment or foam flooring from a nearby building, spread them on the ground where the eating and sleeping areas will be. Even floormats from damaged vehicles can make small areas feel better. These materials are a nice way to add a touch of comfort to your quarters.

☞ Here are a couple ideas for a toilet. (1) From a damaged building remove a toilet and its seat and locate it behind some foliage downwind of camp (set plastic bags in the bowl, then tie and remove them every few times the toilet is used). (2) Set a toilet seat on a large bucket or on a milk crate with a small bucket inside (all these items can be scavenged from a damaged building).

☞ If woods are nearby, find saplings for making walking sticks, tent supports, and other furnishings.

☞ The campsite will need a number of containers to store things. Anything you can rescue from the nearby rubble —small cans, shoe organizers, kitchen cabinets, file cabinets, shelves, drawers, bedstands— can help you organize things and keep animals at bay.

☞ Gather all the firewood you will need before starting a fire. A wheelbarrow load will suffice for a dinner and evening fire. Collect much more if the weather will be cold.

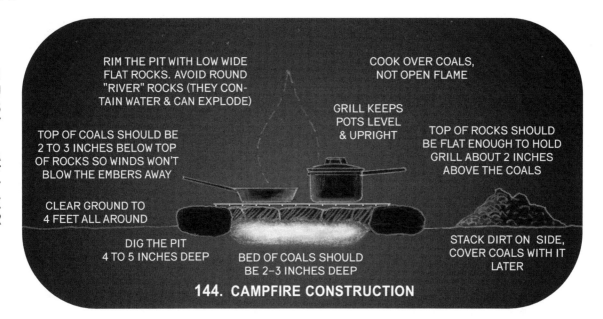

RIM THE PIT WITH LOW WIDE FLAT ROCKS. AVOID ROUND "RIVER" ROCKS (THEY CONTAIN WATER & CAN EXPLODE)

COOK OVER COALS, NOT OPEN FLAME

GRILL KEEPS POTS LEVEL & UPRIGHT

TOP OF COALS SHOULD BE 2 TO 3 INCHES BELOW TOP OF ROCKS SO WINDS WON'T BLOW THE EMBERS AWAY

TOP OF ROCKS SHOULD BE FLAT ENOUGH TO HOLD GRILL ABOUT 2 INCHES ABOVE THE COALS

CLEAR GROUND TO 4 FEET ALL AROUND

DIG THE PIT 4 TO 5 INCHES DEEP

BED OF COALS SHOULD BE 2–3 INCHES DEEP

STACK DIRT ON SIDE, COVER COALS WITH IT LATER

144. CAMPFIRE CONSTRUCTION

If you will need a campfire to cook food, purify water, keep warm, and make life bright at night, here is a recipe for making one …

☞ Clear the ground of any leaf litter and foliage four feet out from the hearth all around.

☞ Rim the firepit with rocks with fairly flat tops that rest a few inches above the ground. Avoid round "river rocks" as they contain water and may explode when heated.

☞ Stack your firewood by the firepit in graduated sizes. Tinder should be dry, about as thick as match sticks, 4 to 6 inches long, and enough to fill a circle made with your hands' thumbs and forefingers. Kindling should no bigger than your thumb and no longer than your forearm, and fuel wood as thick as your ankle and no longer than your lower leg. Use softwood (trees with needles, like pine) for kindling and hardwood (trees with leaves, like oak) for cooking if they are available.

☞ Have a small shovel for moving coals and covering the fire with dirt, a poker (a small forked branch is fine), two long-handled utensils for tending cookware over the coals, and gloves.

☞ When the coals are ready, set a grille flat on the rim of rocks a couple of inches above the coals. Don't cook over an open flame; let the flames die to a bed of coals two to three inches thick.

☞ If it will be cold at night, heat water over the fire, pour the hot water into bottles or other capped containers, and place them in your bed. Warmed rocks are another cozy possibility.

☞ Consider building a dining fly over your dining table and firepit. This is a large (say 12 x 15 feet) tarpaulin whose highest corner overhangs the firepit so it will keep rain off the fire while allowing its smoke to rise and escape outward. The tarp is held aloft by connecting its corners with long ropes or paracords to nearby trees or stakes, with two opposing corners held high and the other two held low to form a soaring saddle-shape that won't flap in the wind. This roof will provide shelter from rain and excessive sun.

145. DINING FLY OVER A CAMPSITE

☞ Know how to tie these three knots: *clove hitch*, *tautline hitch*, and *bowline*. When you are rough-ing it in the rubble these are some of the handiest fasteners you can have.

Tie the *clove hitch* to secure a rope to a post or spar. You can quickly make the holding end longer or shorter by loosening the knot slightly and feeding rope in from one side of the knot and pulling it out the other. This knot works best if the object it is anchored to is round.

Tie the *tautline hitch* to keep a rope tight while letting you easily adjust it. In the knot above, the three loops wrapping around the main line can be slid up and down. If the line sags, slide the loops up until the line is tight. To loosen the line or undo the knot, slide the loops down.

Tie the *bowline* to make a loop that won't slip. In the dining fly above, bowlines were used to tie the four ropes to the corners of the fly, and tautline hitches were used to tie the ropes' other ends to stakes in the ground.

146. THREE USEFUL KNOTS

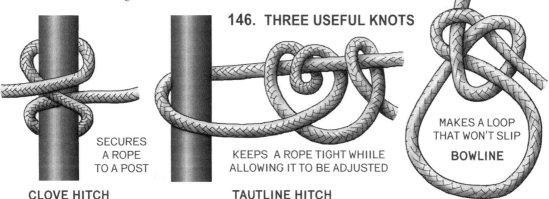

SECURES
A ROPE
TO A POST

CLOVE HITCH

KEEPS A ROPE TIGHT WHIILE
ALLOWING IT TO BE ADJUSTED

TAUTLINE HITCH

MAKES A LOOP
THAT WON'T SLIP

BOWLINE

When living outdoors, you must be constantly on guard for passing marauders, have ready an arsenal of weapons, and be adept at hand-to-hand combat to fend them off. Here I do *not* refer to humans —but ants, mice, rats, flies, ticks, snakes, coons, foxes, coyotes, and other members of an army of pests. A few precautionary measures, similar to what you would do on any vacation camping trip …

☞ Shake your bedding before lying in it.

☞ Empty your shoes and shake out your clothes before putting them on.

☞ Store food in secure containers and set them inside damaged refrigerators or abandoned vehicles where animals from ants to rats to bears can't get at them.

☞ Drape mosquito netting or fine cheesecloth over sleeping and dining areas.

☞ Clean up spills and collect crumbs as soon as possible so they won't lure pests.

☞ On the dining table, clap an inverted sieve over any exposed food while eating.

☞ Each morning, hang your bedding on a clothesline in the sun.

☞ Have a can of insect repellant handy. If you have a bottle of gin, rub handfuls on your exposed skin: bugs hate it (this is a good way to smell of gin).

A particularly formidable pest is the **mosquito.** Though one's legs barely span the top of a thumbtack and its proboscis is thinner than a pin, one stab can make you suffer for days. This insect develops from egg to larva to pupa to adult in as little as four days. Some lay their eggs in cold water in the fall that freezes in winter, then when the ice melts in the spring the eggs hatch,[99] which is why Alaska has swarms of mosquitoes that seemingly come from nowhere when the weather gets warm in late spring. Mosquito larvae look like tiny wiggly white shrimp floating in still water. To minimize their presence, remove any nearby standing water in road ruts, culverts, puddles, old tires, pet dishes, troughs, cans, barrels, buckets, birdbaths, broken bottles, flower pots, clogged gutters, low grassy areas, high tree trunk holes, swimming pools, and the like. Also cover barrels and similar containers with window screen, turn unused boats upside-down, cover water surfaces you can't drain or else fill them with dirt or a film of light oil or larvacide oil, and patch torn screens. But don't think you'll find mosquitoes only in still water that is nearby, because they can fly up to seven miles in one night even over deserts.

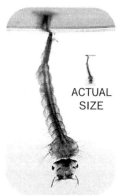

TOP OF WATER

ACTUAL
SIZE

**147. A
MOSQUITO
LARVA** [99]

Snakes are a special concern, both good and bad. When you are roughing it in the rubble, nonvenomous snakes are your friends. If you find one that has vacated its usual premises during a disaster and taken up residence nearby, gently remove it to the outskirts of camp, remembering that it is one of the finest rat traps you can find. If you see a venomous snake, give it a quick karate chop behind its neck with a hoe, then remove it with the hoe or other long-handled tool, not your hands. Avoid the head, because it can bite you hours after it is dead. A good way to catch snakes without getting near them is to tape together several glue boards (the kind that trap mice) and place them across entry ways and along the edges of walls. To release a snake or mouse from a glue board or remove any glue on your hands, pour vegetable oil on it.

Whether you are roughing it in the rubble or sequestered in a livable building, here are a few more precautions that will simplify your life and reduce your suffering until everything returns to normal …

Be careful … The consequences of mistakes so innocuous in normal times —water dripped on the floor, a broken glass, a blister, hair singed by a candle— can be frighteningly magnified in a disaster. Visualize what you will do before doing it. Do everything slowly. Put away things after you use them in order to have more clear area around you, not to be neat but because manual labor and unfamiliar activities require more space than machine-driven and familiar ones. Try to conquer the anxiety that may paralyze you at suddenly having to do old things in new ways. Without electric power, it will take you longer to keep warm or read. Instead of lamenting these limitations, be invigorated by them. Think of all the muscles you have, how strong they are. Take pride in how resourceful you can be, how capably you can deal with adversity. At the other extreme, don't let a few minor successes give you a false sense of security. Keep your guard up. With every move you make, think a few moves in advance, like you're playing a game of chess.

Know what weather to expect … Will it be warmer tomorrow? Colder? Rainy? Sunny? Continue to listen to your radio. If it says the temperature will plummet overnight, you'll know to stack more firewood by your hearth. If it will rain tomorrow, you'll know to cover any belongings outside that dampness would damage. After the October 2011 snowstorm that visited our premises, the overnight weather was forecast to be colder than the inside of our unpowered refrigerator, so my wife and I stored our food in plastic grocery bags on high hooks in the garage. If it would have been sixty degrees outside we wouldn't have done this; if it would have been zero we would have done it with the freezer's food as well. Without a functioning thermostat close by, even minor changes in the weather can make you feel as if you've moved overnight to Alaska or the Amazon. If you prepare for these changes in advance, you'll do less work and be more comfortable.

Get plenty of sleep … No matter how prepared you are for a disaster, the unaccustomed labor may exhaust you and make your muscles ache, and a host of anxieties may drain you mentally. If you feel sleepy, don't drink a cup of coffee: take a nap. This may be hard if children are around and sirens constantly wail, but in figure 148 on the right is a sound snuffer that may help: earmuff hearing protectors. Since sound travels faster through solids than air, much of the sound you hear travels through the side of your head around the hole in your ear to your brain. Ear-buds won't stop this. But earmuff protectors with spongy doughnut pads that enclose your auditory canals will reduce a siren's wail to a low whine while letting you hear someone talking nearby. You can make things even quieter by stuffing the cups with cotton.

148

Network with neighbors … Disaster research indicates it is not ambulances, firetrucks, and police cars that save the most lives during disasters: it is neighbors who are nearest those who need help. But be careful if you decide to check on a neighbor. You wouldn't want to suffer the fate of one victim in our grim list who "died when a tree fell on her while walking to a neighbor's house." If you visit a neighbor after a disaster has ravaged the landscape, wear a helmet and hiking boots, bring a pair of gloves and your personal relief kit, and carry a walking stick. Before you step out the door, leave a note saying where you will go and when you expect to return. With every step you take look everywhere around you, especially overhead and underfoot. Act as if at any moment danger could strike you as swiftly as lightning —because it can.

Protect yourself from outsiders … Many survivalist manuals would have you believe that in a disaster you must know how to use weapons to protect yourself and your family from roving marauders who would take from anyone what they need to survive. While it is *possible* such doomsday behavior could occur, the *truth* is that in all the major disasters that have occurred in America since Mount St. Helens erupted in Oregon in 1980 —earthquakes on the Pacific rim, landslides in the Northwest, tornadoes in the Midwest, hurricanes in the Southeast, blizzards in the Northeast, and all the other calamities in between— hardly any victim has engaged in social violence to obtain what they need to survive. Obviously in such troubled times, dealing with such violent behavior is not the dominant possibility for the majority of the population.

Yet whether in times of turmoil or tranquility, it is always wise to be careful —lest you tempt borderline personalities who would prey on the unwary, or desperate people who would grab what they imagine they need to stay alive, or outlaws who would steal when they think they can get away with it. In any hour, in any place, in any social clime it is prudent for all good citizens to exercise circumspection in protecting what they rightfully have when disaster comes knocking on their door. There are three strategies for doing this: *hiding, barricading,* and *camouflage* …

Hiding involves keeping your food, tools, and other necessities out of view and locked. After using something, put it back in its cabinet or drawer instead of letting it lie around where a passing stranger or unexpected visitor could see it. Don't let anyone indoors or near camp. If anyone approaches, meet them outside. Even if visitors have no ill intentions, they could describe your situation and belongings to others which may lead you to becoming a target for thieves.

Barricading involves placing obstructions between what you have and the covetous eyes of others. Rather than build a stout fort around your encampment, there are ways to erect swifter and subtler battlements. Such as cheesecloth. Cheesecloth curtains mounted over windows will let in light and air while keeping straying eyes from seeing inside, and cheesecloth draped over foods and cookware will hide these items in sunlight as well as darkness. Another barricade against strangers that requires no construction is a barking dog.

Camouflage involves making your encampment look purposefully shabby or blend into its surrounds, or otherwise keeping a low profile and revealing to no one what you have. Remember, the best place to hide a tree is in the forest. You might even try such reverse psychology as posting a sign that says DANGER, CHEMICAL FALLOUT when the only chemical you have is Clorox.

Water

Next to air this is your most vital need. In serious disasters you may have to think mighty hard about where to find it, but such efforts can lead to unexpected dividends. As a sample, during hurricane Sandy I suddenly remembered an old spring deep in the woods near my house. I paid it a visit. The water trickled in from one side of its stone basin and was a half inch deep. I scraped away the sand below, waited for it to settle, and leaned in and took a long drink. It was deliciously cold: a colonial source of water that the citizens of future centuries can enjoy. I told three neighbors about it. These springs should never be destroyed.

There are five kinds of water: *pure, rinse, gray, brown*, and *black*, as follows …

1. ***Pure water*** is drinkable: plumbing water and bottled water. Use it for drinking, cooking, washing dishes, brushing teeth, and making ice. When using bottled water remove the cap briefly, don't drink from the bottle unless you empty it, and never pour any back. Keep the empty containers for storing other things. You can also cut the top off a plastic bottle and use the bottom as a cup and the top (inverted) as a funnel.

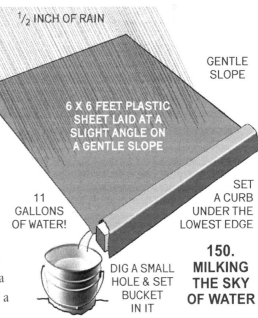

149

2. ***Rinse water*** is fairly clear water that may contain germs that can cause dysentery, cholera, typhoid, and hepatitis. Typical sources are rain, creeks, swimming pools, toilet tanks, baseboard heaters, and waterbeds. You can collect rainwater in cisterns and rain barrels. By laying 6 x 6 feet of clean plastic sheet on sloping terrain and curbing the bottom to channel the water into a container you can collect 11 gallons during a half inch of rainfall. You could also hang a bedsheet or blanket on a clothesline and wring it out after it is soaked with rainwater. If you have snow, fill a bucket with it and set it indoors by some heat, or fill a pillowcase with snow and hang it over a bucket to catch the water that filters through the pillowcase. You can use rinse water to flush toilets, clean counters, wash clothes, and bathe (when washing your face close your eyes and lips). Strain any particles through a tee-shirt folded once over. When rinse water is boiled it is pure enough to drink. If used pure or rinse water is still fairly clean, pour it into a toilet tank for future flushing.

½ INCH OF RAIN

GENTLE SLOPE

6 X 6 FEET PLASTIC SHEET LAID AT A SLIGHT ANGLE ON A GENTLE SLOPE

11 GALLONS OF WATER!

SET A CURB UNDER THE LOWEST EDGE

DIG A SMALL HOLE & SET BUCKET IN IT

150. MILKING THE SKY OF WATER

3. *Gray water* is used bath water, dishwashing water, muddy creek water, rain puddles, and the like. Roof runoff is gray water because it may contain tannin from wood shingles, leachates from asphalt shingles, minerals from ceramic tiles, and toxins from metal roofs. You can use gray water to flush toilets and water plants but not to clean things.

4. *Brown water* is toilet waste. Also known as effluent or sewage, it contains urine, fecal bacteria and other disease microbes. Its smell will warn you away from it.

5. *Black water* contains toxins or harmful chemicals. This includes floodwater which is usually a stew of greases from streets, runoff from fertilized crops, chemicals from factories, leachates from landfills, and the like. Treat this water as though it's poison —because 99 percent of it is. [100]

In the above list you can use water of a lower number for a higher one (e.g. rinse water to flush toilets) but never a higher number for a lower one (e.g. gray water to clean counters). To obtain pure water when the power has failed, try the following ...

Drain the water pressure tank ... If your house has a drilled well, when the water enters indoors it first flows into a pressurized tank that holds perhaps 50 gallons of water at 40 to 50 pounds per square inch (psi). When you open a faucet, the pressure forces the water through the spout. As the water runs, the pressure reduces to a prescribed level that activates the pump in the well which raises the pressure back to 50 psi. If the power fails, the pump can't reraise the pressure in the tank and you don't get more water —but you still may have a tankful of pure water. To use it, set a container under the drain spigot at the tank's base and open the spigot. If the tank holds 50 gallons and each person needs two gallons per day for drinking, cooking, and washing, the tank should have enough pure water to supply a party of five for five days.

Drain the hot water heater ... Turn off the gas or electricity that heats the tank, then set a container under the drain spigot at the base of the tank and, as with pressure tanks, open the spigot. You may collect another 40 gallons.

Drain the plumbing ... (1) Turn off the water supply shutoff valve, usually located near where the water enters the building. (2) Go to the highest plumbing fixture in the building and open the hot and cold faucets to let air in the pipes. (3) Go to the lowest plumbing fixture in the building, open its faucets, and collect the water pouring from them into a container. In most homes you will collect a few quarts.

Boil rinse water ... Boiling water for one minute kills any microbes in it at elevations up to 5,000 feet above sea level. Boil one extra

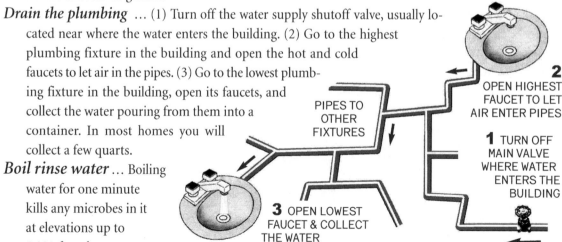

2 OPEN HIGHEST FAUCET TO LET AIR ENTER PIPES

1 TURN OFF MAIN VALVE WHERE WATER ENTERS THE BUILDING

PIPES TO OTHER FIXTURES

3 OPEN LOWEST FAUCET & COLLECT THE WATER

151. DRAINING PLUMBING OF PURE WATER

minute per 1,000 feet of increased elevation. Cover the pot to shorten boiling time and conserve fuel. To make the water taste fresh, add a charcoal briquette and whip with an egg beater for a minute, or pour the water between two containers rinsed with $^3/_4$ cup of bleach per gallon of rinse water.

Filter rinse or gray water … One of the best methods is the *Life-Straw personal water filter,* a tube about 1 inch thick and 7 inches long that you were introduced to on page 36. Dip the lower end in impure water and suck on the top as you would suck a straw and drink pure water.

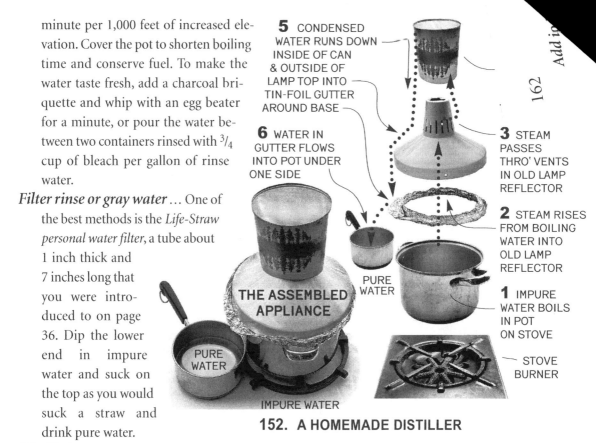

5 CONDENSED WATER RUNS DOWN INSIDE OF CAN & OUTSIDE OF LAMP TOP INTO TIN-FOIL GUTTER AROUND BASE

6 WATER IN GUTTER FLOWS INTO POT UNDER ONE SIDE

3 STEAM PASSES THRO' VENTS IN OLD LAMP REFLECTOR

2 STEAM RISES FROM BOILING WATER INTO OLD LAMP REFLECTOR

1 IMPURE WATER BOILS IN POT ON STOVE

STOVE BURNER

PURE WATER

THE ASSEMBLED APPLIANCE

PURE WATER

IMPURE WATER

152. A HOMEMADE DISTILLER

Distill rinse water or gray water … The apparatus above shows what you can do when you think in terms of principles instead of equipment. By envisioning the process of distilling —rising steam, cool surface, condensation, descending pure water— you can create a life-sustaining appliance out of junk. Any impurities remain in the pot where the water boiled.

153. PURIFYING AND RECYCLING AT THE SAME TIME

Expose to sunshine … You can make pure water by filtering water from a creek or puddle, pouring it into a common 16-ounce clear plastic bottle and placing it on a sheet of black plastic for six hours in the sun. Repeat with sixteen bottles as appears at left, and you have two gallons of pure water: what one person needs each day in a disaster. This method is known as *ultraviolet germicidal irradiation.*

...ine tablets … Two pills in a quart of fairly clear water at room temperature purifies it in 30 minutes. As effective is 8 drops of iodine (which you can buy at a drug store) in a gallon of water. Either method absorbs up to 98 percent of the radioactive iodine in water exposed to nuclear fall-out. Dissolving a vitamin C tablet afterward makes the water taste better.

Add chlorine to rinse water … Add 8 drops of chlorinated bleach per gallon of fairly clear water; if murky add 16 drops. Mix, cover, and let stand for 30 minutes. The treated water should have a slight chlorine odor. If not, add 8 more drops and wait another 15 minutes. If the water has a chloriny taste, add a dash of sugar and the same number of drops of lemon juice that you added of chlorine. What you're making is extremely dilute lemonade.

Add potassium permanganate … This is an oxidizing agent that looks like purple sand. Sprinkle a few grains into a quart of rinse water until it is light pink, and the water will be pure of bacteria and viruses. Add more crystals until the water is purple, and you have a deodorant, a disinfectant for cleaning counters, and an antiseptic for cleansing wounds. Add more crystals and the water becomes a dye, which you can sprinkle a big **SOS** on an area of snow so rescuers can find you. Mix two parts with one part powdered sugar and add a drop of water and it will ignite, which you can use to light a fire. This is a cantankerous chemical. A pharmacist can specially order it for you.

Food

Food is the energy you use to cruise through a disaster. Whether you are roughing it in the rubble or living in luxury, here are a few culinary cues that will make your eating safer…

☞ Avoid opened containers and packages, jars with broken seals, cans that are leaking, bulging, or rusted, as well as food having a strange odor or color. Spoilage is often difficult to detect because the food may have no offensive odor or taste, so don't trust your sense of smell. If any thawed food still contains ice crystals and has no off-odor, you can usually cook, eat, or refreeze it. Foods that can't be refrozen but are still safe to eat can be canned if done so immediately.

WHEW…

OPENED PACKAGES & CONTAINERS   JARS WITH BROKEN SEALS   CANS WITH BULGES OR DENTS   CANS THAT LEAK   FOOD WITH A STRANGE ODOR OR COLOR

154. DON'T EAT THESE FOODS

☞ Avoid meat (especially ground meats like hamburger), poultry, fish (especially seafood sandwich fillings like tuna) and uncured sausage that have been unrefrigerated for more than four hours or above 45°F for two hours, because their spoilage can cause food poisoning. It's best to keep these

UNCURED SASAGE — RAW CHOPPED MEATS — OTHER MEATS — CUSTARDS — PASTRIES WITH CREAM FILLINGS — RAW FISH — VEGETABLES — SOFT CHEESES — OLD FOODS — CREAMED DISHES — SANDWICH FILLINGS — OPENED SPREADS — SOUR CREAMS & YOGURTS — MILK

155. IF LEFT UNREFRIGERATED, DON'T EAT THESE EITHER

foods frozen until you're ready to eat them, then cook before they are completely thawed. If cooked meat can't be cooled below 45°F in two hours, keep it above 140°F to prevent spoiling. You can do this with stews. Large unboned pieces of meat are least susceptible to quick spoilage.

☞ Custards, baked goods with cream fillings, creamed foods, cream cheese, opened cheese spreads, cottage cheese, and milk spoil quickly without refrigeration and should be discarded. Hard cheeses usually keep well at room temperatures, but dispose of any that develop an off-flavor. If surface mold develops on a block of cheese, slice $1/8$ inch below its surface and discard.

☞ Fresh produce and cold salad fixings will keep in an ice chest for about four hours. If you put ice in the chest these foods will remain safe until the ice melts, then eat the food right away. If any is left, throw it away.

☞ If rice, beans, or other dried foods get wet, rinse and dry quickly to prevent mold. Spread on a sheet of insect screen or a screen door raised a foot above the ground where the sun will shine on them. Do this at ten in the morning on a sunny day, and by three the food should be dry.

☞ If containers with screw or twist caps, flip tops, or snap lids have contacted floodwater, scrub their tops in pure or rinse water, immerse the containers for 10 minutes in a solution of 2 tablespoons of bleach per gallon of water, and air-dry before opening (this allows oxygen in the air to kill any remaining germs).

☞ Open only enough food for one meal, save liquids from canned foods and use or drink them right away, and eat food in its original containers to reduce dishwashing. If you heat a can of food, remove the label first, then leave the label nearby in case you want to refer to it later.

☞ Keep garbage in closed containers outdoors or away from camp. If animals could be an annoyance, bury the garbage so its top is at least 15 inches deep, put a flat rock on it, and cover with earth.

☞ A small propane refrigerator will run for two to three weeks on a 5-gallon jug of propane. To read how to extend the time foods will remain safe in refrigerators, go to **J** on page 110.

164

Here are some handy tips on preparing meat, fish, and fowl …

Meat … Almost any mammal from mice to moose is edible except skunks, armadillos (they carry leprosy), and porcupines. If possible, within 15 minutes after killing the animal sever the jugular vein and let the blood drain from the body. Then …

1. Remove the musk glands. Most look like brown scabs in the fur. If you can't find them, cut the legs off at the shoulders and the head off at the neck, then carefully skin the body and roll up the skin with the fur side in.

2. It's usually a good idea to skin the animal before opening the body cavity. If the fur smells or is dirty, scrub with 1 tablespoon of bleach and 2 of dish detergent per gallon of warm water and rinse.

3. If the animal is large, hang it as follows. Cut a hole in each hind leg between the tendon and the bone above the ankles, slip a stout stick through the two holes, tie some rope around the stick between the legs, throw the rope over a strong branch 8 to 10 feet above the ground, hoist the animal (either by tying the rope to a car and driving forward or by several people pulling the rope) until the animal's neck is 18 inches off the ground, then set a wheelbarrow under it. Small animals can be laid on a flat surface.

4. Slit the body from sternum to anus, remove the entrails without puncturing any organs, and (with large animals) let them fall into the wheelbarrow. If a bullet passed through an organ, remove the organ carefully without letting its contents taint the carcass.

5. Cut off the legs and head with a hacksaw.

6. Wash the body inside and out with cold water and pat dry.

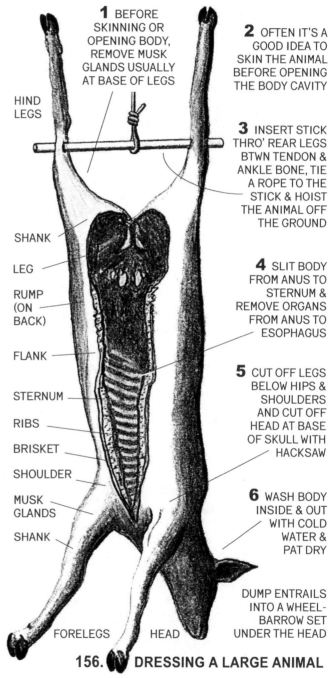

1 BEFORE SKINNING OR OPENING BODY, REMOVE MUSK GLANDS USUALLY AT BASE OF LEGS

2 OFTEN IT'S A GOOD IDEA TO SKIN THE ANIMAL BEFORE OPENING THE BODY CAVITY

3 INSERT STICK THRO' REAR LEGS BTWN TENDON & ANKLE BONE, TIE A ROPE TO THE STICK & HOIST THE ANIMAL OFF THE GROUND

4 SLIT BODY FROM ANUS TO STERNUM & REMOVE ORGANS FROM ANUS TO ESOPHAGUS

5 CUT OFF LEGS BELOW HIPS & SHOULDERS AND CUT OFF HEAD AT BASE OF SKULL WITH HACKSAW

6 WASH BODY INSIDE & OUT WITH COLD WATER & PAT DRY

DUMP ENTRAILS INTO A WHEEL-BARROW SET UNDER THE HEAD

HIND LEGS

SHANK

LEG

RUMP (ON BACK)

FLANK

STERNUM

RIBS

BRISKET

SHOULDER

MUSK GLANDS

SHANK

FORELEGS   HEAD

156. **DRESSING A LARGE ANIMAL**

Fish … Try to catch them Huck Finn-style. If you use a net, try a hair net or coarse sieve for small fry. For larger fare use cheesecloth, bridal veil fabric, insect screen, or part of a badminton net. When you've caught a fish, kill it quickly with a sharp rap on top of its head, then prepare as follows…

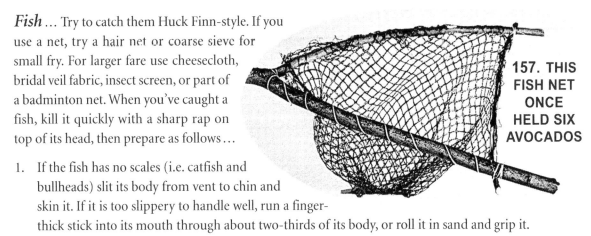

157. THIS FISH NET ONCE HELD SIX AVOCADOS

1. If the fish has no scales (i.e. catfish and bullheads) slit its body from vent to chin and skin it. If it is too slippery to handle well, run a finger-thick stick into its mouth through about two-thirds of its body, or roll it in sand and grip it.

2. Lay the fish on a board and plunge a knife, fork, or nail through its tail.

3. If the fish has scales, while firmly holding the head scrape the skin from tail to head with a fish scaler or slightly dull knife (a butterknife is too dull and a razor is too sharp). You can make a fine fish scaler by nailing a bottle cap to a piece of wood as appears below.

4. Cut the body open from vent to chin and remove the entrails. Scrape the clotted blood from the backbone.

5. Cut off the head behind the gills, slice off the fins, and cut off the tail (optional).

6. Wash inside and out in cold water, and pat dry.

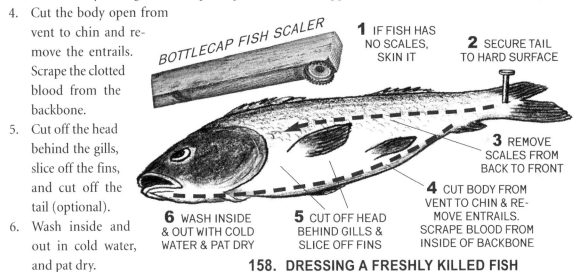

158. DRESSING A FRESHLY KILLED FISH

Fowl … If you have no firearm, try catching birds by baiting a small fishhook with a kernel of corn or felling them with a slingshot. For ammunition use pea gravel, marbles, ball bearings, or similar spheroids.

1. If the bird is alive, wrap its neck in a towel with its head exposed, and hit it sharply on the head to kill it. Hold its neck firmly and slice its head off at the neck with a long knife (if you chop the neck off with a hatchet or cleaver you could cut your hand). If you don't hold the bird firmly, after its head is removed it may fly around and spurt blood all over the place.

2. Remove the feathers. (A) Heat a pot of water to 150° and add a teaspoon of dish detergent to dissolve the oil in the feathers. (B) Immerse the bird in the scalding water and swish it around until

the water penetrates the feathers to the skin. If you don't do this enough the feathers won't pull out; if you do it too much the skin will come off with the feathers, which may be what you want. (C) Pluck the feathers by grasping a few at a time close to the skin and pulling with a slight jerk.

3. Remove the oil gland at the base of the tail.
4. Open the body from sternum to anus & remove the entrails.
5. From the head end remove the windpipe, crop, and neck.
6. Remove the feet.
7. Wash the body inside and out with cold water.

All this requires experience. It may take you a few practices —or disasters— to get it right.

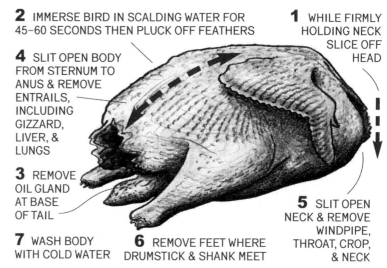

2 IMMERSE BIRD IN SCALDING WATER FOR 45–60 SECONDS THEN PLUCK OFF FEATHERS

1 WHILE FIRMLY HOLDING NECK SLICE OFF HEAD

4 SLIT OPEN BODY FROM STERNUM TO ANUS & REMOVE ENTRAILS, INCLUDING GIZZARD, LIVER, & LUNGS

3 REMOVE OIL GLAND AT BASE OF TAIL

5 SLIT OPEN NECK & REMOVE WINDPIPE, THROAT, CROP, & NECK

7 WASH BODY WITH COLD WATER

6 REMOVE FEET WHERE DRUMSTICK & SHANK MEET

159. DRESSING A FRESHLY KILLED FOWL

Heat

If a disaster strikes in cold weather you must keep your body warm. Fail to do this, and you can die of *hypothermia*. This occurs differently than what many think. You don't just get colder and colder, perhaps thinking that when you need help you can call 911. What happens is that first you shiver, which is your body's way of keeping warm. But as your body gets colder, this defense no longer works and you begin to feel *warmer*, and the colder you get the warmer you feel! Listen to how one doctor described this: "Many severely hypothermic people experience a tingling sensation of feeling overheated. This false sensation prompts many terminal victims to disrobe just before they lose consciousness." [102] The doctor described a victim who had "disrobed and piled his clothing and possessions in a neat pile," and also a rescuer on a bridge who dropped a rope to a hypothermic victim in a cold river below —but the victim "pawed the rope away" because he was too far gone to see it as his lifeline! [103] Such reactions are why four victims in our grim list "died in their homes due to hypothermia from exposure to cold," though the temperature never went below 40 degrees Fahrenheit the week the power was out. Here are a few ways to avoid this fate …

☞ Cocoon yourself in coats, snugglies, blankets, tarps —whatever it takes to keep the shivers away.
☞ Wear a hat (a lot of your body's heat escapes through your head) and slip on two pair of socks.
☞ Since your arms don't need as much heat as your body, wear two or three down vests and snap these layers open and closed as the temperature rises and falls.
☞ If several people are in your party, stay in a small room with the doors closed, try dancing or other light exercise to keep warm, and eat warm high-calorie foods to heat you from the inside.

If you are indoors and the power has failed, use a fireplace or other heat source (not a gas oven) to maintain indoor temps at a cool 50 degrees (this will also increase the time your food will stay frozen in the fridge). If you have a fireplace or woodstove, keep a set of tongs, poker, small shovel, little broom, bucket of water, and a fire extinguisher close by, and set a firescreen in front of the fire when no one is nearby.

Sanitation

In a disaster everything needs to be kept clean, lest germs sicken everyone in your party. The best disinfectant is fire. Its intense heat will kill any germ on contact. Into its flames dump greasy food wrappers, soiled napkins, gnawed chicken bones, and empty food cans (when these are burned fish them out, flatten, and dispose). Incineration also cleans up trash, keeps you warm, and lets you see in the dark. For killing other germs have soap, dish detergent, isopropyl alcohol, and/or chlorinated bleach. The use of bleach throughout this book is encapsulated in the table below. Here are a few more ways to keep evil germs at bay ...

☞ Keep your body, face, hands, and all cooking and eating utensils clean.

☞ Wash and peel all fruits and vegetables, keep food in tightly covered containers, prepare only what you'll eat right away, and eat from original food containers when you can to reduce dishwashing.

☞ Keep living areas free of garbage, debris, refuse, and body waste.

☞ If you're indoors, close holes and openings where rodents, flies, ants, and other insects could enter.

☞ If your clothes become dirty, change them and wash them.

To see the sanitary materials you should have in a disaster, look at figure 48 on page 46.

160. EFFECTIVE CHLORINATED BLEACH-TO-WATER RATIOS FOR CLEANING [101]

8 drops bleach or $1/12$ teaspoon (tsp) in 1 gallon of fairly clear water ... *purifies rinse water* (page 162)

16 drops ($1/6$ tsp) to 24 drops ($1/4$ tsp) in 1 gal ... *purifies murky water* (page 162)

1 tsp in a tub of laundry water (about 5 gal) ... *cleans clothes* (page 169)

$1/4$ tsp per gal of boiled water ... *cleans tables, counters, food prep areas* (page 169)

2 tbsp per gal of water ... *purifies unopened cans exposed to floodwater* (page 163)

5 tbsp per gal ... *cleans surfaces contacted by a dead body* (page 177)

$1/4$ cup per gal ... *cleans rugs and surfaces of flooded appliances* (page 191)

$3/4$ cup per gal ... *sanitizes a container used to purify water* (page 161)

1 cup per gal ... *sanitizes basement walls & floors exposed to sewage & toxins* (page 187)

$1\frac{1}{2}$ cups per gal ... *cleanses skin exposed to hazardous chemicals or biological agents* (page 139)

1 quart per gal ... *cleans surfaces with blood on them* (page 177)

1 tbsp bleach + 2 tbsp dish detergent per gal of warm water ... *cleans fur of killed animals* (page 164)

2 tbsp of bleach & dish detergent per gal ... *cleans walls, floors, & furniture exposed to floodwater* (page 188, 192)

$1/2$ cup of bleach & isopropyl alcohol per gal ... *kills mildew* (page 180)

1 cup bleach to clothes washer cycle at "hot water" setting ... *sanitizes washer after a flood* (page 187)

NOTE
100 drops ≈ 1 tsp
3 tsp = 1 tbsp
16 tbsp = 1 cup
4 cups = 1 qt
4 qt = 1 gal

PAPA POT
HERE IMPURE WATER IS
PURIFIED BY BOILING ON
A STOVE OR FIRE

MAMMA POT
THIS IS THE SUPPLY
OF PURE WATER
BESIDE THE SINK

BABY POT THIS IS THE PURE
WATER YOU
USE TO
CLEAN THE
DISHES

SCRUBBING
SPONGE

SCRUB EACH
PLATE WITH THE
SPONGE, THEN
RINSE CLEAN

DISH
SOAP

SINK WITH
DRAIN

161.

DIRTY DISHES

Washing the dishes

During a disaster the biggest battle of sanitation is waged around the kitchen sink. Here three times a day brigades of bacteria feast on the leftovers of their larger but occasionally careless adversaries, who to minimize their own suffering must wage unremitting warfare against them. Here's how to keep your dinnerware free of these hordes of microbes …

1. Begin with a stove or fire, a big "pappa" pot at least 10 inches across and 8 inches deep, a "mamma" pot about 10 by 6 inches, a "baby" pot maybe 6 by 4 inches, a kitchen sink or equal basin, sponge, and rubber gloves. Fill the pappa pot with rinse water and put on the stove or fire.
2. Set the mamma pot by the sink on the side of the pappa pot, and the baby pot by the mamma pot.
3. When the water in the pappa pot is boiling, carefully pour water into the mamma pot until it is two-thirds full. Add more water to the pappa pot so you'll have enough boiled water to keep working.
4. From the mamma pot pour water into the baby pot until it is about half full.
5. Drip a few drops of dish detergent onto the sponge by the sink.
6. Hold a dirty dish over the sink with one hand and pour a little water from the baby pot on it, then scrub both sides sudsy clean with the sponge. Next, hold the dish at a tilt over the sink and with the baby pot rinse the suds off both sides. Inspect the dish to make sure it is clean. If not, try again.
7. If you need more water on the sponge, *do not dip it into the baby pot*: pour water from the baby pot onto the sponge. The baby pot must *always* contain only pure boiled water. Any time it runs out, *do not dip the baby pot into the momma pot* (the baby pot's possibly dirty underside could contaminate the water in the mamma pot), pour water from the mamma pot into it. And *never dip the sponge in the mamma pot*. The idea is that sterilized water always flows "downstream" from the

pappa pot on the stove, to the mamma pot by the sink, to the baby pot close by, to the work in the sink —and *never* a drop flows "upstream". After a few dishes you'll feel like a pro.

8. Air-dry each item. Do not use a towel, which could contain germs. Save your towels for other things. If the weather is warm you may want to drape some cheesecloth a few inches above the dishes to keep flies from undoing your diligent labor.

Other battlefields in this endless war with germs are tabletops, countertops, and food prep surfaces. After using each, clean with a solution of $1/4$ teaspoon of bleach per gallon of boiled water, perhaps from the papa pot on the stove after you've washed the dishes.

Washing clothes

Dirty clothes carry germs, so clean them regularly, especially underclothes. If your source of energy is "Armstrong Power", here's a way to clean your clothes outdoors …

1. Set a washtub or equal container on eight concrete blocks or equal support that are high enough to build a fire under the tub, and build a fire.
2. Fill the tub with an armload of dirty clothes and add water to 3 inches from the top.
3. Add only a little detergent, because your clothes don't need to be squeaky clean when you're roughing it in the rubble, and if you add too much detergent it will take several rinses to wash out the soap. Add a teaspoon of bleach.
4. Bring the water to a near boil.
5. Occasionally agitate the clothes with a toilet plunger, paddle, or similar stirrer. Wear latex gloves, and be careful you don't spatter yourself with hot water.

5 OCCASIONALLY AGITATE THE CLOTHES WITH TOILET PLUNGER

2 FILL TUB WITH ARMLOAD OF DIRTY CLOTHES & ADD WATER TO 3 INCHES FROM TOP

3 ADD ONLY A LITTLE DETERGENT & A TEASPOON OF BLEACH

4 BRING WATER TO A NEAR BOIL

6 SOAK 10 MINUTES, EMPTY WATER, REFILL & RINSE

7 HAND-RING CLOTHES AS DRY AS YOU CAN, THEN HANG TO DRY

1 SET TUB ON 8 CONCRETE BLOCKS OR EQUAL SUPPORT

162. WASHING CLOTHES WHEN YOU'RE ROUGHING IT IN THE RUBBLE

6. Soak for 10 minutes, then tilt the water out of the tub and refill with pure water or clear rinse water to rinse the clothes. It may take two or three rinses before all the soap is out.
7. Hand-wring the clothes as dry as you can, then hang them on a clothesline or spread over some bushes or clean plastic sheet until they are dry.

Washing yourself

If the power is out and your plumbing has a pressure tank, you don't want to use this pure water for bathing. Better is to sit in the bathtub and have a small pot and two buckets of very warm water close by. With the pot scoop some water from a bucket onto your head and work your way down. If you have a woodstove with a flat top or a fireplace with a crane alongside (like the one below), you can set a washtub on the hearth before the fire and a kettle of water over the flames. I have bathed like this during several power failures since 1975. My washtub is an old tin sitz bath that years ago I found in a secondhand store. After drawing two 5-gallon buckets of water from the pond below my house, I place the sitz bath on the hearth, hang a kettle filled with water on the crane over the fire, and wait till the water is cozily warm. The dirty water ends up in the bottom of the sitz bath, and afterward my wife and I carry this container over to the kitchen sink and tilt the water into the drain. Another picture of these facilities appears in figure 108 on page 96.

TOWEL

A CRANE HOLDS THE KETTLE OVER THE FIRE

FIREWOOD

CLOTHES SET ON TABLE

SOAP & WASHCLOTH

SLIPPERS SET ON FLOOR

OLD-TIMEY SITZ BATH

SHAMPOO

163. BATHING WHEN YOU'RE ROUGHING IT IN THE RUBBLE

Going to the bathroom

Here are a few ways to go to the bathroom in reasonable comfort if the power is out. If you want to use an existing toilet, select one for communal use. While the tank is full, reach under it and turn off the water supply valve (it's an oval handle on a thin vertical pipe). This may be so hard to reach that you can't get a good grip on it, or it may have corroded and you can't turn it without a wrench, or there may not be room enough to turn the wrench —or maybe all three. It happens. If so, another way to turn the water off is as follows. Remove the top from the toilet tank, lift the float inside, and prop something under it so it won't descend when the toilet is flushed, as appears in figure 164 on the right. You can use the toilet once with the water still in the tank, then afterwards fill the tank with rinse water scooped from a bathtub (if you've filled the tub earlier). Do not flush the toilet with pure water, as this commodity is too precious to waste here. Otherwise, use the toilet pretty much as normal. Flush every third time a male urinates, every second time a female does the same (because she uses toilet paper), and every time someone defecates. After each flush refill the tank.

A way to use a regular toilet if you have no water at all is as follows. lift the seat, fit a plastic garbage bag in the bowl, lower the seat onto the bag, then sit on the seat in normal fashion. After a few uses raise the seat, tie the bag's top, remove, and dispose. Here are a few more ways to go to the bathroom when you have no power or pure water …

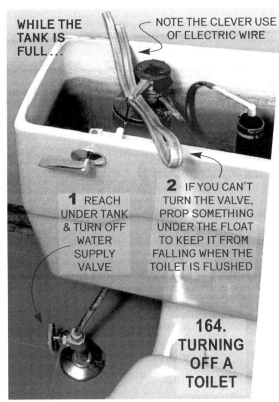

WHILE THE TANK IS FULL...

NOTE THE CLEVER USE OF ELECTRIC WIRE

1 REACH UNDER TANK & TURN OFF WATER SUPPLY VALVE

2 IF YOU CAN'T TURN THE VALVE, PROP SOMETHING UNDER THE FLOAT TO KEEP IT FROM FALLING WHEN THE TOILET IS FLUSHED

164. TURNING OFF A TOILET

165. CHAMBER POT

☞ Use a chamber pot. Vintage models have a wide round rim that's comfortable to sit on, a bowl deep enough to contain urine without splashing, a secure lid that stifles the smell, handles that make it easy to carry outside, and attractive decor around the sides. This potty was usually stored beneath a high-legged bed or under a nearby stool where it could be used at night and emptied the next morning.

☞ Line a 5-gallon joint compound bucket with a plastic bag, then after using it a few times tie the bag's top, remove, and dispose. This method is portable, which helps if you want to go to the bathroom outside and the ground is rocky or frozen. Use a bucket that doesn't have handle flanges on top (if it does, cut them off).

☞ Make a "luxury latrine" depending on what resources you have. As a sample, when Sandy blew through here, I found a 12 x 12 inch chimney flue in the back yard and set it near a small tree with a broken branch (my pertinent TP holder). Since the flue's top was a little rough, I got a piece of cardboard, slipped it under a toilet seat in the house, traced the seat on the cardboard, and on each trip outdoors I toted my bun cushion along with a roll of paper to my *toilette en plein air*.

NICE VIEW

166

TOILET SEAT ON OLD 12 x 12 CHIMNEY FLUE

☞ Build a latrine. In hard times this may be your only choice. It certainly was common before plumbing was invented. If so ...

1. Select a secluded place where the ground is soft and a user will have some privacy.
2. Dig a trench 12 inches deep, 8 inches wide, and at least 18 inches long.
3. Pile the shoveled earth close by and stab it with a trowel or small shovel. After each use, cover with a trowelful of dirt.

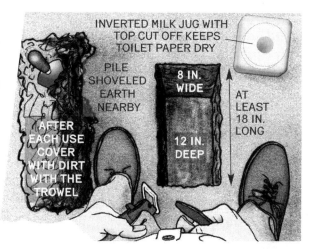

167. WHEN TIMES ARE HARD ...

Keeping the kids happy

In a disaster, children require extra attention because the experience can leave them frightened, confused, and insecure. Grownups can help them by being alert, well-organized, and calm. A few more cues ...

☞ Explain simply and matter-of-factly what has happened and how things will be handled. Ask if they understand. Listen to their responses, and guide them to safe feelings as best as you can. Listen with them to radio and TV broadcasts of the latest updates and advisories. Never leave them alone unless absolutely necessary. Be careful how you reveal your own fears.

☞ Establish normal routines as best as you can. Give children roles, clear instructions, and simple steps to follow. Have them help with cooking, serving meals, cleaning, getting and storing things, and caring for pets. Show them how to seek emergency help, either by calling 911 or going to a neighbor or other trusted adult. Help them feel important and useful.

☞ Give them a favorite object —a doll or teddy bear?— and let them take it wherever they want. If a child has lost a favorite pet or toy, commiserate with their feelings rather than minimize them.

☞ Do not punish a child for such crisis behavior as bedwetting, thumbsucking, and crying. Commiserate with such exhibits of insecurity. Be understanding and patient.

☞ Spend extra moments with them at bedtime. Leave the child's door partly open and a night light on if you can. Let the child sleep close to you if s/he wants.

☞ If you must leave a child with friends or relatives, let the child know where and how long you will be gone and how you will keep in touch. Keep your promises. Give the "sitter" explicit directions on how to care for your children in your absence. When you return, ask the sitter if everything went well, and determine if s/he acted as advised.

☞ Once children are out of danger they still may be afraid, because they may have been traumatized by what they've experienced and may be unable to understand that the worst is over. Continue to encourage them to express their feelings.

Caring for guests

Whether you are a guest in another's home or host guests in yours, here are some tips that will make everyone more comfortable …

If you are a guest … Don't try to be involved in everything. Ask if you can help, then stay out of the way. Don't allay your anxieties with excessive talking, and allow your hosts some privacy and freedom.

☞ Find your own "space" (sleeping area, etc.) and stay there as much as possible. Involve yourself unobtrusively with your own activities and routines.

☞ Don't interfere with your hosts' decisions about their children, pets, or other aspects of their lives.

☞ If you can, check with your insuror to see if they will pay for temporary living arrangements.

If you are a host … Help your guest contribute to running the household while being clear about your role as decision maker.

☞ Remind each guest of positive things, help them feel independent, and give them a "space" of their own to settle into.

☞ Be patient and understanding of your guest's anxieties. If they are upset and need someone to listen to them, do so intently. Talk to them and learn their concerns. Some may be relieved by spiritual support such as prayer and reading the Bible or Koran.

☞ If the guest is grieved, alone, or afraid, try to contact a trained counselor.

☞ Be available and offer support after the crisis is over.

Caring for pets

In disasters pets can be an asset. Dogs can keep prowlers away, cats can keep rats at bay, and both can be a soothing presence if you and your family are wrought with anxiety. For identification purposes, photograph each pet you have once a year or before a disaster arrives. You may need such ID if you must leave your pet somewhere. Some cautions …

If you stay at home with your pets, or after you return home with them …

☞ Be vigilant about removing any debris such as cut glass, nails, and sharp metals that could harm their tender paws.

☞ If your property has suffered extensive damage, familiar scents may be altered and pets could become confused and lost. The first time you take them outdoors, lead them around the property and let them refamiliarize themselves with the territory. Possibly keep them on a long leash and carry a walking stick to uncover pieces of debris and possibly to protect them from other animals.

M FROM **114**

☞ Beware of downed power lines and wild animals. Everything from snakes to alligators may have found a safe haven under fallen debris or other hiding place on your property —and they may attack if discovered.

If you evacuate and take your pets …

☞ Try to leave three days before the disaster will occur, so you will have plenty of time to shop for needed pet supplies along the way.

☞ Know which lodgers or boarders along the way will take your pets. Locate several in case your first choices are closed or full. Make reservations well in advance if you can, as in times of disaster they may fill rapidly.

☞ If you take your pet to a kennel or vet, (1) bring leashes, obedience aids, and medications; (2) make sure the pet's vaccinations are up-to-date and have records with you; (3) ask if someone stays at the kennel overnight, and what would happen if it must evacuate.

☞ If you go to an emergency shelter, be aware that pets are usually not permitted due to health and safety reasons (service animals excepted).

☞ If you transport a pet in a carrier or crate, make sure it is large enough for the animal to stand up and turn around in. Keep small pets (hamsters, birds, etc.) in cages away from dogs and cats.

☞ Make sure each dog and cat has a leash and a snug collar with ID tags on it.

☞ If car sickness could be a problem, administer 1 milligram of Dramamine per pound of the pet's weight every 12 hours.

☞ Bring plenty of food (dry, canned, or packaged semi-moist), clean water in unbreakable containers, and bowls to put them in. Bring litter or sand for cats.

☞ Bring newspapers, plastic bags, cleaners, and disinfectants to maintain sanitary conditions wherever you go.

If you evacuate and leave your pets at home ...

☞ Many people, especially children and the elderly, are reluctant to leave their pets behind as disaster approaches. With them you may need to be tactful and persuasive.

☞ Leave a note on the door that describes the pet, where you plan to go, and when you plan to return.

☞ Designate a friend in the area to care for your pets and replenish food and water if needed.

☞ If you leave a dog or cat indoors, leave interior doors open, and leave plenty of water and a day's supply of dry food in containers that won't tip or spill. A dog or cat can get by for two days without food. Raise the toilet seats, and/or pour some water in the bathtubs. If the pet is small don't fill the tub deeper than its chest, lest it fall in and drown. A good place to leave a dog or cat is in a two-car garage with the door down,

so they will have room to move around. Later the floor can be easily cleaned. If the floor could flood, provide inclined walks to the tops of nearby tables, counters, or workbenches.

☞ A parakeet or other bird must eat daily to survive. Provide them with ample water and an automatic food dispenser.

☞ Never leave a cat with a dog, even if they are normally friendly, unless the cat has a secure place to which it can escape.

☞ Post a notice by the front door, visible to rescuers, that says pets are inside. Include the type and number of pets plus the name and phone number of the veterinarian.

☞ If you leave a dog or cat outdoors, do not tie it up. It might not be able to defend itself, and it could get tangled and panic and even die. Place it in a penned area that is large enough for it to run around in and has plenty of food in an automatic dispenser, ample water in bowls that won't tip, and a doghouse or other shelter. The pet should be unable to crawl under or climb over the fence.

☞ If you have a rowboat or canoe in the yard, fill it with water. It will serve as drinking water for your pets and the water's weight may keep the boat from blowing away. A pond or swimming pool is another source of drinking water for pets, but a danger with pools is that the animal could fall in and drown.

Dealing with the dead [104]

In disaster in which many die, emergency services may be so overwhelmed that they cannot speedily dispose of dead bodies, which may create offensive odors, be visually revulsive, obstruct activities of the living, and attract carrion feeders. Outdoors their decomposition can pollute surface and ground waters, and if left indoors any materials beneath them must be removed and discarded. In such times, non-professionals may have to do all or part of this work.

Before touching anything, try to contact the police, lest you destroy any evidence that would indicate how the victim died. The police typically assign detectives to investigate the scene and after-death cleaners to restore it, as well as contact the coroner and the next of kin.

Before you handle a dead body, dress sanitarily. Wear a hat and a face mask (like the ones nurses wear in hospitals), thick rubber gloves, high rubber boots, and a long raincoat or impermeable full-body suit that can be easily washed afterward. You don't want to be spattered by pathogens in fluids from a decomposed body. A dead body can spread disease if it was contagiously ill when the disaster struck, but usually not if it died from fire, trauma, or drowning.

To satisfy any concerns of the police, coroners, insurers, and the next of kin, before moving anything do the following …

☞ *If you have a camera, take detailed photos of the scene.* If this is in the victim's home, take pictures of the kitchen, bathroom, and bedroom. Photograph the tops of desks, tables, bedstands, bureaus, bookcases, and other places where a number of the deceased's belongings appear. Open medicine cabinets, drawers, and cabinet doors, and photograph the contents inside without touching them. If some important items are hidden under the ones on top, take two photos: one of the items untouched, and one of them rearranged. Write a description of what you find.

☞ *Photograph the victim.* On a floor or other low level surface lay the body on its back with its arms by its sides and its legs straight. The body should be unclothed but for the genitals and any mutilated areas. If you know the victim's name, write it on a waterproof label in dark letters an inch high and lay the label on the victim's chest. Photograph the victim's face, upper body, and lower body from the front and photograph the whole body while standing by its waist, not by its head or feet as this would create a distorted view.

IF YOU KNOW VICTIM'S NAME, WRITE IT IN INCH-HIGH LETTERS ON A LARGE WATERPROOF LABEL

NAME OF DECEASED

LAY BODY ON ITS BACK ON A LOW LEVEL SURFACE

LAY ARMS BESIDE BODY & LEGS STRAIGHT BELOW

PHOTO VICTIM'S FACE & TORSO FROM THE FRONT

BODY SHOULD BE UNCLOTHED EXCEPT FOR GENITALS & MUTILATED AREAS

PHOTO VICTIM'S WHOLE BODY WHILE STANDING BY THE WAIST

168. PHOTOGRAPHING THE DEAD

☞ *Identify the body thoroughly*… This will help relatives and friends identify their loved ones and provide legal ID for inheritance and insurance purposes. Unless the corpse is fresh, touch it only with hoes, long-handled shovels, and the like. Identify the following as best as you can…

- Apparent sex, approximate age.
- Approximate height and weight (slim, average, or plump is adequate).
- Color of hair, eyes, skin.
- Clothing and personal items the victim wore: watch, rings, jewelry, items in pockets, etc.
- Skin features: scars, moles, tattoos, piercings, large ears, amputations, etc.
- Dental features: prominent or missing teeth, gold crowns, fillings, dentures, etc.
- Glasses, hearing aids, etc.

☞ *Give all the above information to the police* … If you can't do this immediately, keep the information in a safe place until you can give it to the proper authorities.

☞ *Gather the victim's personal effects* … Remove everything from where the body was found and any significant areas nearby. Put everything in sealed bags, boxes, or other safe containers. Offer the contents to the police so they can examine them, or give them to the next of kin or a close friend for safekeeping.

☞ *Clean the area where the victim was found* … When a person dies, in hours the decomposing body can saturate the materials it lies on with biological matter that can contaminate the materials and fill the air with bacteria that can threaten the health of other occupants. Within a few days even nearby books, clothes, and furniture may be irretrievably lost. Hence the victim's body must be removed quickly, yet

this should not be done until the other procedures described above have been accomplished. If the body has lain for days or weeks, the materials beneath and around it —known by coroners as the death zone— are contaminated and must be removed. This includes any mattresses or carpets, any plywood subfloor, and any tainted construction below, all of which must be disposed of as medical waste. This work is typically performed by professional after-death cleaners wearing respirators, double gloves, and HAZMAT suits designed for biohazard recovery who cordon off the death zone and meticulously remediate the area. If professional cleaners are so overwhelmed with work that they cannot reach the scene promptly and you must do something before conditions rapidly worsen, you may need to do this work yourself.

☞ *Be attentive to the deceased's social and religious preferences* … If you can, seek a religious leader's guidance. Your dignified and caring manner of handling these matters could profoundly effect the feelings of the bereaved.

☞ *Keep journalists informed* to ensure accurate reportage in the news media.

☞ *Conduct the final arrangements* … This may involve transporting the victim to a coroner or the next of kin, or the victim's burial.

☞ *If you must bury the body*, do as follows

1. Wrap the body in cloth or plastic sheeting, seal with duct tape, and attach the earlier-prepared waterproof identification label to it.
2. Dig a grave at least 5 feet deep and 5 feet above the water table. If the ground slopes

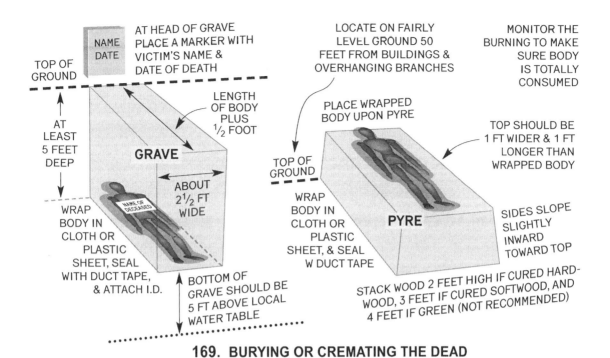

TOP OF GROUND

AT HEAD OF GRAVE PLACE A MARKER WITH VICTIM'S NAME & DATE OF DEATH

NAME DATE

LENGTH OF BODY PLUS ½ FOOT

AT LEAST 5 FEET DEEP

GRAVE

ABOUT 2½ FT WIDE

WRAP BODY IN CLOTH OR PLASTIC SHEET, SEAL WITH DUCT TAPE, & ATTACH I.D.

NAME OF DECEASED

BOTTOM OF GRAVE SHOULD BE 5 FT ABOVE LOCAL WATER TABLE

LOCATE ON FAIRLY LEVEL GROUND 50 FEET FROM BUILDINGS & OVERHANGING BRANCHES

MONITOR THE BURNING TO MAKE SURE BODY IS TOTALLY CONSUMED

PLACE WRAPPED BODY UPON PYRE

TOP OF GROUND

WRAP BODY IN CLOTH OR PLASTIC SHEET, & SEAL W DUCT TAPE

PYRE

TOP SHOULD BE 1 FT WIDER & 1 FT LONGER THAN WRAPPED BODY

SIDES SLOPE SLIGHTLY INWARD TOWARD TOP

STACK WOOD 2 FEET HIGH IF CURED HARDWOOD, 3 FEET IF CURED SOFTWOOD, AND 4 FEET IF GREEN (NOT RECOMMENDED)

169. BURYING OR CREMATING THE DEAD

gently and isn't soggy to at least ten vertical feet below the grave site, the water table is probably low enough. If the ground is soggy or is level and near a marsh, seek a higher elevation. The grave should also be 200 feet from any creeks or lakes or other surface water, and where rainfall runoff from the grave will not enter nearby inhabited areas. When the grave is filled, place a marker above the head. This will make the body easier to locate by relatives and friends, and also by the police if it needs to be exhumed.

3. Wash your hands frequently. Don't touch your face.
4. Afterward, clean any hard surface (i.e. a truck bed) the body has touched with a solution of 5 tablespoons of bleach per gallon of water. If blood is present, increase the solution to 1 quart per gallon, or 1 cup per quart.

☞ If the ground is hard or saturated with water, *consider cremation as follows* ...

1. Build a pyre whose sides slope slightly inward and whose top is a foot longer and wider than the body.
2. Stack the wood two feet high if cured hardwood, 3 feet if cured softwood, and 4 feet if the wood is green (not recommended).
3. Place the wrapped body on top. The burning produces lots of smoke, takes up to 4 hours, and the corpse will be ashes.
4. Monitor the burning to make sure the body is totally consumed so that later you won't need to bury any partial remains. [104]

Well After [105]

After the power is back on and the roads are clear, you can safely return to your home or place of work, if you aren't already there, and begin to restore everything to nearly normal. Before you make your first foray about these premises, you should dress safely…

☞ In normal weather, wear comfortable work clothes and hiking boots.

☞ Add a bandana and a camera around your neck, a pencil and notepad in one pocket, a flashlight and an old toothbrush in another.

☞ Put on your protective helmet, goggles, shoulderpads if you have them, back brace, and work gloves.

☞ Bring a tall-handled shovel you will also use as a walking stick.

☞ If you have binoculars, loop them around your neck.

This is your soldierly uniform for inspecting your home or place of work.

[122]

Grounds and yards …Your first act of restoration is to make an initial survey of the land around the house. This foray is one of your greatest moments of danger, because you may have no idea what damage has been done. With every step, constantly look overhead and on the ground. Dangling branches? Unstable earth? Standing water you should drain? Broken glass or sharp pieces of metal anywhere? Small pieces of debris here and there? Flip them over with the shovel. You don't want to step near any copperheads lurking under them. Investigate up to 100 feet away from the house and any outbuildings, 50 feet from each side of the driveway, and 50 feet in from the street. Take photographs, possibly for the family scrapbook, insurance adjusters, and any contractors who may repair any damage. If the damage is serious, leave everything in place until the insurer has inspected and documented the damage and given you the go-ahead to clean up. On your notepad list the debris that needs to be cleared, damage that needs to be repaired, and other items that require attention. Don't trust anything to memory. Also …

☞ Stay away from fallen or damaged power lines, because they may still be alive. Remember the woman you read about back on page 144 who stepped from her house to see how much a thunderstorm had damaged it? When she stepped into a rivulet of water beside the road fifty feet from where a power line had fallen into it, she was electrocuted.

☞ If a wildfire passed nearby, check the yard for sparks or embers that could blossom into flame. Never take chances with fire: it can flare up days afterward from a spark.

☞ If any trees or branches are obscured by foliage, look at them closely, with binoculars if necessary. Make sure none are broken, or you may join the company of five victims in our grim list who "died when a storm-damaged tree fell on them while clearing debris." I almost suffered this fate the morning after the record snowfall of October 2011. Outside my front door a huge branch laden with tons of wet snow was dangling upside-down 30 feet up the trunk, its leafy crown hovering a foot above the ground. I got a 100-foot length of half-inch thick rope and stepped under the branch, tied one end to the branch as high as

I could reach, played the rope out to the driveway to pull down the branch with my truck. After I tied the rope to the truck's trailer hitch I gave it a little yank to see how tight it was —and the branch's top snapped like a twig and fell where I had stood. If a breeze had blown while I was under it I could have been killed. I also wasn't wearing a protective helmet, shoulderpads, or any of the other armor urged here. Of course I believed my many years' experience at this sort of labor immunized me from harm. On your notepad describe any trees, shrubs, plants, fences, and other construction that may have been damaged. This information will help arborists, contractors, and insurors to assess and repair the damage.

☞ If you have a lawn that has been flooded, the degree of damage will depend on the depth and duration of flooding, temperature, whether the weather has been sunny or cloudy, species of grass, and its condition prior to flooding. Most grasses will survive 4 to 6 days' inundation at normal summer temperatures, and longer if temperatures are cooler.

☞ If the building's water comes from a drilled well, examine the wellhead. If it was inundated by floods, the supply water may be contaminated, and you may need to have the well pumped out and the water tested and treated before drinking. Also, floating debris could have banged into the casing and damaged it, allowing silt in the floodwater to enter the casing and clog the pump —a rare occurrence, but the stakes are too high not to check.

☞ If the building has a *septic system* and the ground above the tank and leaching field was flooded, make sure the septic tank still isn't full, as follows. Walk downhill from where it is located (you might need a site plan of the house and grounds to determine exactly where it is)

until you are about six vertical feet below the septic tank's top and look at the ground at your feet. Is it soggy? With your shovel dig a bucket-size hole and see if water oozes into it. No water? Good. There is water? Go indoors and pour a bucket of water into the lowest plumbing fixture in the building to see if the fixture drains. It drains? Good. It doesn't drain? Floodwater has probably filled the septic system and risen inside the waste plumbing. If so, don't turn on any faucets or flush any toilets and call a plumber. If your septic system is soaked, it may take a week or so of dry weather for the surrounding water table to lower enough to let the building's effluent drain into its septic tank and leaching stems.

☞ When you have finished looking around, estimate the garbage cans you'll need. You may want to rent a dumpster.

The house, outside …After examining the property, stroll around the house. If you smell gas, walk away and call the gas company. Otherwise do the following…

☞ Check the roof, facades, and foundation for damage. Start at the top and work your way down. Get out your pencil and notepad. If the building has a roof (some don't after a disaster), see if it has any torn shingles, bent gutters, or missing trim. Cracks in the chimney? Make a note.

☞ If the building had a fire, do any wisps of smoke appear anywhere? Look with your nose. Any smoky odors? A tiny ember could have fallen into the framing onto a mouse nest, which makes perfect tinder for a fire. This has happened. Check the roof for sparks or embers. Look at the attic vents. Could any embers lay smoldering there? A long shot —but many disasters are long shots that nobody believed would happen. Any smoldering remains or scorched trim? If a fire broke through the roof and left a charred hole, firefighters may have poured a ton of water through the opening and flooded the construction below. Keep a close eye on the house for two days lest a flame reappear. Also make a note to buy some plywood to cover the hole and protect the building from rain damage.

☞ If any part of the roof is sloped, step back or forward until you can just sight across its surface and see if it is perfectly flat like it ought to be. In a similar manner walk around the house and sight across the surface of each facade. Any bulges or indents? This is a quick way to see if any serious damage has been done to the building. If a surface isn't flat, something is wrong. It could be due to age and been there before the disaster occurred, or it could be due to a blow the building took from which it couldn't bounce back —like a sucker punch from an earthquake, tornado, or hurricane. If anything scares you, call a contractor.

☞ Look at the shingles or siding. Any missing? Make a note. Do they lie flat? If they don't, or the siding is warped or cracked, make a note to remove and replace them. Get a crowbar and remove a few damaged shingles or lengths of siding and examine the plywood sheathing behind. Any sheets buckled? Make a note to replace them one sheet at a time. Never remove several sheets of plywood at once, because this membrane thin as your finger holds up the whole building. Any mold or mildew? Make a note to wipe it off with a sponge moistened with a solution of $1/2$ cup bleach and $1/2$ cup isopropyl alcohol per gallon of water, spray with fungicide or other mildew killer, and allow to dry thoroughly.

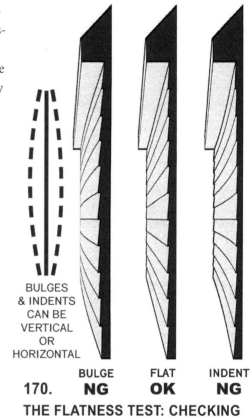

BULGES & INDENTS CAN BE VERTICAL OR HORIZONTAL

| 170. | BULGE NG | FLAT OK | INDENT NG |

THE FLATNESS TEST: CHECKING A FACADE FOR STABILITY

☞ While examining the sheathing, check for silt deposits behind the siding. Are there any? Make a note to remove them and any siding that imprisons them because the silt will absorb moisture which will spawn the growth of mold which will cause decay which will cause the house to fall apart someday. If a lot of the siding is warped or silted, it may take less labor to remove it all and replace it. It's rarely a good idea to install new siding over old, because if the old siding is lumpy the new siding will be lumpier. If the old siding is flat, it probably doesn't need to be replaced.

☞ Examine the foundation. Look for any cracks in the walls. If they are concrete block and you can see them, kneel at a corner and sight along a horizontal mortar joint to see if it is straight as it ought to be. Is it straight? Good. Does it tilt up and down a little here and there? Does the wall have a crack that is a little wider at one end? If so, part of the foundation may have been knocked out of alignment and could be seriously damaged. Sight across the surface of each foundation wall and see if it is perfectly flat. Any bulges? Indents? Look around the foundation's base and see if any earth has washed away, an all-too-common occurrence in floods. Make a note of these damages for your insurance adjuster and building professionals who will repair them.

☞ Look inside the foundation. If there is a crawlspace, is any water in it? Take a photo with a flashbulb, and make a note to remove the water, usually by pumping or siphoning; or it will spawn the growth of mold in any wood construction above and cause it to decay.

ANY CROOKED MORTAR JOINTS?

ANY INDENTS OR BULGES IN THE WALL'S SURFACE?

FROM A CORNER SIGHT DOWN THE FACE OF THE WALL

ANY EARTH WASHED AWAY FROM THE WALL'S BASE?

ANY LONG CRACKS IN THAT ARE WIDER AT ONE END THAN THE OTHER?

171. CHECKING A FOUNDATION FOR STABILITY

If/while the water is being removed, open any doors or crawlspace vents into this space and use ventilating fans to increase the circulation until the area is dry.

☞ If the foundation encloses a basement that has flooded, wait until any floodwaters outside are below the level of the basement floor before draining. Then drain only one-third of the water per day. If you pump all the water out while the surrounding earth is waterlogged, the basement floor could buckle or the walls could cave in —then there goes the house.

If your notetaking indicates that any construction should be rebuilt, follow the *Golden Rule of Remedying*: ***Don't rebuild mistakes.*** If something broke or malfunctioned, don't fix it the way it was before. Either strengthen it, relocate it, or forget it. A possible exception is if something has become damaged due to long-term wear and tear.

The house, inside … Now you are ready to enter the building. Do so during daylight hours, as this light brightens from every direction, while at night a flashlight casts a narrow beam of light in only one direction. Change your leather gloves and boots for rubber ones, keep your helmet on, slip an empty water bottle in your pocket, and hold the shovel/walking stick in one hand and your flashlight in the other. Turn the flashlight on outdoors, as indoors the switch contacting the battery could create a spark and ignite any leaking gas and cause an explosion …

☞ While standing just inside the door, look carefully around. Don't turn on any electrical switches just yet. If you smell gas or hear a hiss, exit quickly, leave the door open for ventilation, turn off the main gas valve if you can, and call the gas company.

Have the gas turned back on by a professional.

☞ Kneel until your eyes are just above the floor and look across it to see if it is perfectly flat. Do this with every room you enter. Step close to each wall and look across its surface and see if it's flat. As with the roofs and facades outside, this little trick will tell you if something big is wrong with the construction.

☞ Be wary of wild animals that may have entered during your absence. Herd them out the doors with the shovel. Do not corner or try to rescue them. If you can't shoo them away, call a local animal control or wildlife center. If any dead animals larger than what you can lift with your shovel are present, call a professional. If you have room to bury large animals on your property and no rendering company is nearby, you should bury the bodies at least five feet deep (you may need a backhoe) in an area approved by a local soil conservation officer.

☞ Unless it's freezing cold outdoors, open all the doors and windows to allow any moisture, odors, and flammable or toxic fumes to escape. If any windows are stuck, perhaps because water has swelled their frames or an impactful force has wracked the surrounding construction, get a small crowbar and remove the strips of molding around the sash if you can, then remove the sash. If a door is stuck, get a hammer and nailset and knock out the hinge pins and remove the door. Make a note of the damages.

☞ Watch for loose carpeting and slippery floors. Poke the shovel through any debris. Open cabinets and cupboards slowly. Keep an eye overhead for any loose construction that could fall on you.

☞ Test the electricity. If you see broken or frayed wires or smell hot insulation, turn off the main circuit breaker at the entrance panel if you can and call an electrician. Otherwise, turn on a light switch. The light

works? Good. It doesn't? Again, turn off the main circuit breaker and call an electrician.

☞ Check the plumbing. If any pipes are damaged, turn the supply water valve off. Turn on a faucet to see if the water runs. Does the spout sputter and gasp? A pipe may be damaged. Call a plumber. Does the faucet run? If so, dip your hand in the water and lift it to your nose. Does it smell funny? Call a plumber. If the water smells okay, fill the bottle in your pocket and have the water tested by a public health laboratory before drinking it. Step over to a toilet and flush it. Does the water rise ominously in the bowl rather than swirl down the drain? If so, your plumbing may need some "drain surgery". Call a plumber.

☞ If the house experienced a fire and is heated by a furnace with ducts that deliver warm air to interior spaces, smoke may have entered the ducts. If so, you may be smelling smoke in your living room every time your furnace turns on for years to come. Have a professional turn on the furnace, even if it is summer, and smell the air entering through a few registers. You want to learn this now, when your insurance company can pay to have the ducts restored.

☞ Clean up any spilled medicines, bleaches, gasoline or other flammable liquids.

During these preliminary investigations you will act like a detective trying to sleuth out a crime —in this case the assault and battery of a disaster. Soon your observations and notes may coalesce into a coherent picture of how the building and adjacent grounds or yards have been damaged. As a sample, if a facade you examined outside bulges outward and the same wall seen from the inside indents inward, you won't need fifty years of construction experience to know the wall is damaged. Such an understanding will also help you select a competent professional when it comes to correcting the construction.

Repairing buildings

If your home or workplace is so damaged that it is uninhabitable, you must first decide whether the whole building should be demolished, or whether parts or all of it are still sturdy enough to be restored. If the latter, you may need to hire a professional designer and contractor to perform this labor.

Easier said than done. After a disaster, when many victims may vie for the services of a few professionals, you may find it difficult to find the help you seek. Like flies drawn to honey, designers and builders will be drawn to the most lucrative opportunities. But here are a few guidelines to help you …

☞ It is easy to say, obtain references from each candidate. But these can be inflated well beyond the bounds of truth by a friend for such recommendations to be valid. Consider only a detailed reference of a candidate given by someone you personally know and trust.

☞ Don't overestimate experience. It takes only five or six years to be a good carpenter, and some who have done it for thirty years still don't know what they are doing. Another possibility is a youthful "inexperienced" person who has done little previous work and has no references to speak of, but who has a real passion for the work and will go to almost any extreme to do it well to gain a reputation for oneself.

☞ Visit the address where a candidate lives. How well a person takes care of his own property may hint at how well he will take care of your property.

☞ Select someone who is familiar with the work to be done. If you have a solar house, don't retain the services of an architect who specializes in antebellum homes.

☞ Obtain each candidate's address and phone number, handed to you by the candidate. Emails can come from anywhere, and a well-designed website often speaks more for its designer than its subject.

☞ Make sure the candidate has liability insurance. Uninsured workers can sue you if they are injured on your property.

☞ Ask if the candidate has a license. Many professionals today must have a license to work in their locality.

☞ Finally, if all the above goes well, obtain a written contract. This includes building plans, a schedule of the work to be performed, its estimated cost, schedule of payments, approximate starting date, and estimated time the work will take to complete. Know that bad weather, unavailable materials, and "acts of god" may affect these details.

Whatever you do, don't be rushed, try to get estimates from two to four candidates, and have a lawyer who specializes in real estate review all contracts before you sign them.

If you rent a residence that is damaged, its repairs are the responsibility of the landlord. Notify the landlord of any damage to your tenancy and make reasonable efforts to protect it from further damage. If repairs are not made within a reasonable time, you can legally sue for damages due to inconvenience plus reduced rent and termination of your lease.

While you are doing the above, keep a record and a receipt of every cost you incur. Send a copy to your insurer, and also your accountant in case any damage is tax-deductible.

If you need assistance with any of the above, contact FEMA, the American Red Cross, the Salvation Army, and local volunteer organizations. In severe disasters they may offer food, first aid, clothing, temporary housing, low-interest loans, and other assistance for families and small businesses. Often local radio, TV, and newspapers report where you can obtain these services.

Repairing grounds and yards

Unless the building will be demolished, your initial act of restoration should be to restore the building's surrounding grounds or yards, as follows …

☞ If debris blocks your driveway or impairs the building's function, or if any lumber, broken glass, nails and other sharp or dangerous objects appear on your property, remove as much as you can with the tools described on pages 57 to 60 of this book. For larger work you may need a contractor who has a bulldozer or backhoe. Backhoes are better on pavement and lawns you don't want to ruin, and bulldozers are better for heavier work and where tearing up the ground is not a concern. Some debris, like fallen trees you want to cut into firewood, you may want to leave on your property; or you may want everything removed, which will require a truck and cost appreciably more. If any large trees are damaged, call an arborist. If you are unaccustomed to working on tall ladders or using chainsaws, hire a professional to perform this labor.

☞ If you burn debris on your property, obtain a fire permit if required.

☞ If you clean any debris along the street, keep a wary eye for oncoming traffic —lest you suffer the fate of another victim in our grim list who died after he "was hit by a truck while cleaning up storm debris."

☞ Drain any standing water in cans, barrels, bird baths, puddles, tree holes, and other depressions where mosquitoes may breed. Cover any cisterns, cesspools, fire barrels and rain barrels so their water won't spawn these bloodsuckers.

☞ If any silt is deposited on your property, examine every part for sharp pieces of metal, shards of broken glass, or other dangerous debris. Measure the silt's depth. If this is one inch or less, any grass below has a good chance of recovering if you (1) wash, shovel, or use a metal-tine rake to remove enough silt so the grass shows through, then (2) aerate and lightly fertilize the area soon after the water recedes. If the silt is deeper than one inch, it may take less labor to plant a new lawn on top. Either way, have a sample of the silt tested by a laboratory to determine if any toxic chemicals have been deposited in your yard. If any topsoil has eroded away, replace it to a depth of 4 to 6 inches. If topsoil is unavailable or too expensive, work the proper amount of peat, manure, or other organic matter into the top 4 inches of subsoil as recommended by a local county extention agent or horticulturalist.

☞ If you have a swimming pool, remove any submerged debris with a long rake, and remove surface debris with a skimmer before restarting the pump so you won't ruin it. If the pump was flooded, have it reconditioned by a professional. Test the water for proper chlorine concentration and intrusion of any toxic chemicals that could damage the pool's finish and its operating equipment. When everything is running properly, run the filter until the water is clear.

Repairing interiors

If your house has suffered damage inside but is sturdy enough to restore, a good plan is to move all the furnishings outdoors (cover them if rain is a threat), get the utilities operating again, clean every surface indoors, clean the furnishings outdoors, then move the furnishings back inside. To see a few common cleaners, go to figure 48 on page 46. In addition to clorox and its dirt-killing kin you'll need a bevy of brushes, rags, rubber gloves, fans, dehumidifiers, a hose with a nozzle, and a squarepoint shovel. Read every label for specific directions and precautions, and protect your hands with waterproof gloves and your eyes with safety glasses or goggles. If you splash or spill any cleaners on your skin, quickly wash them off.

If the building has been closed up for awhile or suffered any flooding, unless it's freezing cold outside get the air moving indoors by opening all the doors and windows. If you have electricity, install one or more fans to increase the circulation of air. If the floors are covered with debris or mud, pick up the debris and shovel up the mud and sweep the floors so you won't trip over anything or track dirt around while you're doing everything else. Remember that mud is heavy. Wear your back brace. If this labor raises dust, wear a dust mask and cover undamaged objects or areas with plastic sheathing or equal material. If any erosion has occurred outside, dump any dirt removed from inside into the eroded areas.

When you can easily walk around inside, first restore your utilities. If you have no electricity, begin with this, because once this is running you can use it to help with everything else. Then get the plumbing running (so you'll have water to drink, clean, and use the bathroom), next the refrigerator (so you can keep foods from spoiling), and finally the clothes washer and dryer (so you can clean soiled fabrics and bedding).

Electricity … If the electrical service panel is in a flooded basement, stay out of the water lest you be electrocuted. Wait till the water is pumped out and the floor is dry and an electrician has examined the entrance panel and its circuits. If any electric outlet indoors could have been damaged and you have a safe path to the entrance panel, turn off the master switch, then walk through the rooms and note any electrical outlets —plugs, switches, lights— that are damaged. On your notepad sketch a little plan of each room with damaged outlets in it and mark where they are, Tape-measure the horizontal distance between each damaged outlet and the nearest corner and its vertical distance above the floor. The more you can show an electrician exactly what and where the damage is, the less you'll pay him. If any outlet was damaged by something banging into it or by smoke or fire, let the electrician fix it. If a flood submerged it, the submerged outlet boxes likely have silt in them. Here, if you want to save some money, put on your rubber gloves and rubber-soled boots and do the following …

1. Remove the box's cover with a small screwdriver whose tip fits perfectly into the screw holding the cover and any draft insulation behind. Mounted in the wall behind the cover is a *switch* (this is a small on–off lever that opens or closes a circuit) or a *receptacle* (this contains two plug holes), both of which here we will call a *connector*.

2. Remove the screws that hold the connector in the box, and pull the connector a few inches from the box.

3. Clean the connector's outside and box's inside with an old toothbrush and some clean water. A plastic-tipped paint scraper may help. You can move the wires around a little, but don't loosen any connections. Leave each box open so the wiring can dry and an electrician can inspect or repair it later.

Plumbing ... If the building's water supply comes from a drilled well whose head has been damaged by something banging into it or the casing has filled with floodwater, call a plumber with a boom truck. S/he will raise the pump and fix it, flush the casing, and disinfect the well. If the building's pressure tank and piping are contaminated, have a plumber flush the entire system with chlorinated water. This involves opening every faucet and running the water until the chlorine odor is gone from each faucet. If any impure water flowed through the water heater, disconnect its piping and flush the tank with clean water. If any of the heater's electronics were damaged or the insulation was soaked, you may need a new water heater. Otherwise clean and dry the unit's thermostat and wiring and apply rust inhibitor to all metal parts. If you have a water softener, a service person may need to regenerate it and backwash the filter bed with chlorinated water before you can use it.

Washer and dryer ... If seriously damaged by impact, fire, or smoke, replace them. If flooded, sanitize them as follows ...

1. Clean the outsides of each, then lay it on its side and look underneath to see if it is clean. If not, hose it clean, let dry, and tilt it up.

2. Clean inside the washer and dryer drums with a wet sponge.

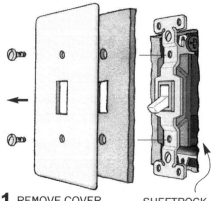

WEAR GOGGLES OR A VISOR OVER YOUR EYES, AND WEAR LATEX GLOVES TO PROTECT FROM SHOCK

1 REMOVE COVER PLATE & ANY DRAFT INSULATION BEHIND

SHEETROCK OR OTHER FINISH AROUND BOX

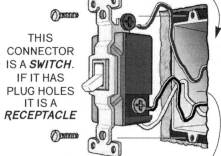

THIS CONNECTOR IS A **SWITCH**. IF IT HAS PLUG HOLES IT IS A **RECEPTACLE**

2 PULL THE CONNECTOR A FEW INCHES FROM THE BOX

BOX BEHIND FINISH MATERIAL

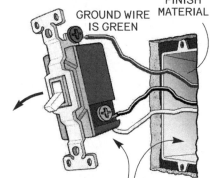

GROUND WIRE IS GREEN

3 CLEAN OUTSIDE OF CONNECTOR & INSIDE OF BOX

172. CLEANING AN ELECTRICAL OUTLET

3. To sanitize the washer, pour a cup of bleach into the empty drum and operate a 15-minute cycle at the "hot" water setting.

4. To sanitize the dryer, soak two bath towels with 1 cup of bleach per gallon of water, put the towels in the dryer, turn it on, and let run until no chlorine smell exits the exhaust vent.

Refrigerator … If it has been submerged in floodwater and is cased in batt insulation (the fluffy kind), junk it because the batts are impregnated with microbes and toxins. If is cased in rigid insulation (the styrofoam kind) and doesn't smell, have a service person check every component. If any don't work, replace them or junk the whole thing. Otherwise, clean it inside and out and sanitize as follows …

1. Remove the shelves, racks, drawers, and trays and wash in hot soapy water. Rinse in a solution of one teaspoon of bleach per gallon of water.

2. Wash every surface inside and out with a solution of one cup baking soda in a gallon of warm water. Leave the door open until the inside is dry.

3. If the interior has a musty odor, either place an open box of baking soda inside; or set several pieces of activated charcoal in an open container, close the door, and don't use until the odor is gone.

Lights … If any don't work, remove the bulbs and examine the plug, wires, and switch. Clean every part, especially inside the socket, and replace anything that is damaged. Reassemble, replug, and switch it on. It lights up? Good. If not, take to a service center or junk it.

Now that the electricity, plumbing, refrigerator, washer, and dryer are running, you can clean everything inside, day and night. Clean each room one at a time from the ceilings down through the walls, windows, and doors, letting any debris and dust settle on the floor. You may want to cover the floor and any open doorways with dropclothes to keep dust from entering adjacent rooms and make it easier to finish-clean the floor when you're done. When doing this work, wear rubber gloves, a baseball cap, a visor that fits over the cap and protects your whole face, and something waterproof on your shoulders. Not only do you want to protect your skin and hair from noxious or dangerous chemicals, you don't want drops of bleach to make little spots in your fine work clothes.

Basements … If the building has a basement that has flooded and the floodwaters outside have receded to below the level of the basement floor, Mother Nature may have drained this area for you. If not, as said earlier, remove only one-third of the water per day to keep the floor from buckling or the walls from caving in. Use a garden hose as a siphon, which is slow but cheap. While the water is being removed, watch the walls. Make sure they don't tilt or shift, that they stay exactly where they belong. After the basement is drained, shovel out any mud and debris on the floor while it is moist and hose the silt off the walls before it dries. If sewage or toxins have tainted these surfaces, scrub the floors and walls with a solution of 1 cup bleach per gallon of water.

Ceilings and walls … If these are only dirty, simply clean their surfaces. For small areas you may need a stepladder, but for large areas you'll need scaffolding so you can see what you're doing and your arms won't tire so fast. The following text and figure 173 describe how to erect a scaffolding that is easy to build, economical, and useful for cleaning large ceiling areas …

1. Build a 4 x 8 foot rectangular frame out of 2 x 4s.
2. On this frame nail a 4 x 8 foot sheet of $^3/_4$ inch thick plywood.
3. Arrange four piers of bricks and/or concrete blocks beneath the frame's four corners until the top of your head is an inch under the ceiling as you stand on the plywood.

On this platform two people can easily move around, and one person can move the platform from one room to another by tilting it upright and sliding it across the floor.

If a ceiling or upper wall finish is soaked due to water damage, perhaps from a tornado or hurricane or from putting out a fire, it may take weeks to dry. If the finish is drywall (also known as sheetrock) or plaster, it may be so warped or crumbly it should be replaced. If the finish material is salvageable, clean dirty surfaces with a large sponge laden with a solution of 2 tablespoons each of bleach and dish detergent per gallon of warm water, then rinse with clean warm water. Don't use a water-based cleaner on bare drywall or joint compound; it will dissolve these materials. Open the windows and use an electric fan to increase ventilation. If it's cold outside, wear an old coat. If these surfaces are covered with soot, special chemical sponges are available for removing it. If mildew appears (possibly due to leaks in the roof above), first eliminate the source of the moisture, then take a sponge laden with a solution of $^1/_2$ cup bleach per quart of water, press the sponge against the mildew until the solution saturates it, then scrub lightly.

As for walls, clean them much the same as ceilings. If you can't remove any dirt or other damage as detailed above, you may have to cut out the surface and replace it. If the lower walls have been flooded (the upper walls will rarely be so because if the water rose this high the building will likely be condemned), they are probably saturated with sewage and toxins. If so, draw a line a foot above the level of highest flooding, remove all finishes and any batt or fill insulation behind from this line down, and schedule these materials for carting to a landfill. This work will expose the building's structure beneath the finished surfaces. Most likely it is wood framing or concrete. Inspect it carefully. If concrete, you may only need to clean its surface. If wood framing, does the plywood sheathing lie flat against the outsides of

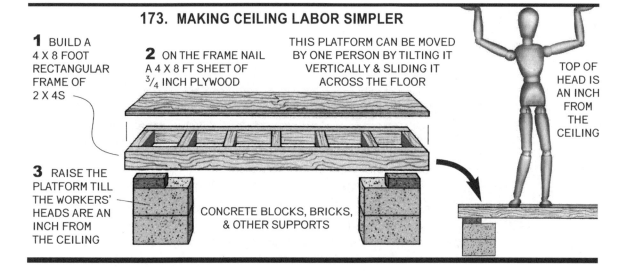

173. MAKING CEILING LABOR SIMPLER

1 BUILD A 4 X 8 FOOT RECTANGULAR FRAME OF 2 X 4S

2 ON THE FRAME NAIL A 4 X 8 FT SHEET OF $^3/_4$ INCH PLYWOOD

THIS PLATFORM CAN BE MOVED BY ONE PERSON BY TILTING IT VERTICALLY & SLIDING IT ACROSS THE FLOOR

TOP OF HEAD IS AN INCH FROM THE CEILING

3 RAISE THE PLATFORM TILL THE WORKERS' HEADS ARE AN INCH FROM THE CEILING

CONCRETE BLOCKS, BRICKS, & OTHER SUPPORTS

the studs? If not, you may be standing in a house that should be condemned. Have this inspected by a professional and repaired before you do anything else. You might want to invite your insurance adjuster to this party. The sheathing is flat? *Whew.* But don't let your guard down yet, because every surface of this structure —vertical studs, horizontal plates, and areas of sheathing— must be cleaned, disinfected and dried, as follows …

Cleaning … If mud, silt, mildew, or debris is on any surface, scrape or wipe it off.

Disinfecting … One way to do this is with a spray nozzle mounted on a tank filled with a solution of 1 cup of bleach per gallon of water. Cover every surface and get into every crack and crevice.

Drying … Speed this up by opening the windows and doors, operating ventilation fans, and/or turning on the heating or cooling. While waiting, clean the windows, doors, and floors as detailed below. You may have plenty of time before the structure is dry enough to reinstall the building's insulation and finish.

Windows … Windows have three parts: *panes* of glass, *sashes* that the panes fit into, and *frames* that the sashes fit into. Each is restored differently as follows …

Panes … If dirty, clean with a commercial cleaner. If broken and you don't know how to replace them, call a carpenter. If you want to replace them, several websites describe this work on the internet.

Sashes … If they are merely dirty and ride smoothly in their frames, clean their surfaces with $1/4$ cup of dish detergent per gallon of warm water. If they are broken or stick in their frames, remove the trim that holds the sashes in the frames, the tracks the

sashes slide in, and the handles and other hardware, then remove each sash and repair it.

Frames … If dirty, clean the same as sashes. If damaged, call a carpenter.

Doors … If an interior door is damaged by impact, fire, smoke, or water, it is usually not worth keeping. Remove the door from its frame, strip the hardware (knobs, latches, locks, and hinges), buy a new door, and reinstall the hardware. If the door is a little dirty, stained, or mildewed, remove it and clean the sams as ceilings. To save a slightly soaked exterior door, lay it on a pair of sawhorses and clamp its ends to the horses' spines to keep the door from warping as it dries.

Floors … Most have two layers: a *finish floor* on top (usually wood, tile, carpet, or linoleum: what you see and walk on) and a *subfloor* just below (usually a layer of plywood that strengthens the joists below and supports the finish floor above). Since structure trumps function (i.e. if structure fails function fails), knowing what to do with a damaged finish floor begins with knowing how damaged the subfloor is. Therefore, if part of the finish floor is moldy, soaked, warped, humped, buckled, punctured, scorched, or otherwise damaged or deformed, pull it up and look below. Any similar damage to the subfloor? Is any of the damage due to moisture? Moisture is a haven for molds, mildews, termites, and carpenter ants —and hidden by the finished floor above, these destructors will spread like a cancer until the whole floor caves in. So if any moisture exists in the subfloor, remove it until a ring of solid dry subfloor appears around the hole you've made. Look at the joists or other structure below. Is it dry and undamaged? If not, have a professional repair it before doing anything else. Once you've gotten to the bottom of the problem, work your way back up:

construction, subflooring, finish floor. If any part is merely dirty, scrub it with $^1/_4$ cup of dish detergent per gallon of warm water and rinse afterward. If it's stained or mildewed, spray it with $^1/_2$ cup bleach per quart of water. If the subfloor is mostly dry but warped or buckled a little, try to nail down any lifts or bulges with long roofing nails (these are galvanized so they won't rust and they have large heads which will hold the wood down). *Never* install a new finish floor over a moist, warped, buckled, or lumpy subfloor.

If a concrete floor is badly damaged, break it up and pour a new floor. If the damage is minor, patch with a mixture of concrete containing only a sand aggregate. To remove mildew from a concrete floor, sweep up the dirt and debris, scrub the afflicted area with the usual $^1/_2$ cup bleach per quart of water and let dry. If the mildew odor persists, repeat the application.

Repairing furnishings

Now let's clean everything you may have taken outdoors while you restored the house. What you do with each piece will depend on its initial cost, extent of damage, how much you need it, sentimental value, and cost of restoration. Antiques may be worth the effort and expense, while thrift shop favorites may not. Wear your goggles, rubber gloves, and old clothes.

Food … Discard any foods that have been exposed to fire, heat, smoke, soot, or floods. A good guideline for what foods to keep and discard after a disaster is the text and pictures on page 162–63. Also discard …

☞ Cans found far from where they were stored (they may have been banged around and their seams may be damaged) and home-canned foods sealed with paraffin (the seals may have been jarred loose). These may be kept if close inspection indicates they are still in perfect condition. Label them with a warning that their food should be inspected carefully when opened.

☞ Damaged paper or cardboard containers of crackers, cereals, pastas, cookies, rice, cake mixes, and the like. Unbroken packages that are a little wet may be wiped dry.

☞ Containers with non-sealed or fitted lids, such as cocoa and baking powder.

☞ Powdered or granulated foods that are discolored or caked.

☞ Any wooden spoons, bowls, and chopping blocks that contact food.

Some flooded food cans are safe if you sanitize them as follows. (1) After removing the labels, either boil for 10 minutes, dry the cans to prevent rusting, and relabel; or (2) scrub in a strong detergent solution, immerse for 15 minutes in 60–70°F water containing 2 tablespoons of bleach per gallon of water, air-dry, and relabel.

If a garden has flooded, don't harvest any foods from it for a month. Even then look carefully for silt and other matter that may be embedded in the crevices of such leafy foods as lettuce, cabbage, kale, collards, spinach, celery and the like. Also examine berry fruits as tomatoes, cucumbers, summer squash, strawberries and peppers. If the floodwaters were deep, lasted several days, and may have contained concentrations of sewage or toxins, take a sample of your garden soil to a public health laboratory and have it tested. Hopefully you won't have to remove your plants and the top few inches of soil and start over next spring.

Kitchenware … If any metal, ceramic, plastic, or glass cookware or silverware has been exposed to fire, smoke, or floods, scrape off any debris, remove any handles or other parts that can be disassembled, and clean each part in a dishwasher or boil for ten minutes. If boiled, air-dry them, hopefully where the sun can shine on them. If flies are a concern, cover with cheesecloth. Also …

☞ If any cupboards and food preparation areas were exposed to fire, smoke, soot, or floods, clean them with $1/2$ cup bleach per quart of water, then rinse with clean water.

☞ If any cast-iron implements need to be reseasoned, coat all surfaces with a thin layer of vegetable oil, heat in a 350-degree oven for an hour, and wipe clean.

☞ Cover hinges, latches, and other metal moving parts with a thin coat of machine oil.

☞ Wash and polish silver, brass, or copper.

Appliances … If any are damaged, do the following …

1. Disassemble the unit if wet or dirty inside, clean any controls and wiring, and let dry.
2. Clean the outside with dish detergent and hot water, and rinse with a solution of $1/4$ cup of bleach per gallon of water.
3. Do any minor and obvious repairs, then reassemble, plug it in, and turn it on. If it works, fine. If it doesn't, junk it or take to a service center.

Rugs and carpets … Restoring these fabrics is delicate work on a large scale, especially if they are fragile or valuable. If they rest on tack strips, foam pads, and underlayments that are soiled, soaked, or seriously damaged, remove these items and replace them. If the fabric is only slightly damaged and is not soaked and the floor underneath is not wood, you may be able to restore it in place. Otherwise, to avoid dust, moisture and smells, take the fabric outdoors or to an open roofed area such as a carport or garage with the doors open. Restoring takes three steps …

1. *Cleaning* … Removing crusted dirt, sediment, and other particulate matter by vacuuming, shaking, or sweeping the fabric. A solution of 1 part Lysol to ten parts warm water kills bacteria, mold, and mildew if you wet (not soak) the area with a sponge; but wear goggles and arm-length rubber gloves when doing this work, then rinse the area and quickly dry. If the fabric has a musty smell, lay it flat, sprinkle baking soda on it, work the soda in with a broom or sponge mop, leave overnight, and vacuum the soda out the next day; then repeat the above and vacuum the area in a direction opposite to the first. If a fabric must be disinfected, you can dip a sponge mop in a solution of $1/4$ cup of bleach per gallon of water and scrub the fabric lightly; but beware that bleach may discolor it, especially if made of nylon. Fabrics soaked by rain are more salvageable than ones soaked by floods.

2. *Drying* … Removing moisture from the fabric. If it is soaked, this work can be done with a dry-wet vacuum cleaner. Do this quickly to keep mold and mildew from staining and rotting the fabric.

3. *Washing* … Removing stains, odors, and contaminants with soaps, shampoos, steam-cleaners and the like until the fabric is clean, then rinsing it several times until the rinse water is fairly clear. If the fabric is large and washed in place or a surface nearby, it is usually shampooed. Otherwise it is often sent to a professional cleaner. Do not wash a rug or carpet

unless completely dry. After washing, it must again be dried quickly. It's also good to vacuum it when dry in the direction of the nap. Other tips …

☞ Some rugs and carpets may shrink when shampooed. If this could adversely affect the fabric, don't shampoo it. Do not use electric shampooers on shag rugs, as the long piles can get tangled in the brushes.

☞ If a small rug is soaked, lay a few towels on a dry floor and the rug on the towels, roll up the two and wring them dry, then lay the rug in the sun until dry. You can clean a small throw rug in a washing machine.

☞ Soot requires special attention. It easily stains carpets, curtains, drapes and other fabrics, but the stains usually remain on the fabrics' surface. If you try to wash them out, you'll usually dissolve them and drive them into the weave. Instead, hold a narrow nozzle of a vacuum cleaner $1/8$ inch above the texture's surface and suck as much of the soot as you can. Do not use a vacuum cleaner's brush attachment as this will tend to rub the soot into the weave. A professional restorer does this work with special tools.

Curtains and drapes … If exposed to soot, treat the same as for rugs. If exposed to smoke whose odor remains in the fabric, send to a professional to remove the odor, then dry-clean them. Remove any mechanisms that open and close them, and separate the cords from their metal or plastic assemblies. Clean the fabrics and cords as you would laundry, and clean the assemblies with a solution of $1/4$ cup of dish detergent per gallon of warm water. You can use products known as ***counteractants*** to eliminate smoke odors from carpets, tapestries, curtains, drapes, bedding, and clothes; but most of these chemicals should not be applied to paint or plastic. Professional fire restorers and dry cleaners often have several counteractants depending on the material damaged. Several paints are also available that seal smoke odors.

Furniture … If it has been scorched, flooded, or damaged by debris, you may have many decisions to make. Antiques and heirlooms may be worth saving, then you must decide whether to do the work yourself or send it to a professional.

Clean the surfaces of dirty furniture with 2 tablespoons each of bleach and dish detergent per gallon of warm water. To save a piece of upholstered furniture whose surface is mildewed, remove the fungus promptly because it can spread rapidly. Take the furnishing outdoors to avoid scattering spores indoors and spawning new growths. Lightly brush loose mold from outer surfaces, vacuum fabrics and crevices to remove embedded mold, and wipe with a damp cloth dipped in 1 cup isopropyl alcohol per 1 cup water. If mold or floodwaters have penetrated the stuffing, replace it. The fabric can often be saved by dry-cleaning. This applies to cushions and pillows as well.

If a wood furnishing has suffered smoke or flood damage, take it outside and remove as many drawers and other removable parts as you can. If a drawer or door is swollen shut, don't force them open from the front (you could pull off the handles). Let them dry, and if they still won't open remove the furnishing's back and push them open from behind. Removing the back of a cabinet or bureau will also help it dry. If any joinery is loose, take it apart, clean away any mud and dirt, using a hose if necessary. Thoroughly dry each piece in a shaded area (drying wood too fast in the sun can cause it to warp), and reassemble.

To flatten a warped board as a dresser or table top, remove the board, strip its finish, then remove the moisture from its wet (convex) side by placing it on a heat source and add moisture to its dry (concave) side by laying moist cloths on it and ironing them. When the board is fairly flat, clamp it flat until dry. Loosen and move the clamps slightly each day to prevent splitting. Afterwards, refinish the board on both sides to keep it from reabsorbing moisture and rewarping.

When cleaning or finishing fine wood furniture don't use sandpaper; use steel wool. Sandpaper makes tiny scratches in the wood which feel "smooth" only because its scratches are less rough than the original ones, while the fibers of steel wool plane the surfaces smooth. Try sandpaper and steel wool on two pieces of wood and you'll feel the difference. For a lustrous finish, dip 000 steel wool in boiled linseed oil. When using steel wool wear gloves, or tiny metal splinters may embed in your skin.

If any veneer is bubbled or loose, carefully remove it, scrape away the glue underneath, reglue it, place wax paper over it, and place a weight on it so it will dry flat.

If a furnishing has a metal mechanism (i.e. the underside of an office chair) invert the furnishing or open the mechanism, pour some bleach solution into it, flush with a hose, and let dry. Lightly coat the mechanism with WD-40.

Give special attention to cleaning children's toys and play equipment. Boil any items a baby or toddler might put in one's mouth. Discard waterlogged and noncleanable toys.

If you have a safe or strong box whose outside has experienced a fire, do not try to open its door or top for at least a day after everything else has cooled. If you open it before its inside has cooled, the entering air combined with the high internal temperature could cause the contents to burst into flames.

Mattresses and bedding ... If a mattress is soaked, junk it, though a good boxspring may be worth the cost of reconditioning. If the outside of a mattress is slightly damp, dry it first. If it is dirty, vacuum it, gently wash with a sponge dipped in a solution of equal amounts of isopropyl alcohol and water, and turn it occasionally as it dries. Household fans may speed the drying.

If any blanket, quilt, or comforter is seriously damaged, have a professional advise you whether to restore it or throw it away. If the fabric is slightly wet or dirty, launder according to manufacturer's instructions. Otherwise soak it for 15 minutes in a solution of a teaspoon of dish or other mild detergent per quart of lukewarm water, agitate slightly every five minutes or so, and gently wring dry. If it is still dirty, change the water and resoak as above. When clean, hang the fabric over two clotheslines so it forms a somewhat **M**-shape, or place it in a preheated dryer with several large dry bath towels until it is nearly dry. Then lay it on a flat surface, stretch it gently into shape, and let thoroughly dry. If any odors persist, do the final drying outdoors. Blankets may need to be brushed on both sides to raise the nap.

If an electric blanket is slightly soiled, clean according to the manufacturer's instructions. If seriously damaged and you want to keep it, tape a heavy cloth around the plug, gently clean the soiled areas with a solution of 1 teaspoon of mild detergent per quart of warm water, rinse clean, and dry on a clothesline in the sun.

If a feather pillow is a little dirty, slip it into a pillowcase and secure its opening to keep the feathers from coming out, then wash one or two pillows at a time in a machine or by hand in warm water. If you wash them by hand, rinse one to three times in warm water or until the rinse water is clean. To dry, place one or two pillows with a clean tennis shoe or tennis ball in a dryer set at low heat and gently spin dry. This may take two or three hours. Wash and dry polyester and foam pillows the same as feather pillows, minus inserting them into a pillowcase. If a pillow was submerged in floodwater, junk it.

Clothing ... Most clothes can be laundered or dry-cleaned as usual. Scrub out any seriously soiled areas before washing and wash within a day or so to kill any mildew. If cleaned in a clothes washer, add extra detergent if they were submerged in floodwater. Each belt, handbag, suede garment, embroidered apparel, and the like must be cleaned differently depending on the damage and its value.

If shoes are worth saving, remove the laces, flush any dirt inside with a hose fitted with a nozzle, hand-wash in a solution of one tablespoon of bleach and two tablespoons of dish or mild detergent per gallon of warm water, and let dry in a ventilated room or the sun. You may want to wash the outsides of leather shoes with saddle soap, then lightly rub neatsfoot oil into the leather.

Books and Papers ... Dry, disinfect, and repair water-damaged books as described below. If you have a large library, this may take a team of helpers several days.

To dry ... If the pages are soaked, place each book on end with its pages opened and expose them to gently flowing fresh air. You can use a fan to hasten drying. If any pages are damp, sprinkle corn starch or talcum powder between them to absorb the moisture, leave for a day, then shake or brush the powder off. If a page is wet or soaked, slip a paper towel or some cheesecloth behind it, and dry it with an electric iron set on low.

To disinfect ... If a book was submerged in floodwater, you can dry and disinfect it at the same time by setting it on end with its pages separated in an oven turned to 250°F for an hour. If the pages are still damp, allow them to air-dry. After the pages are disinfected and dry, clamp the book between two pieces of plywood to help retain its shape and keep its pages from wrinkling. If you have so many soaked books that you can't dry them all in a day or so, to prevent mildew from spreading in them either freeze them or slip each into a sealed container with a few mothballs or some moth crystals. If a book's pages have been exposed to floodwaters, even if they have been dried and disinfected they still may disintegrate over time due to substances in the floodwater. If the book has leather covers, take it to a professional.

To repair ... If a book's contents are important and it is badly damaged, consider photocopying its pages and binding them to make a new book. If the pages are dirty, dampen a sponge with a solution of one tablespoon of mild detergent per quart of warm water and gently blot (don't rub) the dirt from each page, then let dry. If a page is torn, much depends what kind of paper it is (glossy, matte, newsprint?) and what is on the page (blank space, text, photos, drawings?). Three methods of repairing such pages are *rice paper* (this is nearly transparent, is strong for its thinness, is pH neutral, and contains no chemical that could discolor the paper over time), *mending tissue* (this tissue-like paper is strong, thin, transparent, and designed for this purpose), and *3M 845 book tape* (this is a stretchable transparent tape that won't crack or dry out). A reliable source for archival and repair products as well as library-related supplies, equipment, and furnishings is Gaylord Brothers of Syracuse, New York. Two helpful book-repair websites are

http://usgenweb.org/research/documents.html
http://www.shopbrodart.com/book-care-repair/

Repairing Vehicles

If a vehicle you own was partly submerged in floodwater, repair it as follows …

☞ Clean the exterior thoroughly with a hose, scrub greasy deposits with solvent, then slide under the chassis and hose-wash the underside as thoroughly as you can.

☞ Open the doors, remove the interior panels, wash behind them, and lube the latches and window-raising mechanisms. Remove the seats and floor mats, clean, and vacuum thoroughly. If the seats were flooded, steam-clean or replace. Wash every inundated interior surface you can reach.

☞ Clean the leaf springs. Raise the vehicle on a lift until the leaves open, hose-clean the spaces between, let dry, then spray WD-40 in the spaces.

☞ Remove and clean unsealed wheel bearings with solvent, then lubricate and reinstall.

☞ Check the steering and brakes.

☞ Drain the crankcase and transmission, flush each with solvent, and refill. Drain the cooling system, flush with fresh water, and hose-clean the radiator.

☞ Take apart the fuel system (tank, pump, and lines) and flush with #1 diesel fuel.

☞ If the starter, generator, or battery was submerged, junk them.

☞ Examine the belts for frays, peels, and cracks; replace as needed.

☞ Replace all filters (engine, fuel, hydraulic).

☞ Remove the spark plugs, air cleaner, and carburetor, and clean each with solvent. Finally, turn the crankcase slowly with the spark plugs removed to force any water out of the cylinders, squirt light oil into each cylinder, let stand for five minutes, then turn the crankcase again to lubricate the cylinder walls and rings. If everything turns smoothly, reinsert the spark plugs and try starting the engine. It starts? Run it slowly a few minutes. After you've driven a hundred miles, change the oil.

At all times pace yourself, get plenty of rest, drink lots of pure water, eat heartily, wash your hands frequently with soap and clean water, and be well.

Addenda

The following pages include sections on several disasters that cannot easily be categorized in other parts of this book, mostly because their occurrence has little relation to one's home, workplace, or specific buildings one frequently visits. As such, they could be called random public disasters.

If you are in a plane crash, train wreck, sinking ship, shooting, or other sudden emergency, *act quickly!* When the planes struck the World Trade Center only one in ten people inside acted immediately. Many *took eight minutes* to respond to the emergency. Almost every one of these people died. If an alarm suddenly goes off —don't finish writing your note, don't finish your phone call, don't finish eating your doughnut. If you've just bought lunch, don't finish eating it —get up and grab your jacket (hopefully with gloves in its pockets) and *move out fast!*

To survive a plane crash [109]

Commercial plane crash safety begins a few weeks before you board the plane, when you book your flight. Statistics show that you have a slightly greater chance of survival if you select an aisle seat behind the wings within five rows of an exit.

Next, before you board, dress practically. You want to protect your body from flames and sharp objects and be able to run from a burning plane, possibly over rough terrain and at night. Don't wear flammable fabrics like polyester or nylon: wear natural fabrics like cotton or wool. Wool is better if you'll fly over cold regions because this fabric will keep you warm if it is wet. Wear long-sleeve shirts (cotton turtlenecks are a good choice) and long pants. Wear shoes with tie-on laces or velcro that have flat soles (you can't run fast in loafers or high heels). Wear a baseball cap or other wide-brimmed hat (the bill or brim will help shield your head, eyes, and face from damage), a large scarf, and a jacket (light in summer, heavy in winter) with light work gloves in its pockets. Carry a small flashlight in a pocket (i.e. an LED key light). If you bring a carry-all it should be small enough fit under the seat in front of you.

Don't drink before or after you board; you want to be as clearheaded as possible in an emergency.

As you enter the plane, look up and down the aisles. Note the exits. Look carefully at an exit door. Imagine opening it. If the flight crew is incapacitated in a crash, a passenger —possibly you— might have to open this portal. As you near your seat, count the rows between you and the nearest exits front and back; you may need to know this if the cabin fills with smoke or it is night. Note any obese passengers. Sad to say, in a plane crash they impede the escapes of others. There have been instances of obese persons being unable to squeeze through a 20-inch-wide exit door and several people trapped behind have died because they couldn't escape.

As you nestle into your seat, note the nearest exits in front, behind, and on the other side. Slip your carry-all under the seat in front, stuff your jacket on top if it is too warm to wear, and ask an attendant for a pillow and blanket if available. Nestle your seat belt low on your hips until you can feel the ridge of your pelvis above the belt. If the belt rests against your stomach, you could suffer serious internal injuries. Remove from your pockets any sharp objects —pens, keys— and slip them into your carry-all.

Next, read the safety card. Study its text and pictures. When it describes the oxygen mask (the cupped device that drops from the ceiling panel above your seat), the flotation device (usually the cushion you're sitting on), and the life vest (a yellow rubberized fabric folded into a book-size packet and stored under your seat), locate these items. Know exactly where they are, and how to use them quickly if necessary.

When a flight attendant gives the preflight safety instructions, listen carefully.

The most dangerous parts of a flight are the first three minutes after takeoff and the last eight minutes before landing —so be attentive during takeoff and landing. Keep your shoes tied and your tray up, don't doze off, and keep your jacket and blanket and pillow in your lap or close by.

If at any time the oxygen mask drops from the ceiling panel, slip it on quickly before assisting others (you can help them better if you can breathe comfortably). If the plane will crash, make sure your seat belt is fastened snugly and your shoes are tied, slip on your jacket and zip up its front, put on the gloves, place the pillow on your knees, wrap the scarf around your head and face, cover your head and upper

TURTLENECK OR OTHER *LONGSLEEVE SHIRT*; COVER AS MUCH OF YOUR SKIN AS POSSIBLE

WEAR NATURAL FABRICS LIKE COTTON & WOOL. AVOID SYNTHETICS, BECAUSE THEY WILL MELT ON YOUR SKIN IF THEY BURN

WINDBREAKER TYPE *JACKET* THAT IS FUNCTIONAL, LIGHT, ATTRACTIVE, AND HAS SIDE & INSIDE BREAST POCKETS. IN THE SIDE POCKETS KEEP LIGHT WORK *GLOVES* TO PROTECT YOUR HANDS FROM BURNS & DIRT. ALSO CARRY A SMALL *FLASHLIGHT* TO SEE IN THE DARK, IN SMOKE, OR AT NIGHT.

BASEBALL *CAP*, OR OTHER BEAKED OR BRIMMED HAT. THIS WILL HELP SHIELD YOUR HEAD, EYES AND UPPER FACE FROM DAMAGE

LARGE *SCARF* AROUND NECK, TO PROTECT YOUR SKIN, KEEP WARM, AND COVER YOUR EYES WHEN SLEEPING

WEAR *LONG PANTS*: TROUSERS FOR MEN, SLACKS FOR WOMEN

WEAR *SHOES WITH LACES & LOW HEELS*. NO LOAFERS, HIGH HEELS, OR FLIP-FLOPS. WEAR SHOES YOU CAN RUN IN OVER ROUGH TERRAIN

KEEP TRAVEL ITEMS IN A SMALL CARRY-ALL THAT FITS UNDER THE SEAT IN FRONT OF YOUR FEET

174. FASHIONABLE APPAREL FOR AIR TRAVEL (AND TRAINS AND SHIPS AS WELL)

body with the blanket, set your feet flat on the floor a few inches behind your knees, lean forward and hug your knees with your arms, bury your face in the pillow, and brace yourself.

After the impact, remain still until the plane completely stops —sometimes it bounces, or experiences a second or third impact, or makes a long rough slide to a stop. If you can, *leave the plane quickly* —in many instances you have *90 seconds* before the cabin fills with smoke or fire. As you rise from your seat look through the windows. Any fire outside? You don't want to jump out an exit door into a fire. Any rough terrain? Look *before* you reach the door so you know what to expect or can turn to another door if necessary. Any water? If so, slip on your life vest but don't inflate it (its bulk could keep you from reaching an exit). Bring your scarf and blanket —*nothing else*— and wrap them around your lower face and upper torso so your hands are free. The narrow aisle may be strewn with luggage and wreckage.

Outside, run at least 500 feet from the aircraft, as it could explode at any moment.

To survive a train wreck[110]

A train wreck may be a *head-on collison, rear-end collision,* or *derailment* (the train leaves the tracks sideways and may collide with another train or the ground). Most train wrecks are derailments.

Before boarding, dress practically as you would for planes as appears in figure 174 on page 197. Carry a small flashlight, even during the day (the train could crash in a tunnel and there are other ways it could be dark). While in the station or on the boarding platform, read every map and notice posted in view, and listen to every announcement. Have a pen and notepad and take notes. Don't depend on your memory.

Statistics indicate that the safest seat in a train is an aisle seat facing the rear (if the train crashes your momentum will likely push you into the back of your seat instead of throw you several yards up the aisle) in a car that is one or two cars back from the middle of the train.

When you board, note the emergency escape windows. Sit next to one if you can, and think of how you would open it. To escape through the other windows you'll need a fire axe or sledgehammer to break them because train windows are made of impact-resistant glass. Once on board, stay in your seat as much as possible. If the train crashes your chances of injury greatly increase if you are out of your seat. Especially hazardous is standing in the cafe car near the edges of fixed tables and counters. Rest rooms are fairly safe, because their compartments are small and few objects inside can be tossed about.

If a crash occurs, duck quickly and hold onto an armrest or anything sturdy you can find. If thrown to the floor, grab a seat leg if you can to keep from sliding. Since trains have no seatbelts you could be thrown yards from your seat and other passengers and overhead luggage yards away may fly at you like projectiles. Hold on tightly until everything comes to a complete stop. If you are able, flee in the direction opposite the impact or any smoke. If the car has tipped over you may have to crawl over the seats one at a time. Look out the windows. Is it rocky outside? Rough? Swampy? Steep? Any smoke or fire? Look before you leap. When you reach a door, jump or climb carefully down to safe ground, then run from the train for at least 50 yards if you can. Once you are safe, try to help others. If it is night you'll be glad you have the flashlight, and if it is rainy or cold you will be glad you have a cap, scarf, and jacket. Wait for help. In the United States this will probably arrive within a half hour.

To escape a sinking ship[111]

Usually the bigger a ship, the slower it sinks. Aside from this, there is no typical way that a ship sinks. It depends on the shape of the hull, its center of gravity (this depends on how fully loaded the ship is and how the load is distributed), how the hull was penetrated or is filling with water, and how many bulkheads have been breached. Usually the water drains into the bilges (the lowest interior part of the ship) and is removed by the bilge pumps. However, when the Greek cruise ship MTS Oceanus sank in a storm off the coast of South Africa in 1991, the water entered through a ruptured sewage valve and entered the ship through its commodes, sinks, and showers and the bilge pumps were useless. If water flows in faster than the pumps can discharge it or the pumps fail, the ship will eventually sink.

Before boarding a sea vessel, even if a short trip across a harbor, dress practically as you would for planes as described on page 197 and assemble a *ditch bag*, a maritime go-bag, which is a small waterproof knapsack you wear on your back or a carry-all with a wrist strap. This bag should float. If not, fill it with pieces of styrofoam until it floats and test its buoyancy in a bathtub. This bag should contain …

☞ A pencil or pen and a notepad.
☞ A flashlight and extra batteries. Waterproof these by keeping them in a sealed clear plastic bag. You can operate the light and keep it dry while it's in the bag.
☞ Drinking water and energy foods.
☞ First-aid kit, including sunscreen.
☞ 100 feet of paracord and a small roll of duct tape.
☞ Signal mirror and Swiss army knife (or equal).
☞ A hooded raincoat (wear this) with waterproof gloves in its pockets.
☞ Compass and map of your route and nearby lands.

Know what language the crew speaks. If you can't speak their language, find an onboard authority who speaks your language and can advise you in an emergency.

Immediately after boarding, find the life vests. Lift one. See how to put it on. Then find a lifeboat. Note how it suspends from its davits (the curved supports that hang over the edge of the ship). See how you could enter the boat from the deck. Modern lifeboats are usually large, covered, and have motors. They are usually loaded with passengers from the ship's deck and mechanically lowered into the water —if the ship is still fairly upright.

Next, walk completely around the ship. Learn the territory. Note every safety exit, especially where the crew boards and leaves the ship. Note the immovable objects you could hold onto if the ship lists. Railings. Ropes or rigging. Wood objects such as tables, counters, furniture, hatch covers. Remember that wood floats. Foam cushions and other floating materials. With your paracord and duct tape, you could fashion a floating counter and a few foam cushions into a small life raft. Imagine these possibilities as you walk around.

If you will stay overnight, familiarize yourself with your cabin. Then take *another* stroll around the ship, and relate your surrounds to your cabin.

If at any time while aboard you feel a jarring sensation or hear a low thud or scraping sound that seems to come from the center of the earth —beware! Stop *everything* you are doing and investigate —the biggest cause of fatalities in a sinking ship is *delayed response*. If something is terribly wrong you may shortly hear an announcement over the captain's intercom or the evacuate signal: seven short horn blasts and one long one —or you may hear nothing. Act quickly and alertly but don't panic. First find a lifejacket. Go to your cabin if you can and dress in light warm clothes, add your cap and coat and gloves, grab your ditch bag, slip on the life jacket, and head for the lifeboats. If you're inside the ship, move upward and outward toward the main deck. Don't strike a match, and try to keep dry. Obey any orders of the captain and the crew.

The biggest danger on a sinking ship is *listing*: the steep tilting of a ship onto its side. Image your whole house tilting 30 to 40 degrees to one side: that's what listing is like. Floors may tilt so steeply that you can't walk on them, furnishings slide to the lowest wall and injure or crush people in the way, and foods and beverages in kitchens and dining rooms fall onto the floors and make them slipperier still. On a listing ship hold onto the handrails, hide behind large fixed objects, and stay away from sliding objects. Here is where a few strands of paracord tied to anchored objects could save your life.

If you have to jump into the water, look first. Avoid landing on people, flotsam, fires, and propellors. In the water, try to find something that floats that you can climb onto, then paddle 100 feet away from the ship (if it goes under, it can suck in objects floating nearby). The sea is usually cold and rough. All the above is even harsher if it happens at night. Here a flashlight slipped inside a sealed clear plastic bag can be lifesaver.

If you have made it into a lifeboat, eat your food and water sparingly. Never drink seawater as this will only worsen your thirst. If it rains, spread out your raincoat or other water-repellent sheeting and collect as much water as you can. Even a towel can be wrung out or a cloth fabric sucked on to quench your thirst. Keep as warm as you can. Use any flares on board only when an approaching rescuer can see you. On sunny days keep every part of your skin covered with fabrics or sunscreen to prevent sunburn.

To survive a shooting [112]

In recent years a number of horrific incidents have occurred when one or more deranged gunmen have entered a public place and began shooting innocent citizens. On June 11, 2014, President Barack Obama spoke at the White House about the latest string of senseless shootings that had occurred across America. He said, "Our levels of gun violence are off the charts. We don't have enough tools right now to really make as big a dent as we need to." [113] The next few pages are a tool with which you can make a dent.

One cold morning in December 2012, Adam Lanza took (some reporters said *stole*) a .223-caliber Bushmaster rifle, a 10mm Glock handgun, and a 9mm Sauer handgun from his mother —a gun enthusiast who legally owned at least seven firearms and 1,400 rounds of ammunition— and shot and killed her in their home, then he drove five miles to Sandy Hook Elementary School in Newtown, Connecticut, where he fired 156 shots in five minutes, killing 26 people. [114]

Whatever your opinion is of gun control, it is undebatable that shooters usually go where people are unarmed. If you are disinclined to wear a gun in public where happenstance could put you in the path of a bullet, your first steps toward protecting yourself from such savagery are *prevention* and *preparation*.

Regarding *prevention* … At the risk of being considered intrusive, report any strange or obsessive behavior by anyone you know or hear about. Shooters often mention their plans in advance, not so much to brag or show off but to vent their resentments and because they are obsessed with such thoughts. After Adam Lanza's rampage, authorities found in his home several videos relating to previous mass murders and a 4-by-7-foot spreadsheet listing 500 mass murderers and the weapons they used which must have taken him years to compile. It would have been nice if somebody —like the mother he murdered— had reported his deranged behavior to an authority.

Regarding *preparation* … In any public area you regularly inhabit, ask the management what lockdown procedures the building has. Note how the doors are locked, where people can quickly hide or escape, how the police would be called, and similar details. In any such place, *know how to escape from where you are in at least two directions.* As you enter a lobby think, "If I hear gunshots where would I go?" Look around. Trace at least two ways you can flee. Do this with every space you pass through. Make it a habit.

If you work in an office, classroom, or other area that has a closeable door to a public area, find a way to keep the door closed even if it has a lock. Since there are many kinds of doors, hopefully the ideas shown herc will spur your imagination to create a simple, clever constrictor that will stymie a shooter from entering and killing you. An effective item may be lying nearby right now, and all you need is to be prompted about it and test it to protect yourself.

If the door swings out and has a hydraulic closer arm on top, you may be able to keep the door from opening more than a few inches by fitting a custom-made flange over the arms as appears at **A** at the top of figure 175. I made this for a friend's office; but it might not work if the door is pulled hard (I couldn't test this at my friend's office). It is $5^{1}/_{2}$ inches long, $1^{1}/_{4}$ inches wide, and nearly $^{1}/_{8}$ inch thick. By enlarging the quarter-size photo of this flange 400 percent on a copier you can make your own. First make a pattern out of cardboard, test the pattern for size on the door you are making it for, make any needed adjustments, then trace the pattern on a piece of metal to make the flange. Another way to keep this kind of door from opening more than a few inches is to wrap a belt or purse strap around the closer arm. If the door swings out and has no closer arm, you could fit a custom-made stop over the knob as appears at **B** in figure 175, or slip an umbrella handle, poker handle, or other hooked object over the knob to keep the shooter from opening it from the outside. Even if he blasts away the knob with a few gunshots, this will cause him to waste precious seconds and bullets that may otherwise do far more harm.

If the door swings in, you could wedge a chair or a notched 2 x 4 under the knob, or a door stop under the base. These methods also appear in figure 175.

Test every method in advance to make sure it will work. Other precautions …

☞ In a theater or at an athletic event, select a seat where you can escape quickly. A seat within three

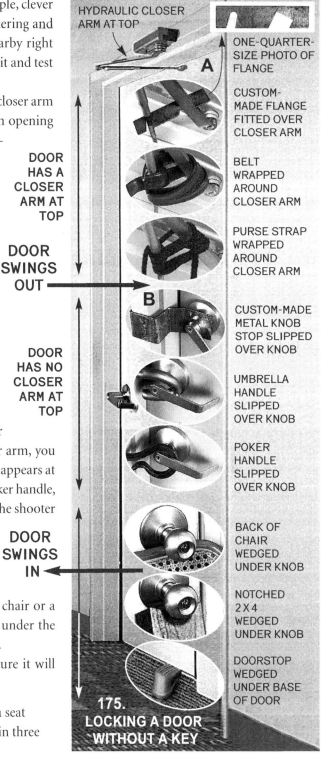

HYDRAULIC CLOSER ARM AT TOP

A

ONE-QUARTER-SIZE PHOTO OF FLANGE

CUSTOM-MADE FLANGE FITTED OVER CLOSER ARM

BELT WRAPPED AROUND CLOSER ARM

PURSE STRAP WRAPPED AROUND CLOSER ARM

B

CUSTOM-MADE METAL KNOB STOP SLIPPED OVER KNOB

UMBRELLA HANDLE SLIPPED OVER KNOB

POKER HANDLE SLIPPED OVER KNOB

BACK OF CHAIR WEDGED UNDER KNOB

NOTCHED 2 X 4 WEDGED UNDER KNOB

DOORSTOP WEDGED UNDER BASE OF DOOR

DOOR HAS A CLOSER ARM AT TOP

DOOR SWINGS OUT

DOOR HAS NO CLOSER ARM AT TOP

DOOR SWINGS IN

175. LOCKING A DOOR WITHOUT A KEY

seats of an aisle is best. Before sitting down, trace your path from your seat to a safe place in two directions. If in a bar or restaurant, try to sit with your back to a wall.

☞ At your workplace keep a supply of water, energy bars and other quick foods, first-aid equipment, bathroom bucket, toiletries including toilet paper, and a change of clothes in case you must hide in a safe place for possibly a few hours until the police arrive.

☞ Some say shine a bright LED flashlight in the killer's eyes — but this works only if you have a very bright and costly light (not the $4.99 kind that appears by the register in a hardware store) and it is dark. In daylight or if any lights are on a normal flashlight will only create after-image spots in the killer's eyes; and in the dark he can't see you anyway, so why shine a light that shows where you are?

☞ Take a class in self-defense. Some police departments also offer crisis response training programs. Visit your town hall and ask if such programs are available in your area.

Now for the tough part. If you hear what sounds like firecrackers going off or balloons popping somewhere nearby, quickly decide whether to *RUN*, *HIDE*, or *FIGHT*. You have two objectives: (1) Save your life, and (2) Slow the killer down so he has less time to shoot others before help arrives.

RUN fast away from the shooter if you safely can. This should be your first option because runners have the highest chance of survival in a shooting.

HIDE if you can't run away but can conceal yourself so the shooter can't see you or will have trouble finding you. Hiding includes barricading an entrance so the killer can't see or reach you. Barricade only if you can do so quickly.

FIGHT if the shooter is so close you can't run or hide, or you are responsible for the safety of others less able than you (as in a classroom of children). If you're going to die anyway, do it in a way that will slow the killer as much as you can so he'll have less time to shoot others before the SWAT teams arrive. There's nothing worse you can do than cower in a corner while the killer mows you down with a few quick shots then moves swiftly to the next victim.

These three options are described in greater detail below.

RUN … If you hear shots, quickly determine their direction and flee the other way. *Don't freeze* —this is like signing your death warrant. Also …

☞ *Take nothing with you* but your cellphone if you can snatch it quickly. You can come back later.

☞ Bring others if you safely can. If others look disoriented or scared, grab them, shout at them, slap them, whatever it takes, and bring them with you. Not only will this increase their chances of fleeing safely, the more people in your group the less likely any one person will be shot, and if you encounter a shooter your greater numbers will be more able to subdue him. Don't cluster —spread as wide as you can.

☞ Run in a random zigzag pattern —not straight or uniformly zigzag— and crouch to reduce your body target. You will decrease your chances of being shot, and you may increase the time the killer must aim at you which would decrease the time he'd have to shoot others before the police arrive. Crouch low below any windows you may pass so the shooter won't see you and possibly open fire on you.

☞ If you see a fire extinguisher and have time to dismount it, create a fog behind you so the shooter can't see you. If you can, spray him in the face then throw the extinguisher at his neck. Don't worry about getting shot if it will happen anyway.

☞ If you are in a room with other people at ground level, possibly break a window with a chair and help others outside.

☞ Once you are safe call 911 and give the location of the gunfire and any other information you have, but make your call short. Warn everyone else you see to get away from the building.

HIDE … If you hear the shooter approach and can't escape but he can't see you, crouch low behind a desk, under a table, in a closet, or other dark place and remain completely quiet —no whimpering, weeping, or heavy breathing that could betray your location. If you have time do the following:

☞ If you are in a room with a door, lock it if you can. If you have a doorstop, hardbacked chair, 2 x 4 of the right height, or any of the other earlier-mentioned deterrent, or if any desks, file cabinets, copiers, or other heavy furnishings are near the door, slide them behind the door. Keep well to the side in case the killer tries to blast away the knob or shoot you through the door. Anything to slow him down and give him less time to shoot others before help arrives.

☞ Turn off the lights, close any curtains or blinds, silence your cellphone, and make the room look as if no one is there. This will make it harder for the killer to see you, he'll be more afraid to enter, or he may think no one is there. Even if he does enter, if it is dark it will be harder for him to find anyone. The longer he lingers the better.

☞ Call 911 if you can. Use a land line if possible so police can trace where you are.

☞ Arm yourself with sharply pointed or clublike weapons —pencils, pens, scissors, umbrella, cane, a piece of broken glass you can brandish, cup of hot coffee, a coat or jacket you can throw in the shooter's face.

☞ Stay close to the floor to offer the smallest target. If you haven't barricaded the door with furniture, lie on the floor against the back of the door to keep it closed.

☞ Wait until help arrives, even if it takes hours.

Here are a few tactics that saved lives at Sandy Hook Elementary School …

☞ When the shooting began someone turned on the public address system so everyone could hear gunshots over the intercom, which "saved a lot of people."

☞ A six-year-old girl, the sole survivor in her class of 18, hid in a corner of the classroom's bathroom and played dead until the police found her.

☞ A school nurse hid under a desk in her office. The door opened and under her desk she saw Lanza's boots and legs facing her 20 feet away. He stood there a few seconds, then turned and left.

BEST

BETTER

BAD

176. HOW TO RUN FROM A SHOOTER

☞ A first-grade teacher hid 14 students in a bathroom, told them to be completely quiet, and barricaded the door. A piece of black construction paper covered a small window in the door of the classroom outside. When Landa walked past the door he apparently believed the room was vacant because the door was closed and the window was covered.

☞ Two librarians hid 18 children in a part of the library used for lockdowns in practice drills, then barricaded the door with a filing cabinet and led the children into a store room.

☞ A music teacher barricaded her fourth-graders in a small supply closet moments before Lanza pounded on the door and yelled, "Let me in!" When he heard nothing he left.

☞ A nurse hid in a first-aid supply closet for three hours before she believed it was safe to leave.

FIGHT ... If you come face to face with the shooter and are sure you will be shot, fight for your life. Even if you die, any way you can slow the killer may reduce the number he kills before the SWAT teams arrive.

Here's something to remember if you're ever shot. If the bullet misses your brain or your spinal cord, if you are aggressive before you are hit you will likely experience a spasm of shock for about two seconds *then you will become enraged and feel no pain as you reflexively attack the killer,* because your instincts are programmed this way. You may be mortally wounded, and may bleed to death in twenty seconds —but in this time you may subdue the shooter and keep him from killing others. If your reaction is fear, when the shots are fired you will cower and fall. [115]

☞ Attack the shooter with any weapon you can find —pencils, pens, scissors, piece of broken glass, umbrella, books and chairs and other objects you can throw. If you have a bladed instrument slice him across the forehead if you can —his eyes will quickly fill with blood and he won't be able to

177

Acknowledgements

This book was largely inspired by my experiences in two disasters, Snowstorm Alfred in late October 2011 and Hurricane Sandy in late October 2012, which gave me opportunity to assess their nature and devise ways to overcome them. Hence, conceptually, my first thanks goes to these normally feared events.

Next, I extend my warmest thanks to the citizens of metropolitan New York who so nobly parried the forces of hurricane Sandy without resorting to social violence. *They* established the ethical foundation for this volume when I went looking for it.

I thank the *New York Times* and the *Reporter-Dispatch* for their excellent reportage of local disasters, Wikipedia for the wonderful variety of information it has posted for the public, and Amazon.com for its see. Some say kick him in the crotch —but unlike what Hollywood scripts say, unless you score a really hard direct hit the assailant will only become more enraged. Stab him in the face, spray a fire extinguisher in his eyes, claw his face with your nails and gouge his eyes, grab the arm that holds the gun, throw a coat in his face, tackle him and hold onto his legs, if he wears a hood grab it and pull it over his face. Butt him with your head and fight ferociously with both arms because while he holds the gun he has only one arm to ward you off. If you're lucky his gun may jam or run out of bullets —then *he* is the defenseless one!

☞ If others are with you, *all of you attack the killer at the same time!* He may shoot one or two of you which will be less than if you do nothing —but one of you may be able to tackle him while others stomp on his face and arms and someone can grab the gun.

Finally... When the police arrive, do not run to them, as they might think you're a threat. Walk alertly with your arms held wide and your hands open, or place your hands on your head. Tell them everything you know. Do quickly what they order you to do.

> You may download for free a .pdf file of *To Survive a Shooting* at this book's website at http://thedisasterhandbook.com. Feel free to send this file or copies of it to all your friends.

customer reviews of the many products it sells— all of which enabled me to make this volume as relevant, informative, accurate, and comprehensive as it can be.

I thank Mike Revenson and Mike Linehan, two local emergency responders, for examining this book for accuracy and thoroughness and making numerous suggestions for improving it.

I thank Harry Wirtz for his invaluable artistic counsel, immeasurable graphic wisdom, and kindly keeping my computer behaving during this arduous literary adventure.

Finally I thank my wife, Janis Butler, my partner in fear, grime, toil, and ultimate triumph during the disasters we experienced, and for her work in editing my floods of errant words into productive prose.

Text notes

1. Cover: *Tornado intensity and damage*; http://en.wikipedia.org/wiki/Tornado_intensity_and_damage; photo 6; image taken by Mike Branick of the U.S. National Oceanic and Atmospheric Administration; as a work of the U.S. federal government this image is in the public domain. **2.** Page 6–7 background: *Effects of Hurricane Sandy in New Jersey*; photo 3, "Damage in Mantoloking"; http://en.wikipedia.org/wiki/Effects_of_Hurricane_Sandy_in_New_Jersey; File 121030-F-AL508-081c, Oct 30, 2012; image taken by Master Sgt. Mark Olsen, USAF. **3.** Page 8–9 background: http://commons.wikimedia.org/wiki/File:US_Navy_110320-M-0145H-063_A_large_ferry_boat_rests_inland, 20 March 2011; image taken by Lance Cpl. Larry Welch, US Navy. **4.** "Mapping Hurricane Sandy's Deadly Toll", Josh Keller (*The New York Times*, Nov. 17, 2012); http://www.nytimes.com/interactive/2012/11/17/nyregion/hurricane-sandy-map.html. **5.** The original Family Contact Card appeared in *Are You ready? An in-depth guide to Citizen Preparedness* (2004, FEMA), p 25; http://www.ready.gov/are-you-ready-guide/pdf. **6.** Void. **7.** *Official Highway and Transportation Map*, ©2011 Georgia Department of Transportation. **8.** void **9.** The photo of the First Alert smoke and fire alarm appears courtesy of First Alert of Aurora, Illinois. **10.** The photo of the Kidde smoke and carbon monoxide alarm appears courtesy of Kidde Fire Safety of Mebane, North Carolina. **11.** http://www.consumerreports.org/cro/co-and-smoke-alarms-buying-guide.htm. **12.** *Travels with Lucy & Flo*; http://travelswithlucy.com_photo20.jpg; posted Jan. 28, 2014 by trav6360. **13.** This drawing is from *Architecture Laid Bare*, Robert Brown Butler (©2012, Robert Brown Butler), p 128. **14.** The photo of figure 20 appears courtesy of Nick Mehl of Element 5 Architecture in Austin, Texas. **15.** The photo in figure 21 is taken from YouTube ➡ http://www.weather.com/video/tornado-picks-up-debris-near-dallas-26761. **16.** The photo of the Avanti compact kitchen is courtesy of Avanti Products of Miami, Florida. **17.** The photo of figure 23 appears courtesy of Abbi Williams, designer, and Hugh Pitts of Kokopelli Builders Inc. of Decatur, Georgia. **18.** The photo of the garage storm shelter that appears in figure 25 is a composite of several similarly constructed models, notably one from http://www.ebay.com/bhp/storm-shelter titled *6x10 Storm Shelter storm cellar*. **19.** *FEMA 320: Taking Shelter from the Storm: Building a Safe Room For Your Home or Small Business* (3rd Edition, 2008), p 14. **20.** The photo of the children's playhouse used as a safe room was found on an internet website of a company that makes this product; the information of this source has been lost. **21.** http://www.amazon.com/Vestergaard-Frandsen-LifeStraw-Personal-Water-Filter. **22.** The photo of the Outdoor Camp Oven 2 Burner Range and Stove appears courtesy of Camp Chef of Hyde Park, Utah. **23.** The woodstove photo appears courtesy of Fireglow of Yorktown, NY. **24.** The photo of the Personal Locator Beacon appears courtesy of ACR Electronics of Fort Lauderdale, Florida. **25.** The photo of the SPOT Gen3 Satellite GPS Messenger appears courtesy of SPOT LLC of Covington, Louisiana. **26.** The photo of the ICOM M802 Digital Marine SSB radio appears courtesy of ICOM America of Kirkland, Washington. **27.** *Cheesecloth*, Wikipedia; http://en.wikipedia .org/wiki/Cheesecloth. **28.** The photo of the Chief AJ HFX Arrow Sling Shot appears courtesy of Armed Mobile Survivor LLC of Newburgh, Indiana. **29.** The photo of the block and tackle appears courtesy of Kevlargaff, its manufacturer. **30.** The photo of the come-along appears courtesy of Garrett Wade Tools of Cincinnati, OH. **31.** The photo of the escape chair appears courtesy of commons.wikimedia .org/wiki/file:Sedia_cardiopatia_Escapechair.png; GNU Free Documentation License ©2009. **32.** The HELP flag appearing in figure 81 is sold by Orion Safety Products of Peru, Indiana; see http://www.orionsignals.com/. **33.** This photo illustration by Robert Brown Butler is a depiction of a real event. **34.** *Bhopal Disaster*, Wikipedia;

http://en.wikipedia.org/wiki/Bhopal_disaster. **35.** *Infrastructure, Safety, and Environment,* a RAND Corporation monograph available as a pdf file at www.rand.org., p 7. Much of the information about the World Trade Center disaster that appears in this section is from this document. **36.** *Bhopal Disaster,* Wikipedia; http://en.wikipedia .org/wiki/Bhopal_disaster. **37.** The photo of the escape hood respirator appears courtesy of ILC Dover of Frederica, Delaware. **38.** Much of the information about respirators is from *Respirator,* Wikipedia; http://en .wikipedia.org/wiki/Respirator. **39.** *The Galveston Hurricane of 1900,* Texas State Historical Association; http://www.tshaonline.org/handbook/online/articles/ydg02. **40.** *FEMA 320: Taking Shelter from the Storm: Building a Safe Room For Your Home or Small Business* (3rd Edition, 2008), p 14. **41.** Figure 94 and the related text on tornados is from *Architecture Laid Bare,* Robert Brown Butler (2012, Robert Brown Butler), p 125–26. **42.** *Tsunami,* Wikipedia; http://en.wikipedia.org/wiki/Tsunami. **43.** *2011 Tohoku Earthquake and Tsunami,* Wikipedia; http://en.wikipedia.org/wiki/2011_Tohoku_earthquake_and_tsunami. **44.** *Halifax Explosion,* Wikipedia; http://en.wikipedia.org/wiki/Halifax_Explosion. **45.** *A Tsunami in Switzerland? Lake Evidence Says Yes,* Henry Fountain (*The New York Times,* Nov. 19, 2012); http://www.nytimes.com/2012/11/20/science/earth .html. **46.** *A History of Road Closures along Highway 1, Big Sur, Monterey, and San Luis Obispo Counties, California;* ©2001 by JRP Historical Consulting Services, Davis, California. **47.** *The Gros Ventre Slide,* National Forestry Service; http://www.ultimatewyoming.com/grosventreslide.html. **48.** *Huascarán,* Wikipedia; http://en .wikipedia.org/wiki/Huascarán. **49.** *Wellington Avalanche,* en.wikipedia.org/wiki/Wellington,Washington. **50.** *Blons, Austria, avalanche,* en.wikipedia.org.wiki/Blons_avalanche. **51.** *The Galen Avalanche,* http://.www .environmental graffit.com/mountains/news-10-worst-avalanches-history?image=8. **52.** The photo of the Wellington, Washington, avalanche taken during early summer of 1910 is in the public domain since its copyright has expired. **53.** The photo of the avalanche transceiver appears in en.wikipedia.org/wiki/avalanche_transceiver and is a file from Wikipedia Commons and is licensed under Creative Commons Attribution 3.0. **54.** en.wikipedia.org/wiki/1980_eruption_of_Mount_St._Helens. **55.** The Mount St. Helens eruption deposits map is taken from en.wikipedia.org/wiki/file/:St_helens_map_showing_1980 _eruption deposits.png; file from Wikipedia Commons; the original image was prepared by the U.S. Geological Survey, an agency of the U.S. Department of the Interior. **56.** Figure 101 and the related text on earthquakes is from *Architectural Engineering Design: Structural Systems,* Robert Brown Butler (2002, McGraw-Hill), p 530–31. **57.** The photo of the flexible connection appears courtesy of SharkBite Plumbing Solutions of Cullman, Alabama. **58.** The photo of the auto gas shutoff valve appears courtesy of Submeter Solutions, Inc. of Issaquah, Washington. **59.** The photo of the auto water shutoff valve appears courtesy of FloLogic, Inc. of Raleigh, North Carolina. **60.** The information about the National Weather Service advisories is taken from http: //www.nws.noaa.gov/view/national .php?prod=ALL. **61.** *Breezy Point: Drowned, Burned, but Unbowed,* Rick Hampton (*USA Today,* Nov. 26, 2012); http://www.usatoday.com/story/news/nation/2012/11/25. **62.** *Oakland Firestorm of 1991,* Wikipedia; http://en.wikipedia.org/wiki/Oakland_firestorm_of_1991. **63.** *The Great Chicago Fire,* en.wikipedia.org/wiki /Great_Chicago_Fire. **64.** *Bhopal Disaster,* Wikipedia; http://en.wikipedia.org/wiki /Bhopal_disaster. **65.** *Fallout Shelters,* Wikipedia; http://en.wikipedia.org/wiki/Fallout_shelter. **66.** http://www.nrc.gov/reading-rm/doc-collections/fact-sheets/emergency-plan-prep-nuclear-power-bg.html. **67.** *Chernobyl disaster,* en.wiki pedia.org/wiki/Chernobyl_disaster. **68.** *Three Mile Island accident,* en.wikipedia.org/wiki/Three_Mile_Island _accident. **69.** The Indian Point Nuclear emergency zone map is taken from http://www.loopny.com/wp-content/uploads/2011/03/IP_PAA_8x11_11_13_2008.jpg. **70.** *National Weather Service*, Wikipedia; http://en.wikipedia.org/wiki/National_Weather_Service. **71.** Some of the information appearing in figure 122 is taken from http://.www.disaster.ifas.ufl.edu/chap9fr.htm, Section 9.5, page 4–5. **72.** *Flood Preparedness and Response: Strategies for Families* (2003, Univ. of Wisconsin Cooperative Extension), "Building Dikes to Prevent Flooding", p 7–8; http://www.uwex.edu/ces/news/info/flood.pdf. **73.** http://www.egu.eu /medialibrary/image14/karymsky-volcano-2004/; image taken by Alexander Belousov of the Earth Observatory of Singapore. **74.** Much of the information on wildfires is from *Architecture Laid Bare*, Robert Brown Butler (©2012, Robert Brown Butler), p 77–80. **75.** *Hail*, Jacque Marshall (UCAR > Communications > Fact Sheet, April 10, 2000); http://www.ucar.edu/communications/factsheets/Hail.html. **76.** *1989 Loma Prieta Earthquake*, Wikipedia; http://en.wikipedia.org/wiki/1989_Loma_Prieta_earthquake. **77.** *In Asteroid's aftermath, a Sigh of Relief*, Henry Fountain (*The New York Times*, Mar. 26, 2013), p D3. **78.** *Meteor strikes Alabama woman*; http://www.history.com/this-day-in-history/meteorite-strikes-alabama-woman. **79.** *Mount Pinatubo*, Wikipedia; http://en.wikipedia.org/wiki/Mount_Pinatubo. **80.** *Mayon Volcano*, wikipedia; http://en.wikipedia.org/wiki/Mayon_Volcano. **81.** The author learned this information in Oct 2002 from the insurance adjustor for the Happy Land Nightclub fire, Larry Savino of Putnam Valley, NY. **82.** *26 Killed in Flash Fire in Westchester Hotel*, Robert D. McFadden (*The New York Times*, Dec. 5, 1980), page A1. **83.** *Hotels could be Hazardous to your Health*, Richard H. Kaufmann, Captain, Los Angeles County Fire Department (1976). **84.** "Atlanta Officials Gamble on Storm and Lose …", Kim Severson (*The New York Times*, Jan. 30, 2014), page A13. **85.** I viewed this story on a television news program the night after this event occurred in early December 2013. **86.** I viewed this story on a Weather Channel video in late summer 2013. **87.** http://www.disaster.ifas.ufl.edu/chap4fr.htm; particularly Sections 4.26 through 4.32. **88.** http://.www.disaster.ifas.ufl.edu/chap3fr.htm; Section 3.12. **89.** Northeast Blackout of 2003, http://.www.en.wikipedia.org/wiki/Northeast_blackout_of_2003. **90.** Tohoku earthquake and tsumani, http://www.en.wikipedia.org/wiki/Tohoku_earthquake_and_tsumani. **91.** *2011 Joplin Tornado*, Wikipedia; http://en.wikipedia.org/wiki/2011_Joplin_tornado. **92.** *1980 Eruption of Mount St. Helens*, Wikipedia; http://en.wikipedia.org/wiki/1980_eruption_of_Mount_St._Helens. **93.** This photo (20 helo CH-146_Griffon.jpg) was taken by TM Wolf and posted to Flickr and is licensed to Creative Commons (http://en.wikipedia.org/wiki/Creative_Commons). **94.** This photo is adapted from one of four rotating images on the homepage of Airlift AS, an emergency search and rescue company in Førde Lufthaven, Norway; http://www.airlift.no/. **95.** The air-lift rescue vest photo appears courtesy of Yates Gear, Inc. of Redding, CA. **96.** Much of the aerial rescue text is from *High Wire Act*, Bill Springer, (*Sail Magazine*, December 2003); http://sailmagazine.com/sailspringer.pdf. **97.** Much of the ground rescue text is from *Light Search & Rescue* (2009, Newport Beach Fire Department Community Emergency Response Team); http://www.nbcert.org/lightsearchrescue.html. **98.** This photo illustration is derived from a FEMA photo taken by Win Henderson that is archived as FEMA library photo 44359. **99.** *Mosquito*, http://.www.en.wikipedia.org/mosquito. **100.** The text on the five kinds of water is from *Architecture Laid Bare*, Robert Brown Butler (©2012, Robert Brown Butler), p 314–15. **101.** Much of this data is from *Bleach: A Cleaning Mainstay*, Marian Gooding (2007); http://www.show catsonline.com/x/bleach .html. **102.** *Over The Edge: Death in Grand Canyon*, Michael P. Ghiglieri and Thomas M. Myers (2012, Puma Press, Flagstaff, AZ), p 99. **103.**

Ibid, p 248. **104.** *Management of Dead Bodies after Disasters: A Field Manual for First Responders*, Oliver Morgan, Morris Tidball-Binz, and Dana van Alphen, editors (Pan American Health Organization, 2009). **105.** Much of this section's text is from *The Disaster Handbook for Extension Agents* (2003, University of Wisconsin Cooperative Extension), particularly pp 22–25, 28–31, 33–37, and 52–53; http://www.uwex.edu/ces/news/info/flood.pdf. **106.** Void. **107.** The photo of the Large Bike Foldable Luggage Cargo Trailer appears courtesy of Aosom LLC of Lake Oswego, OR. **108.** Asteroid belt, wikipedia, http://en.wikipedia.org/wiki/asteroid_b. **109.** Much of this section's text is from http://www.wikihow.com/Survive-a-Plane-Crash. **110.** Much of this section's text is from http://www.wikihow.com/Survive-a-Train-Wreck, and http://www.vocativ.com/usa/nyc/wheres-the-safest-place-to-sit-on-the-train/. **111.** Much of this section's text is from http://www.wikihow.com/Escape-a-Sinking-Ship. **112.** Much of this section's text is from http://www.wikihow.com/Survive-a-School-or-Workplace-Shooting. **113.** "Obama Speaks of Frustrations After Oregon Shooting", Mark Landler and Lee van der Loo (*The New York Times*, Jun 11, 2014), page A12. **114.** The information about the Sandy Hook Elementary School massacre is from http://en.wikipedia.org/wiki/Sandy_Hook_Elementary_School_shooting. **115.** The information about how a person reacts to a bullet wound is from an issue of *Handguns* magazine that I read in the early 1990s. **116.** The map in figure 125 is from http://en.wikipedia.org/wiki/National_Atlas_of_the_United_States, and the location of the nuclear reactors is from http://nuclear.wiki.lovett.org. **117.** The background image on pages 76 and 77 is adapted from a photo taken from en.wikipedia.org/wiki/Collapse_of_the_World_Trade_Center; the image is a U.S. Navy Photo taken by Journalist 1st Class Preston Keres and released by the United States Navy with the ID 010914-N-3995K-015. **118.** The background photo on pages 116 and 117 is adapted from a photo taken from en.wikipedia.org/wiki/Flood; the image's title is "Trapped woman on a car roof during flash flooding in Toowoomba 2" by Kingbob86 (Timothy) - http://www.flickr.com/photos/kingbob86/5341730273/ and the image is licensed under Creative Commons Attribution 2.0 via Wikimedia Commons - http://commons.wikimedia.org/wiki/File:Trapped_woman_on_a_car_roof_during_flash_flooding_in_Toowoomba_2.jpg#mediaviewer. **119.** The background photo on page 145 is adapted from en.wikipedia.org/wiki/United_States_Capitol; the image's title is "US Capitol east side" by Martin Falbisoner - Own work and the image is licensed under Creative Commons Attribution-Share Alike 3.0 via Wikimedia Commons http://commons.wikimedia.org/wiki/File:US_Capitol_east_side.JPG #mediaviewer/File:US_Capitol_east_side.JPG. **120.** The background photo on page 148 and 149 is adapted from commons.wikimedia.org/wiki/File:F4_tornado_damage_example.jpg; the image is in the public domain because it contains materials that came from the U.S. National Oceanic and Atmospheric Administration and was taken or made as part of an employee's official duties; the photo was taken by Mike Branick of the National Weather Service. **121.** The background photo on page 178 and 179 is adapted from en.wikipedia.org/wiki/Flea_market. This image is titled "Fushun Flea Market 03" and is lacking source information. It is licensed under Public domain via Wikimedia Commons - http://commons.wikimedia.org/wiki/File:Fushun_Flea_Market_03.png#mediaviewer. **122.** The background photo of the backhoe on page 148 and 149 is a drawing by the author from *The Ecological House*, Robert Brown Butler (© 1981, Morgan & Morgan, 1981), p 98. **123.** The background photo of the carpentry belt on page 183 is a drawing by the author from *The Ecological House*, Robert Brown Butler (© 1981, Morgan & Morgan, 1981), p 100.

Index ... Main references are in **boldface**; illustrations are in *italics*

Emergency Addresses

_____
_____
_____
_____
_____
_____
_____
_____
_____
_____

Other Important Information

Family Contact Card

Contact Name _____
Address _____
                  Phone _____
Distant Contact Name _____
Address _____
                  Phone _____
Meeting Place _____
                  Phone _____

Dial 9-1-1 for Emergencies!

_____
_____
_____
_____
_____
_____
_____
_____
_____
_____

Other Important Information

Family Contact Card

Contact Name _____
Address _____
                  Phone _____
Distant Contact Name _____
Address _____
                  Phone _____
Meeting Place _____
                  Phone _____

Dial 9-1-1 for Emergencies!

_____
_____
_____
_____
_____
_____
_____
_____
_____
_____

Other Important Information

Family Contact Card

Contact Name _____
Address _____
                  Phone _____
Distant Contact Name _____
Address _____
                  Phone _____
Meeting Place _____
                  Phone _____

Dial 9-1-1 for Emergencies!

_____
_____
_____
_____
_____
_____
_____
_____
_____
_____

Other Important Information

Family Contact Card

Contact Name _____
Address _____
                  Phone _____
Distant Contact Name _____
Address _____
                  Phone _____
Meeting Place _____
                  Phone _____

Dial 9-1-1 for Emergencies!

178. Photocopy these four cards or tear them out and give one to each family member or friend

216